Practical SQL

Practical SQL
The Sequel

Judith S. Bowman

Addison-Wesley

Boston • San Francisco • New York • Toronto • Montreal
London • Munich • Paris • Madrid
Capetown • Sydney • Tokyo • Singapore • Mexico City

Many of the designations used by manufacturers and sellers to distinguish their products are claimed as trademarks. Where those designations appear in this book, and Addison-Wesley was aware of a trademark claim, the designations have been printed with initial capital letters or in all capitals.

The author and publisher have taken care in the preparation of this book, but make no expressed or implied warranty of any kind and assume no responsibility for errors or omissions. No liability is assumed for incidental or consequential damages in connection with or arising out of the use of the information or programs contained herein.

The publisher offers discounts on this book when ordered in quantity for special sales. For more information, please contact:

Pearson Education Corporate Sales Division
One Lake Street
Upper Saddle River, NJ 07458
(800) 382-3419
corpsales@pearsontechgroup.com

Visit AW on the Web: www.awl.com/cseng

Library of Congress Cataloging-in-Publication Data

Bowman, Judith S.
    Practical SQL : the sequel / Judith S. Bowman.
        p. cm.
    Includes bibliographical references and index.
    ISBN 0-201-61638-6 (alk. paper)
    1. SQL (Computer program language) I. Title.
QA76.73.S67 B695 2000
005.75'6—dc21   00-062081

ISBN 0-201-61638-6
Text printed on recycled paper
1 2 3 4 5 6 7 8 9 10–CRS–04 03 02 01 00
First printing, November 2000

Contents

List of Tables

List of Figures

Acknowledgments

I'd like to thank the folks at Addison-Wesley for their help and encouragement while I was working on this book, particularly my wonderful editor, Mary T. O'Brien; her assistant, Mariann Kourafas; and Jacquelyn Doucette, who handled production issues. Sybase generously made a copy of Sybase Adaptive Server Anywhere available for the CD. Mike Radencich handled the details.

I'm also grateful to the many technical reviewers who read and commented on the draft manuscript. Among them are John Viescas, Keith Hare, Amy Sticksel, Michael Blaha, Ashesh Parekh, Sujata Soman, William Grosky, and Carlton Doe. My co-authors from *The Practical SQL Handbook*, Sandy Emerson and Marcy Darnovsky, also gave me useful notes. Thanks to all for the opinions, corrections, pans, and praises. The book benefited greatly. Any errors, of course, are mine.

Chapter 1

Introduction

In This Chapter

- Why This Book?
- Who This Book Is For
- Contents
- Speaking Multiple SQLs
- Following Conventions
- Understanding the `msdpn` Database
- Using the Examples

Why This Book?

SQL (here pronounced "sequel") is the premier language for relational database management systems (RDBMSs). If you work with databases, you need to know it. This book assumes that you have studied the fundamentals and want to move on.

There are lots of books on learning basic SQL, and more are being published all the time. You can find excellent general tutorials, references, and vendor-specific manuals. Classes and videos abound, too. Unfortunately, most working database applications don't use basic SQL. After you read an introductory book or get some training, you're thrown into a world of complex code and told to "maintain this—don't change it, just keep it working" or "fix this." The lines you look at have only a passing similarity to the things you learned from that great book or in class. How do you make the transition?

This book aims to help you over the classroom-to-reality hump in five ways.

- Information is organized by use, rather than by feature.
- The text is code-heavy, and all the examples use the same database.

- Every example was tested on multiple systems—Adaptive Server Anywhere (on the CD), Oracle, Informix, Microsoft SQL Server, and Sybase Adaptive Server Enterprise.
- Legacy systems and inherited problems are given special attention.
- SQL tuning notes help you avoid bad performance.

Use, not Feature

Why is use better than feature? You can always look up syntax specifics. What you really need is a way to attack a problem.

For example, you'll see six methods for finding the top N, rather than six uses of GROUP BY ("Top N: Six Approaches" in Chapter 5). Along the way, you'll dive into self-joins, GROUP BY, HAVING, subqueries, aggregates, and cursors—all areas where new SQL users tend to need practice. In Chapter 4, you look at five ways to work with unconnected master-detail rows ("Locating Disconnected Rows"), including outer joins and MINUS. You'll also work with IS NULL and NOT IN.

Putting features in the context of solving a problem makes learning more useful. You can compare different methods and become familiar with the approach as a whole rather than focusing on isolated features. When you confront a new problem, you'll have the skills for analyzing and attacking it.

Lots of Examples

Explanations and examples are thoroughly worked through, using the same database all the way (the database and the Adaptive Server Anywhere small-footprint RDBMS for managing it are on the CD).

Every piece of code runs—there is nothing in this book you can't produce, given the right system and version. You'll see the same data over and over and become familiar with it. Knowing what you've got makes it easy to set up and run your own experiments. It also helps you troubleshoot your code. You understand what's in the database and what you want to see. This gives you a good place to start in diagnosing your programming errors.

By working through the many code examples, you'll improve your SQL reading and writing skills.

Multiple Systems

Every example was tested on five systems—Adaptive Server Anywhere, Oracle, Informix, Microsoft SQL Server, and Sybase Adaptive Server Enterprise. In most cases, there is no difference in the systems. Vendors work hard to maintain a core of portable commands that represent informal industry practice. However, some areas show wide divergence. Where options vary or results are not the same, you'll find a note or a code comparison.

Nowadays, when many companies are running multiple RDBMSs, you need to be able to apply your expertise in one system to another system. The examples provide a handy way to find out how autonumbering works in Oracle (the section "Comparing Autonumbering Systems" in Chapter 5), understand differences in transaction-related commands ("Experimenting and Transaction Management" in Appendix A), or learn how Microsoft SQL Server handles math on dates ("Dealing with Dates" in Chapter 2). Discussion of each topic includes a table comparing the five systems.

Legacy

In reality, you seldom start "clean." You're stuck with code written by some long-gone employee or a database designed by an intern who didn't have time to put in the constraints that prevent duplicates or force master-detail integrity checks. You need to be able to read and understand code that doesn't use current standards, and you need to get rid of bad data. This means reviewing all kinds of SQL and figuring out what is going on, whether or not you'd do it that way yourself. For this reason, the book includes detailed information on finding and fixing errors, from minor glitches in Chapter 2 to more complex issues in Chapter 4.

You'll also find examples of "old" ways of doing things. After you learn how to use CASE/DECODE to translate fundamentally meaningless values ("1," "X5") to character strings ("Female," "Extended benefit package"), you look at earlier ways to do the same thing (Chapter 3). The methods include point (characteristic) functions, UNION, embedded subqueries, joins and outer joins, and subqueries. When you see this kind of code on the job, you'll understand what it is doing and how to change or maintain it.

Tuning

SQL isn't the only factor in database performance. Database design, hardware configuration, system architecture, and network setup all have profound effects—and all are outside the scope of this book. However, you can learn what elements in a query tend to degrade performance. Often, very simple changes are helpful. Most of the tuning notes are collected in Chapter 6.

Who This Book Is For

This book is for you, the SQL user who understands the basics and wants to know more.

- You've been using a GUI report writer, and you're trying to do things it can't; or you'd like to stop being at the mercy of the system guys by giving them clearer instructions or doing more of the coding yourself.
- Your opportunities for practice are limited and the code templates you find turn out to be based on a specific system or on a theoretical model—not really applicable to your situation.
- The SQL dialect you're using on the job is different from the one you learned in class, or you are working with multiple systems.
- You're supporting code some long-gone employee wrote, which doesn't seem to work right and is full of stuff you've never seen before.
- Some of the queries you see seem more complicated than necessary, and you wonder if you could do anything to improve performance.

This book will help you tackle new assignments, read inherited code, and make improvements to it. Start by looking up a problem. Run the code, then modify a few things to make sure you understand how it works. Try applying the method to similar situations in your own database.

Contents

You don't need to read the book from start to end—you can jump in at any point. If a topic is treated in one chapter and mentioned in another, the shorter treatment refers to the longer one.

Chapters

Here are the chapters and their contents.

1. "Introduction" assumes that you've already started your SQL career. It explains the book approach, organization, and conventions, and lists the SQL systems used. It provides a brief summary of the sample database.

2. "Handling Dirty Data" explores SQL functions and predicates, with suggestions on using them for finding and fixing dirty data—data with case or space or size problems or data containing embedded garbage. You get

practice in UPPER/LOWER, TRIM, CHAR_LENGTH, SUBSTR, concatenate, POSITION, and SOUNDEX. You also examine LIKE variants and some things you can do with BETWEEN. The chapter closes with a section on dates—doing math on them, changing their display format, and matching them.

3. "Translating Values" presents a number of ways to expand a code (display "male" for 1, "female" for 2). Here's where you learn about DECODE and CASE. You'll also find explanations of other methods of doing the same thing—characteristic functions, UNION, joins and outer joins, and embedded subqueries. The chapter includes a summary of other conditional elements, including ISNULL, NVL, COALESCE, and TRANSLATE. Functions include LPAD, REPEAT/REPLICATE, and SPACE.

4. "Managing Multiples" has additional techniques for handling dirty data, but here it is more significant soiling than a few letters or spaces. You'll track down duplicate rows, locate near-duplicate entries, rescue disconnected rows, find out how to group items by some subset of characteristics, and look at distribution. In the process, you'll practice some important techniques, including GROUP BY, aggregates, self-joins, unequal joins, MINUS, HAVING, and outer joins. You'll also work with subqueries. To prevent future problems with multiples, you examine unique indexes and foreign key constraints.

5. "Navigating Numbers" starts out with a comparison of autonumbering mechanisms in the five target systems, with examples of each. These methods include default, column property, sequence object, and datatype. Next, there is an interesting collection of code segments, treated together because all use similar elements, often GROUP BY, COUNT, and unequal joins. Sections include finding the high value, using row numbers, getting the top *N*, locating every *N*th, and calculating a running total. In most cases there are alternative methods that you can compare. The section on top *N*, for example, includes six approaches, from row limits and subqueries to cursors.

6. "Tuning Queries" explores indexes and the optimizer and ways to get information about them from your system. Then it compares WHERE clauses that can take advantage of indexes with those that can't, urging the SQL programmer not to use IN where a range will work or do math on a column unnecessarily. Multicolumn and covering indexes are the next topics, followed by some hints on joins and on eliminating unneeded sorting (as manifested in DISTINCT and UNION). HAVING versus WHERE performance issues and cautions on views fill out the

picture. The chapter concludes with a list of questions you can ask when you have performance problems, and a discussion of forcing indexes.

7. "Using SQL to Write SQL" reviews system catalogs, the tables or views that store meta-data about the system (users, tables, space, permissions, and so on). These catalogs differ greatly from vendor to vendor in specific tables and columns, but they all supply the same kind of information. To use them effectively, you need to find out what system functions your RDBMS offers. Once you have an understanding of the system catalogs and system functions, you can use SQL to generate SQL—a technique often used to write cleanup and permission scripts. You can apply similar skills to the problem of test data.

Appendices

The appendices contain supplementary materials.

A. "Understanding the Sample DB: msdpn" provides information about the sample database, including hard copy of the scripts that create the database for the five test systems. These scripts are on the CD in electronic form. Finally, there are notes on transaction commands—SQL statements you can use to cancel data modifications (if you plan ahead) and on deleting data or dropping tables, should you need to start over again.

B. "Comparing Datatypes and Functions" is all the little SQL dialect variant charts merged into a big one for your convenience. Here you'll see datatype information and tables summarizing variations in character, number, date, convert, conditional, tuning, and system functions. There is also a table on outer join syntax and notes on environment.

C. "Using Resources" includes books, Web sites, and newsgroups you might find interesting.

Speaking Multiple SQLs

This book is about SQL, the language, as it is commercially practiced by relational database management systems. It does not focus on any particular vendor of database software or on the ANSI standard, though neither vendors nor ANSI can be ignored. It assumes that you know the basics—it does not explain them. To fill in holes in your SQL background, see Appendix C.

SQL Engines

Because examples don't mean much unless they actually run, software is provided on the CD: Sybase Adaptive Server Anywhere (ASA, also known as SQL Anywhere Studio). It has a small footprint and relatively few eccentric extensions, as well as being easy to use. It runs on Windows and Windows NT. It comes loaded with the msdpn database, a simple set of tables modeling the business of MegaSysDataProNet Co, an Internet software sales company. All code, unless otherwise noted, is run on ASA.

Examples are also checked on some of the major database players:

- Oracle
- Informix
- Sybase Adaptive Server Enterprise (ASE)
- Microsoft SQL Server

The latter two are sometimes lumped together in the text as Transact-SQL, since both started out with this Sybase dialect of SQL and still have similar features. Adaptive Server Anywhere sometimes supports Transact-SQL features, but it is considered separately, because it often has a different approach. Where interesting differences or incompatibilities come up among different SQL versions, they are noted.

A script to create the tables and other objects used in the examples is included for each SQL engine mentioned in the book (on the CD and, slightly simplified, in "Collecting the CREATE Scripts" in Appendix A), in case you want to either run the examples on your favorite system or just install some practice data. Remember, not all code runs on all systems. For details on the RDBMSs mentioned in the book, see Table 1–1. All systems cited were installed on an NT 4 operating system.

Table 1–1. SQL Engines

Vendor	Software	Version	Tool	Notes
Sybase	Adaptive Server Anywhere (ASA), also known as SQL Anywhere Studio	6.0.3	Interactive SQL	Included on CD
Sybase	Adaptive Server Enterprise (ASE)	11.5	SQL Advantage	Transact-SQL
Microsoft	SQL Server	7.0	Query Analyzer	
Oracle	Personal Oracle	8.03	SQL Plus	
Informix	Informix	7.30	dbaccess	

SQL Dialects

You'll find single-topic variant comparisons dotted through the text (see Table 1–2) and a full chart in the back of the book (Appendix B). In some cases, the SQL-variant table entries give something pretty close to full syntax (Table 1–2). In others, the only entry is the keyword or function name. Why this inconsistency? Well, it's arbitrary—tables for short, simple functions include syntax, while tables with more complex elements include only function names. All details of all major SQL dialects is too big a topic, and one that wiggles all the time. An effort to supply complete syntax in every case is bound to fail. Instead, this book focuses on generic SQL capabilities and tries to save you some pain when you apply these principles to your own system. For example, knowing that CHARINDEX, LOCATE, and INSTR are all pretty much the same function should be enough to get you going. You'll be able to find the precise syntax for your system. (When there are multiple names for identical or similar SQL functions, look for the ANSI or ASA versions in headings and table names.)

Finally, remember that architecture varies greatly from SQL engine to SQL engine. For that reason, you won't find anything in this book on topics such as space use. Chapter 6, "Tuning Queries," considers ways you can improve SQL speed by how you write SQL: it does not discuss other issues that may help or hinder performance.

Following Conventions

The conventions in text and code examples are somewhat different.

Text

In text, object names (database, table, column, and view names) are in fixed-width font, like the customer table, which has wandered into this sentence just

Table 1-2. Names with Syntax

ANSI	ASA	ASE	MS SQL Server	Oracle	Informix
CHAR_LENGTH (expr)	LENGTH (expr) DATALENGTH (expr) CHAR_LENGTH (expr)	DATALENGTH (expr) CHAR_LENGTH (expr)	LEN(expr) DATALENGTH (expr)	LENGTH (expr)	LENGTH (expr)

to illustrate a fixed-width object name. Keywords (SQL verbs and function names) are capitalized. The SUBSTR function is an example.

Because very few people read this kind of work linearly from start to finish, there are many headings and pointers to other sections or chapters. For example, to learn about the SUBSTR function, see "Choosing a Subset" in Chapter 2.

Code

All code runs on the software on the CD (Sybase Adaptive Server Anywhere) unless otherwise noted. Here are the conventions (Figure 1–1).

- A blank line separates the query and the results.
- Code is in a fixed-width (typewriter) font. In code, keywords are not in uppercase letters and object names have no special font.
- Each line starts with a SQL keyword (SELECT, FROM, WHERE) or an indentation, if the line has wrapped.
- Features just described are bold, such as the LENGTH function in Figure 1–1.
- When relevant, the number of rows affected is displayed, usually copied as part of the results, but occasionally added by hand. For Oracle SQL Plus, the command SET FEEDBACK 1 (run for each login session) forces a row tally for all results (the default is for sets of six rows or more).
- NULL displays vary slightly from system to system. You may see NULL or [NULL] or a blank. In Oracle SQL Plus, SET NULL 'text' substitutes 'text' for the blank. In this book, the Oracle NULL display is left in its default state.

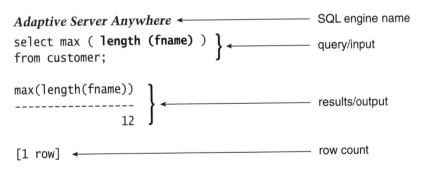

Figure 1–1. Code Conventions

- Occasionally, part of the code is made inactive with comment marks: either two dashes (--, indicating "from here to the end of the line only") or sets of brackets (/* marks the beginning and its reverse marks the end of the not-to-be-processed code, which may include multiple lines */).

Where Oracle, for example, supports a feature differently than ASA or supports a feature that ASA does not have, you'll see "Oracle" in the SQL engine name position and slightly different-looking input and output. (In this example, the only variation is format.)

Oracle

```
SQL> select max ( length (fname) )
  2  from customer;

MAX(LENGTH(FNAME))
------------------
                12

1 row selected.
```

Occasionally, a display is edited to fit on the page. The output of the following query is hard to read because the line wraps.

Adaptive Server Anywhere

```
select custnum, fname, lname, address, city, state, phone
from customer
where fname = 'ruby'

custnum    fname               lname            address
city                state phone
========= ==================== ====================
============================================= ==================== ===== =======
111223333 ruby                 archer           444 37th St #3
Oakland             CA    5551111

[1 row]
```

A little editing, and the output is easier to understand.

Adaptive Server Anywhere

custnum	fname	lname	address	city	state	phone
=========	========	==========	===============	======	=====	======
111223333	ruby	archer	444 37th St #3	Oakland	CA	5551111

[1 row]

Notice that only the format has changed. The data is not edited.

Understanding the msdpn Database

Every example in the book has been run against tables on all five of the relational database management systems included in the test set. The results are the actual output. As you work through the examples, you'll become familiar with the data.

Most people find it easier to follow examples when working with a consistent data set. Here it is the msdpn database, which models the business of MegaSysDataProNet Co, a (completely imaginary) high-tech e-commerce enterprise. There's an entity-relationship diagram in Figure 1–2 and a list of table data in "Table Details." If you don't load the database on the CD, you can still follow along.

MegaSysDataProNet Co (MSDPN Co) sells software, toys, educational materials, minor hardware, and the like over the Internet. Examples use just six tables.

- customer contains customer name, address, phone, and status information. All customers are domestic (USA).
- supplier gives similar information on the product makers, with the addition of columns for country names and international phone numbers. One supplier is Japanese.
- product holds notes about the item, including its supplier, price, weight, type, description, and version.
- ordermaster represents the top level of an order. It includes the order number, the order date, the customer identification number, the credit card information, and the identification number of the employee who made the sale.
- orderdetail is the order line item table, with one row for each line item. The table contains order and product numbers, unit, and shipdate. To get master-detail information on an order, you need to join ordermaster and orderdetail.

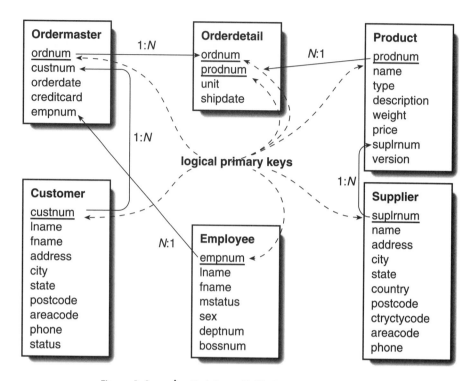

Figure 1-2. msdpn Database Entity-Relationship Diagram

- employee stores worker data, including name, identification number, marital status, sex, and boss's identification number. There is a many-to-many relationship between employee and customer (an employee could serve many different customers, and a customer could place orders with multiple employees). To get the name of an employee who helped a particular customer, you need to do a three-way join: employee-ordermaster-customer.

In the diagram, table names are bold and in slightly larger type than column names. Columns that make up unique identifiers (logical primary keys) are underlined. Each table has a unique index built on its unique identifier. In one case (orderdetail), two columns (ordnum and prodnum) are required for uniqueness, so the index uses both.

The arrows show the relationships between the tables. Checking ordermaster and orderdetail, you can see that each row in ordermaster may have multiple related rows in orderdetail. Each row in orderdetail has only one related row in ordermaster. This parent-child relationship is described as 1:N (one ordermaster row to one-or-many orderdetail rows).

Six tables, each with a handful of rows, are ridiculously few—but they are just a sample database. Because the database is small, it's easy to load and easy to understand. Some tests are built in. For example, customer.postcode is CHAR(10), while supplier.postcode is VARCHAR(10). Both columns contain five characters. This difference in datatype provides a way to compare the effect of a character function on CHAR and VARCHAR data. In real life, you'd try to make identical columns have identical datatypes. In the same way, ordermaster.orderdate is TIMESTAMP datatype (date and time information), and orderdetail.shipdate is plain DATE (date information only).

For the CREATE TABLE and INSERT INTO scripts, see Appendix A (the scripts are also available in electronic form on the CD).

Table Details

Following is all the table data in an easy-to-read format.

Because datatype names vary from system to system (price could be MONEY or NUMBER(8,2) or DECIMAL, depending on the vendor's decisions), you won't see datatype names in these charts. Check the appropriate script (see "Collecting the CREATE Scripts" in Appendix A) or your manuals to find out precisely how each datatype is implemented on your system.

Columns are labeled as to whether or not they allow null. Indexed columns are also noted—the index names are the underlined words below the null–not null line.

customer The customer table contains information about MSDPN customers. The columns are all fixed or variable character datatypes. The unique index on custnum is named custix. The table contains 12 rows.

custnum not null custix	lname not null	fname null	address not null	city not null	state not null	postcode not null	areacode null	phone null	status null
111222222	McBaird	geoff lowell	89 Hillcrest St.	Berkeley	CA	94608	510	5552234	(NULL)
111333333	aziz	phillip	92 Arch St.	reading	MA	01867	617	5551333	1
223456789	khandasamy	SAM	123 Lane St.	NY	NY	10028	212	2231234	2
777777778	mokoperto	merit	Old Foundry Block 2	Boston	MA	02110	617	5557777	1
776667778	Peters	Pete	45 N. Maine	Macedon	NY	14502	800	5557777	2
999456789	WONG	LI-REN	12 Main St.	Silver Spring	MD	20906	301	1231235	3
111223333	archer	ruby	444 37th St #3	Oakland	CA	94609	510	5551111	2
111334444	le blanc	felipe	2 Jacob Way #8	reading	MA	01867	617	5551111	3
111444444	sato	kimiko	the highlands	Seattle	WA	98104	206	5552233	3

777777777	deathmask-z	(NULL)		Old Foundry Block 2	Boston	MA	02110	617	5557777	(NULL)
776677778	rs	pete	pete	New Trail 6	Austin	TX	78730	512	5557777	2
923457789	Menendez	lauren		158 Beach St.	NY	NY	11215	917	1231235	3

supplier Like customer, supplier stores name and address information, but this time for product suppliers. All columns are defined as variable character, except state (fixed character) and suplrnum (whole number). The unique index suppix is on the suplrnum column. There are seven suppliers.

suplrnum	name	address	city	state	country	postcode	ctryctycode	areacode	phone
not null	not null	not null	not null	null	not null	not null	null	null	null
suppix									
========	================	===============	==========	=======	=======	=============	============	=========	=======
111	Connectix Co.	333 North Ave	S.F.	CA	USA	94130	(NULL)	(NULL)	(NULL)
222	Soft Stuff	373 Java Ave	San Jose	CA	USA	95128	(NULL)	408	5554223
333	Total Recall	42 Norton St.	Tokyo	(NULL)	JAPAN	143	81-3	376	1311
444	Hi Finance!	53 5th Ave	NY	NY	USA	10028	(NULL)	201	5554434
555	TrendMaster	9 Nopar Ct.	Seattle	WA	USA	98104	(NULL)	206	5552233
666	Above Average Arts	33 West St.	Boston	MA	USA	02110	(NULL)	617	5554223
777	Emu Sister Prdctns	7 Forge Ave	Philadelphia	PA	USA	97212	(NULL)	215	5557433

product The product table stores information about products. The product number is an integer, while name, type, description, and version are all variable character columns. The weight and price columns are decimal values (price may be a MONEY data type, if that is available). There is a unique index on prodnum called prodix and a nonunique index on price named pricex. Undecided weights are flagged with a negative one (–1.00). There are 21 products.

prodnum	name	type	description	weight	price	suplrnum	version
not null	not null	null	null	not null	null	not null	null
prodix							
					pricex		
======	==================	===========	=======================	======	=======	========	========
2000	cook & book	application	record your recipes	2.50	19.99	555	Super 6.
2047	paper dolls	game	create & dress dolls	2.50	19.99	666	10.1.01
2049	more paper dolls	game	create & dress dolls	2.50	19.99	666	10.1.01
2050	tax time	application	1995 edition	2.50	49.99	444	(NULL)
2111	memory tripler	application	50% or more	-1.00	119.99	333	6.5_a
1084	memory manager	application	(NULL)	-1.00	19.99	333	10.1_6.5
1099	typing test	education	(NULL)	2.50	29.99	666	(NULL)
1105	home poll kit	game	take the pulse of america	2.50	19.99	555	Super 6.
1110	star systems	education	scientific horoscopes	1.50	39.99	555	Super 6.
2113	bugbane	application	(NULL)	1.00	49.00	222	(NULL)
1794	memory8	hardware	8 Meg mem	-1.00	400.00	333	6.5_a
1083	money master	application	pers checking	5.80	29.00	444	1.2
1104	teach yourself greek	education	(NULL)	2.50	49.99	666	(NULL)
1107	mortgage minder	application	know where you stand	1.50	39.99	444	(NULL)
1108	blood & guts	game	(NULL)	2.50	29.99	666	(NULL)
1109	C++ for kids	education	(NULL)	2.50	39.99	666	1.1
1255	bug stories	book	(NULL)	3.00	20.00	777	2.2
1357	nt guru	book	(NULL)	3.00	20.00	777	2.2

1457	how multi is media?	book	(NULL)	3.00	20.00	777	10.1
2110	landlord logs	application	(NULL)	2.50	89.99	444	1.3
1106	z_connector	hardware	(NULL)	2.20	149.00	111	1.1

ordermaster This table contains the top-level order information: order number, customer number, order date, and credit card number. Both ordnum and custnum are whole numbers: orderdate holds date and time data. The next to last column, creditcard, is variable character. There is a unique index on ordnum. The table has 12 rows.

ordnum not null ordix	custnum not null	orderdate not null	creditcard not null	empnum not null
81	223456789	Jan 02 1999 02:30:00	1222222232224222	123232345
85	111334444	Jan 02 1999 00:00:00	7777 7777 7777 7777	123232345
86	777777779	Jan 02 1999 00:00:00	7777 7777 6663	111223333
87	111333333	Jan 02 1999 00:00:00	00001111222233334444	111223333
89	111222222	Jan 02 1999 00:00:00	1234333331114123	923457789
90	111444444	Jan 02 1999 00:00:00	111112111121111	923457789
91	111223333	Jan 02 1999 00:00:00	1111222233334444	923457789
92	777777778	Jan 02 1999 00:00:00	777766661234X	222222221
93	111334444	Jan 05 1999 14:30:00	X7777 7777	222222221
94	777777778	Jan 02 1999 00:00:00	777766661234X	222222221
95	923456789	Jan 03 1999 00:00:00	3131 7777 7777 7777	443232366
99	776677778	Jan 02 1999 00:00:00	1222222232224222	923457789

orderdetail This table contains the line (detail) information for the orders. Three columns (ordnum, prodnum, and unit) are whole numbers. The fourth column is a date. Only shipdate may be null. The unique index (ordprodix) is on the ordnum and prodnum columns. There are 33 rows.

ordnum not null ordprodix	prodnum not null	unit not null	shipdate null
84	1099	1	(NULL)
84	1255	1	(NULL)
86	2000	2	(NULL)
81	1357	1	(NULL)
87	1106	1	(NULL)
87	2113	1	Jan 04 1999

87	1794	1	(NULL)
87	1083	1	(NULL)
91	2111	5	Jan 03 1999
89	1099	1	Jan 04 1999
89	2050	2	Jan 04 1999
85	1794	1	Jan 02 1999
90	2110	1	Jan 02 1999
95	1255	1	(NULL)
95	1108	1	(NULL)
95	1105	1	(NULL)
99	2047	6	(NULL)
99	2050	2222	(NULL)
92	2050	3333	(NULL)
93	1105	1	(NULL)
94	1108	1	(NULL)
81	2050	5	Jan 01 1999
84	2050	1	Jan 05 1999
85	2050	25	Jan 05 1999
86	1083	7	Jan 05 1999
91	1107	7	Jan 05 1999
93	2050	5	Jan 05 1999
94	1083	5	Jan 05 1999
95	1083	2	Jan 05 1999
86	1105	20	Jan 05 1999
87	1105	20	Jan 05 1999
87	2000	20	Jan 05 1999
81	1106	2	Jan 05 1999

employee   This table contains some employee information—name, ID number, sex, marital status, department, and boss's ID number. Names are variable character, IDs are fixed character, and the other columns are numeric. There is a unique index on empnum. MegaSysDataProNet Co has six employees.

empnum not null empix	lname not null	fname null	mstatus null	sex null	deptnum not null	bossnum not null
123232345	Miller	Hamid	1	1	1	223232366
223232366	Chang	laurna	1	2	1	443232366
111223333	archer	ruby	1	2	1	223232366
923457789	Menendez	lauren	1	1	1	223232366
222222221	Bloomfeld	Bill	2	1	1	443232366
443232366	Blake-Pipps	Scorley	2	2	1	443232366

Using the Examples

The best way to learn is by trying the examples yourself. You'll come to recognize the kind of errors you often make and become skilled at correcting yourself.

While you're reading the book (and typing code), focus on the general principle illustrated. Take what you see as a starting point, and go on from there. Be aware that you may be using a later (or earlier) version than the one tested here and that not all examples work on all systems. You may have to modify the code quite a bit to get it to run in a different environment.

Here's where the scripts in Appendix A (and on the CD) may come in handy. If your favorite system is one of those included, you can load the example tables onto your system and go to town using your system rather than (or in addition to) the Adaptive Server Anywhere software on the CD. If there is no script for your system, you'll be able to tailor one of the included scripts to meet your needs. The best place to start is checking datatypes and null use in the CREATE TABLE statements (see "Datatype Comparison" in Appendix B for some hints). Once you get the tables set up, create unique indexes on the primary keys to prevent duplicate rows, and try inserting data.

Summary

This chapter is a reference for use in the rest of the book. It describes:

- The book's scope
- The target reader
- The chapter contents
- The appendix contents
- The SQL dialects used for developing and testing queries, including versions and tools for each
- The conventions used in text and queries
- The structure of the sample `msdpn` database
- The method for using the book

Chapter 2

Handling Dirty Data

In This Chapter

- Case
- Space
- Size
- Matching Patterns
- Locating Patterns
- Sounds Like . . .
- BETWEEN
- Dealing with Dates

Dirty Data

Why look at dirty data? Often, databases grow from a casual collection of information to a huge system before anyone notices how messy the data is. Because developing the database is a rush job or a project for a newbie, few or no constraints are built in—sometimes even unique indexes are lacking! Everyone on the team *means* to be very careful. Over time, so many errors show up, the data becomes hard to use. Inconsistent cases make it hard to find a particular item (WIDGET? widget? Widget?). Leading spaces cause sort anomalies. Embedded junk throws everything into doubt, and similar names cause confusion. Illegal entries creep in if there is no check on upper and lower values.

To make the data useful and cut down on the amount of ad hoc grooming you do, you go through steps like these:

1. Find all questionable data.

2. Figure out the business rules that govern how the data should be stored.

3. Clean up the data so that it meets these standards.

4. Create controls (unique indexes, check constraints, stored procedures, data entry applications) that prevent bad data from getting in.

This chapter reviews SQL functions you can use to find and fix dirty data.

Case

The well-managed database has no case problems. The designer sets clear standards and the front-end application checks data when it is entered to make sure it conforms to these standards. Constraints (PRIMARY KEY, UNIQUE, CHECK, REFERENCES), stored procedures, and triggers in the SQL engine prevent dirty data from taking up residence.

Unfortunately, most of us inherit data that was collected, not managed. As time goes on and the data grows, case problems may emerge. Some names are entered in uppercase letters, some in lowercase letters, and some in mixed-case letters. For databases with case-sensitive sort orders (or collating sequences), inconsistent use of case leads to ordering and matching anomalies. Data essentially vanishes, because you can't predict where it will be in an ordered list.

Fortunately, a couple of widely used string functions provide some relief. UPPER converts a string to uppercase. LOWER converts to lowercase. But before looking at the functions, consider your sort order.

Sort Order

How uppercase and lowercase letters are handled depends on two things:

- Character set—a list of letters and special characters ($, #, @, and the like) that may include non-English characters (i.e., the tilde in Spanish, accents in French, and the non-Roman symbols of Hebrew and Chinese)
- Sort order (also called the *collating sequence* or the *collation*)—the arrangement of the characters in the character set. A sort order may handle uppercase letters before lowercase letters or may consider them equivalent, for example.

Character sets and collating sequences are set up when the RDBMS software is installed, and they should not be changed lightly. SQL-92 provides some commands relevant to picking among available character sets and sort orders (CREATE CHARACTER SET, DROP CHARACTER SET, CREATE COLLATION, DROP COLLATION, COLLATE, and COLLATION FROM), but they are not widely implemented. Check your system manuals for specifics.

If you're curious about which character set/sort order your system is using, you can run some simple experiments yourself or see if your vendor provides a tool or command or system table that shows your collation sequence or character set. These commands vary from system to system. Here are a couple of examples.

Adaptive Server Anywhere stores information about the character set and sort order in a system catalog, syscollation (for more on system catalogs, see "Getting Meta-Data from System Catalogs" in Chapter 7). It uses the collation Latin1, which is case insensitive.

Adaptive Server Anywhere

```
select collation_id, collation_label, collation_name
from syscollation

collation_id collation_label collation_name
=============================================================================
          46 1252LATIN1     Code Page 1252, Windows Latin 1, Western

[1 row]
```

Microsoft SQL Server and Adaptive Server Enterprise offer the sp_helpsort system procedure. The output from the two systems is not the same. In this case, MS SQL Server is also using Latin1, so it is case insensitive.

MS SQL Server

exec sp_helpsort

```
Unicode data sorting
--------------------
Locale ID = 1033  case insensitive, kana type insensitive, width insensitive

Sort Order Description
-------------------------------------------------------------------
Character Set = 1, iso_1
  ISO 8859-1 (Latin-1) - Western European 8-bit character set.
Sort Order = 52, nocase_iso
    Case-insensitive dictionary sort order for use with several
    Western-European languages including English, French, and German.
      Uses the ISO 8859-1 character set.
```

Characters, in Order

```
------------------------------------------------------------------------------
   ! " # $ % & ' ( ) * + , - . / : ; < = > ? @ [ \ ] ^ _ ` { | }
   ~  ¡ ¢ £   ¥ ≠ §  ¨ © ª « ¬    ®  ‾  ° ±Σ ∏ ´ µ ¶  ·  ,  ∂ º » π ∫  Ω
   ¿  ∞ ÷ 0 1 2 3 4 5 6 7 8 9 A=a À=à Á=á Â=â Ã=ã Ä=ä Å=å Æ=æ B=b C
   =c Ç=ç D=d E=e È=è É=é Ê=ê Ë=ë F=f G=g H=h I=i Ì=ì Í=í Î=î Ï=ï J
   =j K=k L=l M=m N=n Ñ=ñ O=o Ò=ò Ó=ó Ô=ô Õ=õ Ö=ö Ø=ø P=p Q=q R=r S
   =s ß T=t U=u Ù=ù Ú=ú Û=û Ü=ü V=v W=w X=x Y=y ≈=∆ ÿ Z=z √=≤ ◊=
```

To compare the effect of case-insensitive (ASA or Microsoft in this set) versus case-sensitive character sets (ASE or Oracle), look at the output of the same
query on two different systems, as shown in Figure 2–1. The case-insensitive
collation ASA uses in this installation makes names sort according to the first
letter, ignoring case. The case-sensitive sort order Oracle uses shows uppercase
first, then lowercase.

Adaptive Server Anywhere

```
select fname
from customer
order by fname


fname
====================
(NULL)
 pete pete
 SAM
felipe
geoff lowell
kimiko
lauren
LI-REN
merit
Pete
phillip
ruby


[12 rows]
```

Oracle

```
SQL> select fname
  2   from customer
  3   order by fname;


FNAME
--------------------
 SAM
 pete pete
LI-REN
Pete
felipe
geoff lowell
kimiko
lauren
merit
phillip
ruby


12 rows selected.
```

Figure 2–1. Sort Order Differences

UPPER and LOWER in Searches

So how do the UPPER and LOWER functions come in? Their utility has something to do with your character set/collation setup.

Let's say you're looking for a customer whose name is Le Blanc—or is it le Blanc, LeBlanc, or Leblanc? Without case functions, you write a query as in Figure 2–2, with the percent sign wildcard (representing 0 or more characters) standing in for the possible space. Depending on the character set, you'd get a match—or not. (There's more on LIKE later in this chapter.)

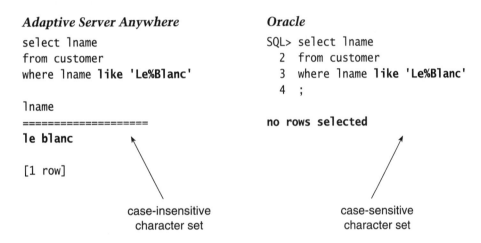

Figure 2-2. Sorting and Case

For a universal solution, try this variant, using UPPER on one side and an uppercase character on the other.

Adaptive Server Anywhere

```
select lname
from customer
where upper(lname) like '%P%'

lname
====================
mokoperto
Peters

[2 rows]
```

As long as the expression and character string are both uppercase (or lowercase), you'll always find the right answer, no matter what the character set. But what if you are matching two columns and aren't sure of the case of either? Here's where you use UPPER and/or LOWER in *two* places.

In this example, you're looking for a possible mistake: first names that are the same as or subsets of last names. Once you find them, a human eye will check the list and decide which are OK and which require further investigation.

The code instructs your SQL engine to find all customers whose last name consists of an unknown (possibly zero) number of characters followed by the first name and an unknown (possibly zero) number of characters. Notice the quotation marks: they enclose the wildcard ('%'), not the fname column. The double pipe (||) is the concatenation operator for slapping character expressions together. Table 2–1 lists variants.

Adaptive Server Anywhere

```
select fname, lname
from customer
where upper (lname) like '%' || upper(fname) || '%'
```

fname	lname
=======================	=======================
Pete	**Peters**
(NULL)	deathmask-z

[2 rows]

Why do you need two instances of UPPER for a complete solution? Because you're comparing the uppercase last name to an uppercase pattern. If only one element is uppercase, you can't count on a match.

Some systems may not return the deathmask-z row, depending on whether they handle the first name as a NULL or as an empty string. If the columns are fixed rather than variable character datatype, you'll need to trim the trailing blanks (see "Space" in this chapter)—except for ASA, which treats CHAR and VARCHAR data the same.

Where the concatenation sign is "+" rather than "||," use code like this:

Sybase Adaptive Server Enterprise

```
select fname, lname
from customer
where upper(lname) like '%' + upper(fname) + '%'
```

Table 2-1. Concatenation

ANSI	ASA	ASE	MS SQL Server	Oracle	Informix
char_expr || char_expr	char_expr + char_expr char_expr || char_expr STRING (char_expr, char_expr)	char_expr + char_expr	char_expr + char_expr	char_expr || char_expr CONCAT (char_expr , char_expr)	char_expr || char_expr

UPPER and LOWER in UPDATE

The case functions also let you modify data. For example, to change all state names to uppercase, use code like this:

Adaptive Server Anywhere
```
update customer
set state = upper (state)
```

```
[12 rows updated]
```

Now all state names are stored in uppercase letters. If you want to change only some of the data, add a WHERE clause.

Adaptive Server Anywhere
```
update customer
set state = lower (state)
where state = 'NY'
```

```
[3 rows updated]
```

```
select distinct state
from customer
```

```
state
=====
CA
MA
ny
MD
WA
TX

[6 rows]
```

Restore the state data to uppercase with another UPDATE statement.

Adaptive Server Anywhere

```
update customer
set state = upper(state)
where state <> upper(state)

[3 rows updated]
```

UPPER and LOWER with Dates

Some vendors allow you to use UPPER and LOWER on alphabetic elements in date columns.

Adaptive Server Anywhere

```
select ordnum, orderdate, lower ( orderdate )
from ordermaster
```

```
       ordnum orderdate          lower(ordermaster.orderdate)
    =========== ================= ============================
           81 Jan 02 1999 02:30 jan 02 1999 02:30
           85 Jan 02 1999 00:00 jan 02 1999 00:00
           86 Jan 02 1999 00:00 jan 02 1999 00:00
           87 Jan 02 1999 00:00 jan 02 1999 00:00
           89 Jan 02 1999 00:00 jan 02 1999 00:00
           90 Jan 02 1999 00:00 jan 02 1999 00:00
           91 Jan 02 1999 00:00 jan 02 1999 00:00
           92 Jan 02 1999 00:00 jan 02 1999 00:00
           93 Jan 05 1999 14:30 jan 05 1999 14:30
```

```
94 Jan 02 1999 00:00 jan 02 1999 00:00
95 Jan 03 1999 00:00 jan 03 1999 00:00
99 Jan 02 1999 00:00 jan 02 1999 00:00
```

[12 rows]

Other vendors require some kind of conversion of dates to character strings ("Dealing with Dates" in this chapter), or give an error when you use UPPER or LOWER with any string that contains numbers.

INITCAP

Some vendors support an INITCAP function that produces title-style strings (an initial capital letter in each separate word). Use it to display or correct character data that's been entered in the wrong case or in randomly mixed-case letters. Here's how a search for nontitle-style names looks on Oracle.

Oracle
```
SQL> select lname, initcap(lname)
  2  from customer
  3  where lname <> initcap(lname);
```

LNAME	INITCAP(LNAME)
McBaird	Mcbaird
archer	Archer
aziz	Aziz
le blanc	Le Blanc
sato	Sato
khandasamy	Khandasamy
deathmask-z	Deathmask-Z
mokoperto	Mokoperto
rs	Rs
WONG	Wong

```
10 rows selected.
```

If you're happy with these results, you can use INITCAP in an update and change your data to mixed case. Before you go too far with this, familiarize yourself with the function. How does it handle spaces, underbars, dots? Be sure

Table 2-2. Case Functions

ANSI	SQL Anywhere	SAE	MS SQL Server	Oracle	Informix
UPPER(expr) LOWER(expr)	UPPER(expr) LOWER(expr) UCASE(expr) LCASE(expr)	UPPER(expr) LOWER(expr)	UPPER(expr) LOWER(expr)	UPPER(expr) LOWER(expr)	UPPER(expr) LOWER(expr)
				INITCAP(expr)	INITCAP(expr)

you understand the ramifications. Notice, for example, how McBaird turns into Mcbaird, while le blanc becomes Le Blanc.

For information on UPPER, LOWER, and INITCAP, see Table 2–2.

Space

Unwanted spaces can sneak into data. The spaces can cause sort anomalies and make data hard to find. Most systems provide "trim" functions for removing leading and trailing spaces. Some also allow you to specify a character to trim. Let's say you're looking for a particular customer named "Sam."

Adaptive Server Anywhere

```
select custnum, fname
from customer
where upper(fname) = 'SAM'


custnum          fname
=============== ==============

[0 rows]
```

The query ought to work (you even took precautions on case), but it doesn't. Listing the customer names shows why. Sam's name has a leading space.

Adaptive Server Anywhere

```
select custnum, fname
from customer
order by fname
```

```
custnum    fname
========= ====================
777777777 (NULL)
776677778  pete pete
223456789  SAM
111334444 felipe
111222222 geoff lowell
111444444 kimiko
923457789 lauren
999456789 LI-REN
777777778 merit
776667778 Pete
776677778 pete pete
111333333 phillip
111223333 ruby

[12 rows]
```

Using a trim function, you can handle the spaces. Here, LTRIM removes left (leading) spaces. See Table 2–3 later in this chapter for a list of related functions.

Adaptive Server Anywhere
```
select custnum, fname
from customer
where ltrim(fname) = 'SAM'

custnum    fname
========= ====================
223456789  SAM

[1 row]
```

You can find all names beginning with a space or two with either of these pieces of code:

Adaptive Server Anywhere
```
select custnum, fname
from customer
where fname like ' %'
```

```
select custnum, fname
from customer
where fname <> ltrim(fname)

custnum    fname
=========  ====================
223456789  SAM
776677778  pete pete

[2 rows]
```

To show the order without spaces, be sure to use the function in the ORDER BY clause. You'll still see the leading space in the results, but the data will be properly sorted. To show the data without the space, put the trim function in both the SELECT list and the ORDER BY list.

Adaptive Server Anywhere
```
select fname
from customer
order by ltrim(fname)

fname
====================
(NULL)
felipe
geoff lowell
kimiko
lauren
LI-REN
merit
Pete
 pete pete
phillip
ruby
 SAM

[12 rows]
```

Removing Spaces

Using trim functions, you can remove spaces without even looking at them.

Adaptive Server Anywhere
```
update customer
set fname = ltrim(fname)
```

```
[2 rows updated]
```

A select shows the results.

Adaptive Server Anywhere
```
select fname, custnum
from customer
order by fname
```

```
fname                custnum
==================== =========
(NULL)               777777777
felipe               111334444
geoff lowell         111222222
kimiko               111444444
lauren               923457789
LI-REN               999456789
merit                777777778
Pete                 776667778
pete pete            776677778
phillip              111333333
ruby                 111223333
SAM                  223456789
```

```
[12 rows]
```

Subsequent chapters assume you have removed leading blanks from customer.fname. Trailing blanks are less of a problem, but you can get rid of them in the same way, using a function that trims right (trailing) spaces. Here it is called RTRIM. To trim right and left blanks at the same time, nest the functions:

Adaptive Server Anywhere

```
update customer
set fname = ltrim(rtrim (fname) )
```

Adaptive Server Anywhere allows you to remove both right and left spaces at once with another function, called TRIM.

Adaptive Server Anywhere

```
update customer
set fname = trim(fname)
```

Additional Features

Some vendors offer more trim bells and whistles. Informix provides a TRIM function that allows you to remove characters as well as spaces from your choice of three positions (LEADING, TRAILING, or BOTH). ANSI syntax also supports this capability. Oracle keeps the LTRIM and RTRIM structures but trims more than spaces. For a comparison of trim functions, see Table 2–3.

The following examples produce the same results—they remove leading "1" from product versions. All the "release one" products are going to be withdrawn from the market pending more testing.

Informix

```
select name, version, trim (leading '1' from version)
from product
where version not like '10%'
```

Table 2-3. Trim Functions

ANSI	ASA	ASE	MS SQL Server	Oracle	Informix
TRIM ([LEADING | TRAILING | BOTH] ['char'] FROM expr)					TRIM ([LEADING | TRAILING | BOTH] ['char'] FROM expr)
	TRIM (expr) LTRIM (expr)	LTRIM (expr)	LTRIM (expr)	LTRIM (expr [set])	
	RTRIM (expr)	RTRIM(expr)	RTRIM (expr)	RTRIM (expr [set])	

Oracle

```
SQL> select name, version, ltrim (version, '1')
  2    from product
  3    where version not like '10%';

NAME                    VERSION  LTRIM(VE
----------------------  -------- --------
cook & book             Super 6. Super 6.
memory tripler          6.5_a    6.5_a
home poll kit           Super 6. Super 6.
star systems            Super 6. Super 6.
memory8                 6.5_a    6.5_a
money master            1.2      .2
C++ for kids            1.1      .1
bug stories             2.2      2.2
nt guru                 2.2      2.2
landlord logs           1.3      .3
z_connector             1.1      .1

11 rows selected.
```

Oracle allows you to trim sets of characters. The following code trims leading 1, 10, or 0.

Oracle

```
SQL> select name, version, ltrim (version, '10')
  2    from product
  3    where version like '1%';

NAME                    VERSION  LTRIM(VE
----------------------  -------- --------
paper dolls             10.1.01  .1.01
more paper dolls        10.1.01  .1.01
memory manager          10.1_6.5 .1_6.5
money master            1.2      .2
C++ for kids            1.1      .1
how multi is media?     10.1     .1
landlord logs           1.3      .3
z_connector             1.1      .1

8 rows selected.
```

Table 2–4. LENGTH Functions

ANSI	ASA	ASE	MS SQL Server	Oracle	Informix
CHARacter_LENGTH (expr)	LENGTH (expr) DATALENGTH (expr) CHAR_LENGTH (expr)	DATALENGTH (expr) CHAR_LENGTH (expr)	LEN(expr) DATALENGTH (expr)	LENGTH (expr)	LENGTH (expr) CHAR_LENGTH (expr)
	COL_LENGTH ('table', 'column')	COL_LENGTH ('table', 'column')	COL_LENGTH ('table', 'column')		

Size

Most vendors provide a way to find out the length of a variable character expression. Not every vendor uses the same name (or produces precisely the same results—see Table 2–4 for a listing of functions that find actual and defined size). ANSI also includes OCTET_LENGTH and BIT_LENGTH functions, and some systems support these functions or variants.

The size functions let you find items that are unusually small for their columns (and so, perhaps, are errors) and columns that are oversized for data they hold.

Actual Size

For dirty data searches, use the capability in the WHERE clause when looking for strings that are unreasonably short. To get the results shown here, you may need to remove leading blanks, if you haven't done it yet. Try nesting a left trim function (whatever it is called in your system—see Figure 2–3 later in this chapter) inside the function that reports on data length.

Adaptive Server Anywhere
```
select fname
from customer
where length (fname) <=3
```

```
fname
====================
SAM

[1 row]
```

To find null names as well as short ones, add IS NULL.

Adaptive Server Anywhere

```
select fname
from customer
where length (fname) <=3 or fname is null

fname
====================
SAM
(NULL)

[2 rows]
```

LENGTH (or its equivalent) works with complex expressions, too. Here, the SQL programmer needs a sample of names to print on labels and decides to pick just short names (where first and last names together take up fewer than 15 characters).

Adaptive Server Anywhere

```
select 'My name is ' || upper(fname)
from customer
where length ('My name is' || fname) <15

'My name is ' || upper(custom
==============================
My name is SAM
My name is PETE
My name is RUBY
My name is

[4 rows]
```

You may need to trim trailing blanks (previous section) when you use LENGTH with fixed character datatype columns. You should also check how the length function in your system handles null values and and noncharacter data. Refer to Table 2–1 for variations on the double-pipe concatenation symbol.

Defined Size

A related issue is how the defined size of the column and the amount of data it actually holds compare. Are columns too large? Has the data changed since your tables were designed?

You can get the defined size of the column (as opposed to the actual size) from a system function, if one is available, or from system tables or views (see "Getting Meta-Data from System Catalogs" in Chapter 7) or from graphical tools. Adaptive Server Anywhere and Transact-SQL dialects support a function called COL_LENGTH (Table 2–4). It takes the table name and column name in quotes as arguments, and returns the defined size (the one used in CREATE TABLE).

To find the difference in the defined size of a column and the largest amount of data in the column, try something like this, putting the size function inside a MAX:

Adaptive Server Anywhere
```
select col_length ('customer', 'fname') as Defined,
  max( length (fname )) as Actual
from customer
```

```
   Defined      Actual
=========== ===========
        20          12
```

[1 row]

You could even subtract one from the other to get the difference.

Adaptive Server Anywhere

```
select col_length ('customer', 'fname') as Defined,
 max (length (fname ) ) as Actual,
  col_length ('customer', 'fname') - max (length (fname ) ) as Diff
from customer
```

Defined	Actual	**Diff**
20	12	**8**

[1 row]

These numbers are not bad, but if you were to find a column defined with a size of 200 and the largest actual size in a nontrivial data set were 19, you might want to consider making some changes.

Matching Patterns

LIKE, a SQL keyword rather than a function, is a handy tool for finding matches to a pattern in a string. Its implementation varies little from system to system. LIKE works with two wildcards:

- % (percent sign) represents 0 or more unknown characters.
- _ (underbar) represents 1 unknown character.

For example, to find all products with "paper" in the name, use a query like this:

Adaptive Server Anywhere

```
select name, description
from product
where name like '%paper%'
```

name	description
paper dolls	create & dress dolls
more **paper** dolls	create & dress dolls

[2 rows]

Without the initial wildcard, the code would find only the first row. LIKE has some performance implications, described in "Matching with LIKE" in Chapter 6.

To find customer names for customer numbers with blurry values in positions 4 and 5, try this:

Adaptive Server Anywhere

```
select  fname, custnum
from customer
where custnum like '111__3333'

fname                 custnum
==================== =========
ruby                 111223333
phillip              111333333

[2 rows]
```

Quoting Wildcards with ESCAPE

To treat the wildcard as a simple character with no "magic" meaning, use ESCAPE to designate a quotation mark to put in front of the wildcard (here, the quote is a backslash, but it could be anything not used in the search pattern).

Adaptive Server Anywhere

```
select prodnum, name, description
from product
where description like '%\%%' escape '\'

   prodnum name                 description
========== ==================== ==================================
      2111 memory tripler       50% or more

[1 row]
```

LIKE Variants

Informix supports ESCAPE and, in addition, proves the backslash as a built-in quote character for LIKE. The following code is interchangeable with the previous example starring ESCAPE.

Informix

```
select prodnum, name, description
from product
where description like '%\%%'
```

Informix also provides a variant of LIKE called MATCHES. It functions the same way, but it uses a different set of wildcards (* for zero or more characters, ? for any single character, and square brackets for sets and ranges). A search for product names beginning with the letters a through b looks like this:

Informix

```
select prodnum, name, description
from product
where name matches '[a-b]*'
```

Transact-SQL and ASA provide range and set extensions to LIKE with brackets but do not use * and ? as wildcards. The equivalent code looks like this:

Adaptive Server Anywhere

```
select prodnum, name, description
from product
where name like '[a-b]%'
```

prodnum	name	description
2113	bugbane	(NULL)
1108	blood & guts	(NULL)
1255	bug stories	(NULL)

[3 rows]

All these systems with the bracket LIKE variants allow the caret (^) as a negative inside the square brackets. Here's the Informix code for finding lowercase product names *not* in the range a through s.

Informix

```
select prodnum, name, description
from product
where lower(name) matches '[^a-s]*'
```

Table 2-5. LIKE and MATCHES

ANSI	ASA	ASE	MS SQL Server	Oracle	Informix
LIKE %, _	LIKE %, _, [abc], [a-c], [^abc], [^a-c]	LIKE %, _, [abc], [a-c], [^abc], [^a-c]	LIKE %, _, [abc], [a-c], [^abc], [^a-c]	LIKE %, _	LIKE %, _
ESCAPE 'x'	ESCAPE 'x'	ESCAPE 'x'	ESCAPE 'x'	ESCAPE 'x'	ESCAPE 'x' /
					MATCHES *, ?, [abc], [a-c], [^abc], [^a-c]

The equivalent in Transact-SQL and ASA looks like this (the results are the same on all systems):

Adaptive Server Anywhere
```
select prodnum, name, description
from product
where lower( name) like '[^a-s]%'
```

```
    prodnum name                 description
========== ==================== =================================================
      2050 tax time             1995 edition
      1099 typing test          (NULL)
      1104 teach yourself greek (NULL)
      1106 z_connector          (NULL)
```

[4 rows]

Table 2–5 is a summary of LIKE variants.

Datatypes and LIKE

LIKE works with character expressions on all systems. Check your system to see if it works with date or numeric expressions. Our sample system handles the following query:

Adaptive Server Anywhere

```
select prodnum, name, price
from product
where price like '%.00'
```

```
    prodnum name                      price
=========== ===================== ==========
       2113 bugbane                   49.00
       1794 memory8                  400.00
       1083 money master              29.00
       1255 bug stories               20.00
       1357 nt guru                   20.00
       1457 how multi is media?       20.00
       1106 z_connector              149.00
```

```
[7 rows]
```

Other systems may give an error.

Microsoft SQL Server

```
Server: Msg 257, Level 16, State 3, Line 1
Implicit conversion from data type money to varchar is not allowed.
Use the CONVERT function to run this query.
```

Locating Patterns

Most vendors have a function that reports the *position* of one string inside another. ANSI calls it POSITION, but vendors use a wide variety of names. For a list, see Table 2–6. Whatever its name, the function tells you two things:

- Whether or not the match expression exists
- Where the match expression is

Because it returns a number that tells you where one expression starts inside another, you can use this function to find a pattern (as LIKE does) and pass on the location of the pattern to another function.

Table 2-6. String in String

ANSI	ASA	ASE	MS SQL Server	Oracle	Informix
POSITION	LOCATE CHARINDEX	CHARINDEX	CHARINDEX	INSTR	

How LOCATE Works

Because LOCATE is complex, let's go through it step by step. The first few examples don't have much real-world use, they just illustrate how the function works in isolation. Later examples show LOCATE used as an argument to another function, which is its real strength. The following query finds the location of the first occurrence of "45" in the empnum column. The results show two hits.

Adaptive Server Anywhere

```
select fname, empnum, locate (empnum, '45')
from employee
```

```
fname                    empnum      locate(employee.empnum,'45')
====================  =========  =============================
Hamid                    123232345                              8
laurna                   223232366                              0
ruby                     111223333                              0
lauren                   923457789                              4
Bill                     222222221                              0
Scorley                  443232366                              0

[6 rows]
```

If you want to find employees with 45 somewhere in their employee numbers, use LIKE. If you know the first occurrence is somewhere in the second half of the number (but you're not sure where) you could use code like this:

Adaptive Server Anywhere

```
select fname, empnum
from employee
where locate (empnum, '45') > 3
```

```
fname                    empnum
==================== =========
Hamid                    123232345
lauren                   923457789

[2 rows]
```

Using LOCATE Functions

Because it finds a string inside another string and returns its location as a number, LOCATE (by any name) is useful as input to other functions. The code in this section uses LOCATE as the START argument of SUBSTR (or SUBSTRING). Before looking at the LOCATE-SUBSTR code, give SUBSTR a glance.

Choosing a Subset Usually called SUBSTRING or SUBSTR, this useful character function gives you access to a subset of a character column. It takes three arguments: the expression, the start of the substring, and the size of the substring. See Table 2–7 for a list of variants. Notice that Informix supports three versions.

When you're experimenting with substring functions, check to see whether your system allows an optional third argument. If no third argument is required and you leave it out, the SQL engine displays all characters after the start value. Systems that can do without the third argument may accept a negative second argument as instruction to count backward from the end of the expression for that number of characters.

Table 2–7. Substring Functions

ANSI	ASA	ASE	MS SQL Server	Oracle	Informix
SUBSTRING (char_expr FROM start [FOR size])					SUBSTRING (char_expr FROM start FOR size)
	SUBSTR (char_expr, start [, size])			SUBSTR (char_expr, start [, size])	SUBSTR (char_expr, start [, size])
	SUBSTRING (char_expr, start, size)	SUBSTRING (char_expr, start, size)	SUBSTRING (char_expr, start, size)		
					char_expr [start, end]

For example, you want to use the last four digits of each employee number as the employee's default key code for the new electronic locks. Here are three ways you could get the number (the second and third versions require an optional last argument):

- By starting at character 6 of the expression and going forward four characters
- By starting at character 6 of the expression and retrieving all following characters
- By starting at the end of the expression and going backward four characters

Adaptive Server Anywhere

```
select fname, empnum,
    substr (empnum, 6, 4) as ThreeArgs,
    substr (empnum, 6   ) as CountFwd,
    substr (empnum, -4  ) as CountBack
from employee
```

fname	empnum	ThreeArgs	CountFwd	CountBack
=======	========	===========	==========	===========
Hamid	123232345	2345	2345	2345
laurna	223232366	2366	2366	2366
ruby	111223333	3333	3333	3333
lauren	923457789	7789	7789	7789
Bill	222222221	2221	2221	2221
Scorley	443232366	2366	2366	2366

[6 rows]

Another variation in substring functions is the meaning of a zero (0) starting position. Most systems treat 0 and 1 the same: both mean "start from the first character." Transact-SQL does not. Instead, it interprets 0 as "don't start the substring" and 1 as "start from the first character." This can be important in using point functions (more about this in "Getting CASE Effects from Multiple Functions" in Chapter 3).

Changing Data with LOCATE and SUBSTR   Here's an example of using LOCATE as an argument to SUBSTR (Figure 2–3). You need to substitute the word "and" for every ampersand ("&") you find in product names—special characters aren't allowed. Start by testing your logic in a SELECT. When you get the results you want, use an UPDATE to make the changes.

```
select name,
   substr (name, 1, locate( name, '&')-1)        name before '&'
            || 'and' ||
   substr (name, locate( name, '&') +1)
from product                                       name after '&'
where name like '%&%'
```

name	substr("name",1,locate("name"
cook & book	cook **and** book
blood & guts	blood **and** guts

[2 rows]

Figure 2-3. Using LOCATE to Change Text

1. Use LOCATE to find the &. Then use the value of the ampersand loca-
    tion –1 as the SIZE parameter of a SUBSTR. Specify 1 as the START
    value. That translates as "start at the first character and stop at 1 charac-
    ter before the &."

2. In the same way, use the location of the ampersand as the START value
    of another SUBSTR.

3. Concatenate the two strings together, with "and" between them.

To change your data, translate the SELECT into an UPDATE—and don't forget the WHERE clause. If you want to make the change reversible, run a BEGIN
TRAN before the UPDATE and do a ROLLBACK after you check your results
(more on these commands in "Experimenting and Transaction Management"
in Appendix A).

Adaptive Server Anywhere

begin tran;

```
update product
set name = substr (name, 1, locate( name, '&')-1) || 'and'
   || substr (name, locate( name, '&') +1)
where name like '%&%'
```

[2 rows updated]

```
select name
from product
where name like '% and%'

name
====================
cook and book
blood and guts

[2 rows]

rollback

select name
from product
where name like '% and%' or name like '%&%'

name
====================
cook & book
blood & guts

[2 rows]
```

Notice that the LOCATE finds the first &. If there were more than one, you'd have to run the code multiple times. The Oracle version of this function (INSTR) takes four arguments and allows you to specify a starting point and occurrence number, so that you could look for a character in positions four to ten, or the third occurrence of a character.

Sounds Like . . .

Some RDBMSs support a function called SOUNDEX. It returns a value representing the consonant sounds in a word, and it is very handy for finding a person when you know how the name is pronounced but not how it is spelled. It can also get you over case problems—the sound is the same, whether spelled with uppercase, lowercase, or mixed-case letters.

On Adaptive Server Anywhere, SOUNDEX returns a number based on the first letter and the next three consonants (except H, Y, and W). Double consonants are counted as single consonants. In the following example, SOUNDEX translates five names with different spellings (but probably similar pronunciation) into the same numeric value.

Adaptive Server Anywhere

```
select soundex('loren') as loren, soundex('laurin') as laurin,
    soundex('lawrren') as lawrren, soundex('li-ren') as "li-ren",
    soundex('la hran') as "la hran"

 loren laurin lawrren li-ren la hran
====== ====== ======= ====== =======
  5996   5996    5996   5996    5996
```

[1 row]

In other systems, SOUNDEX produces a string of one letter and three numbers. The letter is the first letter in the expression. The numbers represent the first three consonants after that letter.

Joe Celko, in *SQL for Smarties* (Morgan Kaufmann, 1995), explains the original SOUNDEX algorithm, patented in 1918, like this:

1. Take the first letter of the word (vowel or consonant).

2. Ignoring all following vowels and counting double letters (tt) only once (t), assign values to the next three consonant sounds as follows:

   - BPV (bilabial sounds) = 1
   - CGJKQSXZ (labiodental) = 2
   - DT (dental) = 3
   - L (alveolar) = 4
   - MN (velar) = 5
   - R (glottal) = 6

3. Stop at four characters in your code (one letter, three numbers) or add zeros at the end if you don't have four characters.

Here's the Oracle query and results for the Loren query (using the dummy table dual, since Oracle does not allow queries without a FROM clause).

Oracle
```
SQL> select soundex('loren') as loren, soundex('laurin') as laurin,
  2        soundex('lawrren') as lawrren, soundex('li-ren') as "li-ren",
  3        soundex('la hran') as "la hran"
  4  from dual;

LORE LAUR LAWR li-r la h
---- ---- ---- ---- ----
L650 L650 L650 L650 L650
```

Some systems handle spaces and nonalphabetic characters differently. Run a few experiments—you may see a value other than L650 for li-ren and la hran.

So what do you do with this function? Well, suppose you need to find an employee called something like "Micbirdy." You can't find a match, so you decide to try to go by the sound using SOUNDEX, and you write code like this:

Adaptive Server Anywhere
```
select fname, lname
from customer
where soundex (lname) = soundex ('micbirdy')
```

fname	lname
==================	====================
geoff lowell	McBaird
merit	mokoperto

```
[2 rows]
```

Now you have two possibilities for Micbirdy.

But watch out for pairs such as Sheryl and Cheryl, Jeff and Geoff, Karl and Carl. The different initial letters will make the SOUNDEX values nonmatches, even though the pronunciation is identical.

Your system may support additional sound-oriented functions. Transact-SQL and Adaptive Server Anywhere boast DIFFERENCE for comparing the SOUNDEX values of two strings (a difference of 4 means that the strings have the same SOUNDEX value; a difference of 1 means that they are not at all alike) and ASA has an additional function called SIMILAR, discussed in "Finding Near-Duplicates" in Chapter 4.

Table 2-8. Matching Sounds

ANSI	ASA	ASE	MS SQL Server	Oracle	Informix
	SOUNDEX	SOUNDEX	SOUNDEX	SOUNDEX	
	DIFFERENCE	DIFFERENCE	DIFFERENCE		
	SIMILAR				

Adaptive Server Anywhere

```
select fname
from customer
where difference (fname, 'lorna') >=3
```

```
fname
=====================
LI-REN
lauren
```

```
[2 rows]
```

Table 2–8 lists the sound functions. (SQL-1999 has a SIMILAR predicate, but it is not the same as ASA SIMILAR.)

BETWEEN

NOT BETWEEN is a good choice for finding items that are out of range. The first value must be less than the second one or no rows are returned.

Adaptive Server Anywhere

```
select *
from orderdetail
where unit not between 1 and 25
```

```
      ordnum    prodnum    unit shipdate
   =========== =========== ====== ==========
           99       2050    2222 (NULL)
           92       2050    3333 (NULL)
```

```
[2 rows]
```

You might want to compare the unit values in this out-of-range query with the average unit value.

Adaptive Server Anywhere
```
select avg(unit)
from orderdetail
where unit between 1 and 25
```
```
avg(orderdetail.unit)
=====================
                 4.81
```

Dealing with Dates

Dates are often troublesome just because their storage and display can be quite different. In addition, the date functions vary a lot from system to system. This section covers three areas: using convert functions on dates, doing math on dates, and matching dates. (The first two topics are tools you can use for the third.) Here's where to look for other date information:

- System functions for retrieving the current date are in "Finding Today's Date" in Chapter 7.
- Commands for setting the default date format are in "Defining Default Date Format" in Appendix B.

Converting Dates (and Other Datatypes)

Here's a place where knowing one system isn't much help with another. Every SQL engine provides ways to translate one datatype to another, but the commands, models, and methods are quite different. There are three possibilities among the systems used in this book:

- General-purpose CONVERT or CAST function for all possible conversions
- Specific functions for particular conversions, with names like TO_CHAR or TO_DATE or TO_NUM
- Combinations of general and specific convert functions

Table 2–9 shows examples of convert functions (specifically those used with character/date data) but not all possibilities. Oracle, for example, supports

Table 2-9. CAST/Convert

ANSI	ASA	ASE	MS SQL Server	Oracle	Informix
CAST (expr AS [datatype | domain])	CAST (expr AS datatype)		CAST (expr AS datatype)		CAST expr AS datatype
	CONVERT (target datatype, expr [, datestyle])	CONVERT (target datatype, expr [, datestyle])	CONVERT (target datatype. expr [,datestyle])		expr :: datatype
	DATEFORMAT (expr, 'pattern')			TO_CHAR (expr, 'format'))	TO_CHAR (expr, 'format')
				TO_DATE (char_expr, 'format')	TO_DATE (char_expr, 'format')
	DATE ('expr')				DATE ('expr')

many special functions: CHARTOROWID, ROWIDTOCHAR, HEXTORAW, RAWTOHEX, TO_NUMBER, and more.

As if the difference in convert function names and scope were not confusing enough, there is also the question of autoconversion. Some systems allow you to use character functions with numeric expressions. Others require an explicit conversion, as shown in Figure 2–4, where one system allows concatenation of an integer and date value and another insists on conversion before concatenation.

Doing Math on Dates

All systems offer ways to add and subtract units of time, but there is a great deal of variety in method. If you're not sure how your system handles date math, start out by looking for a list of date functions (Table B–4 gathers all the date functions together).

Just as an example, here's how you add five days to a date column in two different systems. Transact-SQL (and Adaptive Server Anywhere) has a consistent model. You specify the unit (days are DD, months MM, weeks WK, and so on), the number of units, and the expression you are changing.

Adaptive Server Anywhere

```
select orderdate, dateadd (dd, 5, orderdate) as newdate
from ordermaster
```

Adaptive Server Anywhere

```
select ordnum ||
     ': '|| orderdate
from ordermaster
where ordnum < 90
```

Microsoft SQL Server

```
select cast (ordnum as char(2)) +
     ': ' + cast (orderdate as char (19) )
from ordermaster
where ordnum <90
```

Some systems require
conversions to use
noncharacter data with
character functions.

```
ordermaster.ordnum || ': ' ||
==============================
81: Jan 02 1999 02:30:00
85: Jan 02 1999 12:00:00
86: Jan 02 1999 12:00:00
87: Jan 02 1999 12:00:00
89: Jan 02 1999 12:00:00

[5 rows]
```

Figure 2-4. Conversions

Oracle uses a different model, making it very easy to add or subtract days (days are the default unit—other units have special syntax). Microsoft SQL Server and Adaptive Server Anywhere also can add and subtract days this way.

Oracle

```
SQL> select orderdate, orderdate + 5 as newdate
  2  from ordermaster;
```

Both queries return the same results, although the format varies. These results are produced by Oracle.

Oracle

```
ORDERDATE NEWDATE
--------- ---------
02-JAN-99 07-JAN-99
02-JAN-99 07-JAN-99
02-JAN-99 07-JAN-99
02-JAN-99 07-JAN-99
02-JAN-99 07-JAN-99
02-JAN-99 07-JAN-99
02-JAN-99 07-JAN-99
```

```
02-JAN-99 07-JAN-99
02-JAN-99 07-JAN-99
05-JAN-99 10-JAN-99
03-JAN-99 08-JAN-99
02-JAN-99 07-JAN-99

12 rows selected.
```

If the date you want to do math on is a string, rather than a column, Oracle requires a TO_DATE conversion. Specify the date string in the current default format so that the engine knows how to interpret it. (Use the Oracle dummy table dual for queries that don't need to get data from existing tables.)

Oracle
```
SQL> select to_date ('14-SEP-99') +8
  2  from dual;

TO_DATE('
---------
22-SEP-99

1 row selected.
```

Transact-SQL offers the same model it used for adding days to orderdate. In this case, the expression is a string, so it is enclosed in quotation marks.

Adaptive Server Anywhere
```
select dateadd (dd, 8, 'Sep 14 1999')

dateadd(dd,8,'Sep 14 1999')
===========================
Sep 22 1999 12:00:00

[1 row]
```

Check your manuals for details on date functions. Table 2–10 summarizes the functions discussed here.

Table 2-10. Date Functions

ANSI	ASA	ASE	MS SQL Server	Oracle	Informix
date_expr + INTERVAL n unit date_expr - INTERVAL n unit	date_expr + n date_expr - n DATEADD DATEDIFF	DATEADD DATEDIFF	date_expr + n date_expr - n DATEADD DATEDIFF	date_expr + n date_expr - n MONTHS_BETWEEN	date_expr + INTERVAL n unit date_expr - INTERVAL n unit
INTERVAL date_expr unit	DAY MONTH YEAR DATENAME DATEPART	DATENAME DATEPART	DAY MONTH YEAR DATENAME DATEPART	TO_CHAR	DAY WEEKDAY MONTH YEAR TO_CHAR

Finding Dates

A problem that comes up all the time for new and not-so-new SQL users is how to match dates. Since you can display dates in many formats, it's easy to forget how they are stored and to try to retrieve them using a display format.

The order dates in the ordermaster table are defined as TIMESTAMP datatype. For contrast, orderdetail.shipdate information is stored as DATE datatype. You can set the display of month, day, and year to a wide variety of formats.

Adaptive Server Anywhere

```
set option dba.timestamp_format = 'Mmm dd yyyy';
set option public.timestamp_format = 'Mmm dd yyyy';
set option dba.date_format = 'Mmm dd yyyy';
set option public.date_format = 'Mmm dd yyyy';
```

There is more on setting date display formats in "Defining Default Date Format" in Appendix B.

Here are the dates in ordermaster, after the SET OPTION command changes the format.

Adaptive Server Anywhere
```
select orderdate
from ordermaster
order by orderdate

orderdate
===========
Jan 02 1999
Jan 02 1999
Jan 02 1999
Jan 02 1999
Jan 02 1999
Jan 02 1999
Jan 02 1999
Jan 02 1999
Jan 02 1999
Jan 02 1999
Jan 03 1999
Jan 05 1999

[12 rows]
```

However, if you query based on this data, you might get no results.

Adaptive Server Anywhere
```
select ordnum
from ordermaster
where orderdate = 'Jan 05 1999'

[no rows]
```

The same query, with data from a different row, works fine. What's going on?

Adaptive Server Anywhere
```
select ordnum
from ordermaster
where orderdate = 'Jan 03 1999'

     ordnum
===========
         95

[1 row]
```

The display is the culprit. Although it looks as if the dates include only day, month, and year, there's actually a time element, too. You can use the ASA DATEFORMAT function (Table 2–9) to specify the date display format you want. Here you add hours (HH), minutes (NN), and A.M./P.M. marking (AA) to your format string.

Adaptive Server Anywhere

```
select ordnum ,orderdate,  dateformat (orderdate, 'Mmm DD YYYY HH:NN AA')
from ordermaster
order by orderdate
```

```
    ordnum orderdate   dateformat(ordermaster.orderd
=========== =========== =============================
        85 Jan 02 1999 Jan 02 1999 12:00 AM
        86 Jan 02 1999 Jan 02 1999 12:00 AM
        87 Jan 02 1999 Jan 02 1999 12:00 AM
        89 Jan 02 1999 Jan 02 1999 12:00 AM
        90 Jan 02 1999 Jan 02 1999 12:00 AM
        91 Jan 02 1999 Jan 02 1999 12:00 AM
        92 Jan 02 1999 Jan 02 1999 12:00 AM
        94 Jan 02 1999 Jan 02 1999 12:00 AM
        99 Jan 02 1999 Jan 02 1999 12:00 AM
        81 Jan 02 1999 Jan 02 1999 02:30 AM
        95 Jan 03 1999 Jan 03 1999 12:00 AM
        93 Jan 05 1999 Jan 05 1999 02:30 PM
```

[12 rows]

Oracle TO_CHAR is much the same, though the format elements are slightly different:

```
SQL> select ordnum, orderdate, to_char (orderdate, 'Mon DD YYYY hh:miAM')
  2  from ordermaster
  3    where ordnum = 93;

  ORDNUM ORDERDATE TO_CHAR(ORDERDATE,'
--------- --------- -------------------
       93 05-JAN-99 Jan 05 1999 02:30PM
```

1 row selected.

You can also use the CONVERT function, which ASA and Transact-SQL support, to view the complete date-time combination. Specify CHAR as the target datatype, and choose a date style (here 109—see the product documentation for a list of possibilities) that produces the format you want.

Adaptive Server Anywhere

```
select ordnum, orderdate, convert(char(20), orderdate, 109)
from ordermaster
where ordnum = 93
```

```
    ordnum orderdate    orderdate
=========== =========== ====================
         93 Jan 05 1999 jan 05 1999 02:30PM
```

[1 row]

When you don't specify a time, the SQL engine assumes a default time. It allows you to retrieve dates specifying only month, day, and year, as long as the time is the default. Once the time varies from the default, you have to use more sophisticated techniques to retrieve the data.

Entering Date Data   First, though, here are some examples of entering dates of this sort, offered only because they are quite different from each other semantically.

Oracle

```
SQL> update ordermaster
  2  set orderdate = to_date ('05-JAN-1999 02:30PM', 'DD-MON-YYYY HH:MIPM')
  3  where ordnum = 93;
```

In Oracle, the first argument is the character string you want to enter as a date. The second argument is the format. It determines not how the date is displayed, just how the string is interpreted. If the character expression is in the current date format, you can get by without the second argument.

Transact-SQL offers a simpler method.

Transact-SQL

```
update ordermaster
set orderdate ='jan 05 1999 02:30PM'
where ordnum = 93
```

Four Solutions   Once you understand the problem in retrieving date data (the hidden time information), the solution becomes easy.

- Use a BETWEEN.
- Use a LIKE.
- Use date functions.
- Convert the dates before comparing stored dates to a literal (character string) date.

BETWEEN   The BETWEEN query finds dates in a range. The only thing you need to check if you are running this query on a different system is the date format. Your system may require the date to be in the default format.

Adaptive Server Anywhere

```
select ordnum, orderdate
from ordermaster
where orderdate  between  'Jan 05 1995'  and  'Jan 06 1995'
```

LIKE   The LIKE query allows you to match the part of the pattern you know and use a wildcard (%) for the part you do not know. Here again, you may need to change the date format to match your system's default date format, and you may need to convert the date to a character format if your system does not support LIKE with dates.

Adaptive Server Anywhere

```
select ordnum, orderdate
from ordermaster
where orderdate like 'Jan 05 1995%'
```

Date Functions   The date function approach varies considerably from system to system, depending on which date functions are available. In this example, you use DATEPART to match the month number (MM) and day (DD). However, these are not ANSI standard functions. Expect to see a lot of variety among vendors for awhile.

Adaptive Server Anywhere

```
select ordnum, orderdate
from ordermaster
where datepart (MM, orderdate) = 1 and datepart (DD, orderdate) = 5
```

Informix functions do much the same but in a different format. The function specifies the date unit (month, day, year, and so on). ASA supports some of the same code. The following example runs on both ASA and Informix.

Informix and Adaptive Server Anywhere

```
select ordnum, orderdate
from ordermaster
where month(orderdate) = 1 and day(orderdate) = 5 and year(orderdate) = 1999
```

Oracle and Informix both use TO_CHAR to convert orderdate to a character string in order to compare it to a value. The function can extract date parts by specifying a date unit in the WHERE clause. The first argument is the date expression and the second is the date format.

Notice the difference in the second argument. Although the name and scope of TO_CHAR are the same, Oracle and Informix have different format elements—another illustration of how tricky date functions can be.

Oracle

```
SQL> select ordnum, orderdate
   2  from ordermaster
   3  where to_char (orderdate, 'yyyy') = '1995'
   4  and to_char  (orderdate, 'mm') = '01'
   5  and to_char (orderdate, 'dd') = '05';
```

Informix

```
select ordnum, orderdate
from ordermaster
where to_char (orderdate, '%Y') = '1995'
    and to_char (orderdate, '%d') = '05'
    and to_char (orderdate, '%m') = '01'
```

Conversions Finally, you can convert the date to a character string. How you do this depends on the conversion functions available to you (Table 2–9). On our demo system, you can use this code:

Adaptive Server Anywhere

```
select ordnum, orderdate
from ordermaster
where dateformat (orderdate, 'Mmm DD YYYY') = 'Jan 05 1995'
```

The Oracle and Informix TO_CHAR also work fine here. Instead of matching individual elements, go for a full date. Remember that Informix TO_CHAR is not identical to Oracle's.

Oracle

```
SQL>  select ordnum, orderdate
   2    from ordermaster
   3    where to_char (orderdate, 'DD Mon yyyy') = '05 Jan 1995';
```

All four methods (BETWEEN, LIKE, date functions, and conversions) return the same results:

> ***Adaptive Server Anywhere***
> ```
>       ordnum orderdate
> =========== ===========
>          93 Jan 05 1995
> ```

[1 row]

For consistency with result listings in other chapters, set ordermaster.orderdate back to its original format.

> ***Adaptive Server Anywhere***
> ```
> set option dba.timestamp_format = 'Mmm dd yyyy HH:NN:SS pp'
> ```

Summary

This chapter focuses on finding and fixing bad data.

- Case functions include UPPER, LOWER (UCASE/LCASE for ASA), and INITCAP. Use these functions in the WHERE clause of a SELECT to find inconsistent data. In an UPDATE, use them to change case.
- Space functions are the various trim functions, usually called LTRIM, RTRIM, and TRIM. They give you the ability to delete leading and trailing spaces. In some cases, you can do the same with other characters.
- LIKE is a SQL keyword (predicate) rather than a function, designed to find data that matches a pattern. Some vendors offer wildcard extensions, but the core set of % (zero or more unknown characters) and _ (one unknown character) is widely supported.

- POSITION (or INSTR or CHARINDEX or . . .) may be the SQL function with the largest number of name variants and concomitant syntax variants. It finds a pattern and tells you where the pattern is in the expression. The function, unlike LIKE, does not use wildcards.
- SOUNDEX helps you find a name (or some other character expression) when you know how it sounds but aren't sure how it is spelled. There are some differences among systems that support this function, so test before you port.
- NOT BETWEEN is also a SQL predicate, rather than a function. It is widely and consistently supported.
- Dates can be scary because of possible differences in the way they are displayed and stored. You can query for dates you know are there and fail to find them. Actually, once you understand the problem and pick up a few date functions, the solution is quite easy.

Chapter 3

Translating Values

In This Chapter

- CASE/DECODE
- Handling NULL
- Point Functions
- UNION
- Joins and Outer Joins
- Subqueries
- TRANSLATE: Another Conditional Expression

Why Translate?

Translation improves the readability of results, displaying an easy-to-understand string of characters in place of an obscure code. Let's say that the `customer.status` column holds a one-character code that summarizes the customer's credit history with your company. Your results may be in a different order.

Adaptive Server Anywhere

```
select fname, lname, status
from customer
```

fname	lname	status
geoff lowell	McBaird	(NULL)
phillip	aziz	1
SAM	khandasamy	2
merit	ou-yang	1
Pete	Peters	2
LI-REN	WONG	3

ruby	archer	2
felipe	le blanc	3
kimiko	sato	3
(NULL)	deathmask-z	(NULL)
pete pete	rs	2
lauren	Menendez	3

[12 rows]

You want to print out a report, but 1–2–3 doesn't give readers enough information—you need a translation of the code. Which is good credit—1 or 3? Which is bad? What does NULL mean here?

You can handle this problem in several ways. They include SQL functions such as CASE and DECODE, now supported by more and more systems. You can also build your own translation systems with characteristic (or point) functions; you can use a UNION or work with joins and outer joins or turn to correlated subqueries. All these approaches are explored in this chapter. Conditional functions for handling NULL are slipped in after the CASE/DECODE section, and the chapter concludes with the TRANSLATE function Oracle supplies.

CASE/DECODE

CASE and DECODE are similar conditional statements. Because the work is in the SELECT clause rather than the WHERE clause, CASE and DECODE offer good performance. Work through some examples—you'll be glad to be fluent in these functions!

CASE

CASE was introduced in the 1992 ANSI standard. There are two forms of syntax. In both cases, the ELSE clause is optional.

```
CASE expr WHEN value1 THEN result1 [WHEN value2 THEN result2]... [ELSE resultn] END
CASE WHEN condition1 THEN result1 [WHEN condition2 THEN result2]...[ELSE resultn] END
```

Here's an example using CASE to interpret the status code. A 1 means that the customer has credit up to $5,000, a 2 indicates credit up to $2,500, and a 3 signifies the need for a credit report check. The ELSE handles all leftover conditions (in this example, NULL), labeling them UNKNOWN.

Adaptive Server Anywhere

```
select fname, lname,
     case status
         when '1' then 'up to 5000'
         when '2' then 'up to 2500'
         when '3' then 'check rept'
         else 'UNKNOWN'
     end
from customer
```

fname	lname	case customer.status when '1'
=======	=======	===============================
geoff lowell	McBaird	UNKNOWN
phillip	aziz	up to 5000
SAM	khandasamy	up to 2500
merit	mokoperto	up to 5000
Pete	Peters	up to 2500
LI-REN	WONG	check rept
ruby	archer	up to 2500
felipe	le blanc	check rept
kimiko	sato	check rept
(NULL)	deathmask-z	UNKNOWN
pete pete	rs	up to 2500
lauren	Menendez	check rept

[12 rows]

The other version of the CASE syntax allows you to set conditions on multiple columns or expressions. The following code involves three columns—status, fname, and state. Notice that the column name follows not CASE, as in the previous example, but WHEN. The display heading NOTES is added at the end of the phrase after the word END.

Adaptive Server Anywhere

```
select fname, lname,
     case
         when status = '1' then   'up to 5000'
         when fname is null then  'no first name'
         when state = 'CA' then   'check address'
     else 'no notes......'
     end as NOTES
from customer
```

fname	lname	NOTES
=======	=======	=======
geoff lowell	McBaird	check address
phillip	aziz	up to 5000
SAM	khandasamy	no notes......
merit	ou-yang	up to 5000
Pete	Peters	no notes......
LI-REN	WONG	no notes......
ruby	archer	check address
felipe	le blanc	no notes......
kimiko	sato	no notes......
(NULL)	deathmask-z	no first name
pete pete	rs	no notes......
lauren	Menendez	no notes......

[12 rows]

Here's another CASE example, showing how you can compare order and ship dates from the ordermaster and orderdetail tables. If the ship date is within two days of the order date, the report shows "on time." It has other messages for negative numbers, orders that shipped more than two days after the order, and orders with a NULL ship date. (DATEDIFF finds the difference between two dates in the unit specified, here days. Refer to Table 2–10 for a list of date functions.)

Adaptive Server Anywhere

```
select od.ordnum, od.prodnum, orderdate, shipdate,
 case
   when datediff(dd, orderdate, shipdate) between 0 and 2 then 'on time'
   when datediff(dd, orderdate, shipdate) < 0 then 'ERROR--NEG NUM'
   when datediff(dd, orderdate, shipdate) > 2  then 'LATE'
   when shipdate is NULL then 'NO DATE'
 end as note
from ordermaster om, orderdetail od
where om.ordnum = od.ordnum
   and od.ordnum between 81 and 85
```

```
ordnum prodnum orderdate           shipdate             note
====== ======= =================== =================== ==============
    81    1357 Jan 02 1999 02:30:00 (NULL)              NO DATE
    85    1794 Jan 02 1999 12:00:00 Jan 02 1999         on time
    81    2050 Jan 02 1999 02:30:00 Jan 01 1999         ERROR--NEG NUM
    85    2050 Jan 02 1999 12:00:00 Jan 05 1999         LATE
    81    1106 Jan 02 1999 02:30:00 Jan 05 1999         LATE
```

[5 rows]

You can do extremely complicated operations with the CASE function. Kevin Kline and colleagues devote a whole chapter to CASE (specifically for Sybase and Microsoft SQL Server) in *Transact-SQL Programming* (O'Reilly, 1999).

DECODE

Oracle and Informix provide the DECODE function (Informix supports both CASE and DECODE). DECODE is parallel to CASE but shows some syntax differences. The syntax is

```
DECODE  (value, if1, then1 [ , if2, then2, ]... , else)
```

To use it to translate the value in the status column into a meaningful string, as in the first CASE example, write code like this:

Oracle

```
SQL> select fname, lname, decode ( status, '1', 'up to 5000',
  2                                          '2', 'up to 2500',
  3                                          '3', 'check rept')
  4  from customer;

FNAME                LNAME                . DECODE(STA
-------------------- -------------------- ----------
geoff lowell         McBaird
ruby                 archer               up to 2500
phillip              aziz                 up to 5000
felipe               le blanc             check rept
kimiko               sato                 check rept
```

```
SAM                     khandasamy           up to 2500
                        deathmask-z
merit                   mokoperto            up to 5000
pete pete               rs                   up to 2500
Pete                    Peters               up to 2500
lauren                  Menendez             check rept
LI-REN                  WONG                 check rept
```

```
12 rows selected.
```

Because Oracle does some autoconversion of datatypes, quotation marks around the character status values (here 1, 2, or 3) are optional. Other systems that offer similar commands may require quotation marks around character values.

If you want to assign a value for null, add UNKNOWN as a final, unmatched else.

Oracle

```
SQL>  select fname, lname, decode(status, '1', 'up to 5000',
  2                                        '2', 'up to 2500',
  3                                        '3', 'check rept',
  4                                        'UNKNOWN')
  5  from customer;
```

```
FNAME                   LNAME                DECODE(STA
--------------------    --------------------  ----------
geoff lowell            McBaird              UNKNOWN
ruby                    archer               up to 2500
phillip                 aziz                 up to 5000
felipe                  le blanc             check rept
kimiko                  sato                 check rept
SAM                     khandasamy           up to 2500
                        deathmask-z          UNKNOWN
merit                   mokoperto            up to 5000
pete pete               rs                   up to 2500
Pete                    Peters               up to 2500
lauren                  Menendez             check rept
LI-REN                  WONG                 check rept
```

```
12 rows selected.
```

George Koch and Kevin Loney give lots of examples of Oracle's DECODE in their *Oracle8: The Complete Reference* (Osborne/McGraw-Hill, 1997). Informix DECODE syntax is identical.

CASE/DECODE Variations

You might want to test how your system implements CASE/DECODE for fixed character columns with variable-length entries.

Here's an example, starring Oracle's DECODE and the five-digit postcode column:

- In supplier (where it is defined as variable character, with a size of up to ten characters)
- In customer (where it is fixed character, with a maximum size of ten)

In both cases, the entries are only three to five characters long, so the fixed-length column (customer.postcode) is padded with trailing spaces.

You want DECODE to print out special notes, based on postcode. On the supplier table you get the results you expect.

Oracle
```
SQL> select postcode, decode (postcode,
  2       '10028', 'Add $3 delivery surcharge',
  3       '143', 'Include customs declaration',
  4       '02110', 'Add .5% local tax' ) as Vari
  5  from supplier
  6   where postcode between '0' and '2';


POSTCODE    VARI
----------  ---------------------------
143         Include customs declaration
10028       Add $3 delivery surcharge
02110       Add .5% local tax

3 rows selected.
```

The same code on the customer table is not so productive. Although three rows appear to qualify, you don't see the translation.

Oracle

```
SQL>  select postcode, decode (postcode,
  2         '10028', 'Add $3 delivery surcharge',
  3         '143', 'Include customs declaration',
  4         '02110', 'Add .5% local tax' )
  5  as Fixed
  6  from customer
  7  where postcode between '0' and '2';

POSTCODE    FIXED
----------  --------------------------
01867
01867
10028
02110
02110
14502
11215

7 rows selected.
```

Trimming the right spaces makes customer.postcode act like supplier.post-code. (See "Space" in Chapter 2 for more about trim functions.)

Oracle

```
SQL>  select postcode, decode ( rtrim (postcode),
  2         '10028', 'Add $3 delivery surcharge',
  3         '143', 'Include customs declaration',
  4  '02110', 'Add .5% local tax' ) as Fixed
  5  from customer
  6   where postcode between '0' and '2';

POSTCODE    FIXED
----------  --------------------------
01867
01867
10028       Add $3 delivery surcharge
02110       Add .5% local tax
02110       Add .5% local tax
14502
11215

7 rows selected.
```

Table 3-1. DECODE and CASE

ANSI	ASA	ASE	MS SQL Server	Oracle	Informix
CASE	CASE	CASE	CASE	DECODE	CASE DECODE

Table 3-1 summarizes DECODE and CASE use. Since the syntax is complex, the table contains only the function names.

Handling NULL

Most systems support functions that allow you to translate or decode NULL. They include COALESCE and NULLIF (both part of the ANSI standard) and the variants ISNULL and NVL. For a distribution summary of these functions, see Table 3-2 at the end of this section.

COALESCE/ISNULL/NVL

COALESCE (meaning to unite or bring together separate parts) can take two or more arguments. The more-than-two meaning is handled in "Finding the First Non-NULL: COALESCE" in the next section.

With two arguments, you can use COALESCE to change the display for NULL. (In Oracle and Informix, NVL serves this function. ISNULL is the Transact-SQL version, also available for Adaptive Server Anywhere.) The syntax is the same for all three functions:

```
ISNULL
COALESCE        ( expr, value-to-substitute-if-null)
NVL
```

Here's an example using COALESCE to substitute STATUS UNKNOWN for null status values.

Adaptive Server Anywhere

```
select status, fname, phone, coalesce (status, 'STATUS UNKNOWN' )
from customer
```

```
status  fname                   phone     coalesce(customer.status,'STA
======  ====================    =======   ==============================
(NULL)  geoff lowell            5552234   STATUS UNKNOWN
1       phillip                 5551333   1
2       SAM                     2231234   2
1       merit                   5557777   1
2       Pete                    5557777   2
3       LI-REN                  1231235   3
2       ruby                    5551111   2
3       felipe                  5551111   3
3       kimiko                  5552233   3
(NULL)  (NULL)                  5557777   STATUS UNKNOWN
2       pete pete               5557777   2
3       lauren                  1231235   3

[12 rows]
```

You get the same results with NVL, supported by both Informix and Oracle.

Oracle

```
SQL> select  status, fname, phone, nvl(status, 'STATUS UNKNOWN' )
  2  from customer;

S FNAME                 PHONE    NVL(STATUS,'ST
- --------------------  -------  --------------
  geoff lowell          5552234  STATUS UNKNOWN
2 ruby                  5551111  2
1 phillip               5551333  1
3 felipe                5551111  3
3 kimiko                5552233  3
2 SAM                   2231234  2
                        5557777  STATUS UNKNOWN
1 merit                 5557777  1
2 pete pete             5557777  2
2 Pete                  5557777  2
3 lauren                1231235  3
3 LI-REN                1231235  3

12 rows selected.
```

Sybase ASA and Transact-SQL support both ISNULL and COALESCE for this "decode NULL" function.

Sybase Adaptive Server Enterprise

```
select status, fname, phone, isnull (status, 'STATUS UNKNOWN' )
from customer
```

status	fname	phone	
NULL	geoff lowell	5552234	**STATUS UNKNOWN**
2	ruby	5551111	2
1	phillip	5551333	1
3	felipe	5551111	3
3	kimiko	5552233	3
2	SAM	2231234	2
NULL	NULL	5557777	**STATUS UNKNOWN**
1	merit	5557777	1
2	pete pete	5557777	2
2	Pete	5557777	2
3	lauren	1231235	3
3	LI-REN	1231235	3

```
(12 rows affected)
```

Finding the First Non-NULL: COALESCE

COALESCE can also act like the following CASE statement, taking any number of arguments and returning the first nonnull value:

```
CASE
  WHEN expr1 IS NOT NULL THEN expr1
  WHEN expr2 IS NOT NULL THEN expr2
  WHEN exprn IS NOT NULL THEN exprn
  ELSE NULL
END
```

Here's an example of COALESCE used this way to find state for U.S. suppliers, or country for international suppliers (the state column holds NULL for them).

Adaptive Server Anywhere

```
select name, coalesce (state, country )
from supplier
```

```
name                  coalesce(supplier.state,suppl
==================== ==============================
Connectix Co.        CA
Soft Stuff           CA
Total Recall         JAPAN
Hi Finance!          NY
TrendMaster          WA
Above Average Arts   MA
Emu Sister Prdctns   PA
```

[7 rows]

If all arguments evaluate to NULL, COALESCE returns NULL. Here's an example looking at phone, area code, and country code for each supplier. One has no entry in any column and returns NULL.

Adaptive Server Anywhere

```
select name, phone, areacode, ctryctycode, coalesce (phone, areacode, ctryctycode )
from supplier
```

```
name                     phone    areacode ctryctycode coalesce(supplier.phone,suppl
======================== ======= ======== =========== =============================
Connectix Co.            (NULL)  (NULL)   (NULL)      (NULL)
Soft Stuff               5554223 408      (NULL)      5554223
Total Recall             13111   376      81-3        13111
Hi Finance!              5554434 201      (NULL)      5554434
TrendMaster              5552233 206      (NULL)      5552233
Above Average Arts       5554223 617      (NULL)      5554223
Emu Sister Prdctns       5557433 215      (NULL)      5557433
```

[7 rows]

NULLIF

Another function involving NULL and conditional logic is NULLIF. The syntax is

```
NULLIF ( expr1, expr2)
```

IF expr1 and expr2 are equal, NULLIF returns NULL. Otherwise, NULLIF returns expr1. NULLIF is like this CASE statement:

```
CASE
    WHEN expr1 = expr2 THEN NULL
    ELSE expr1
END
```

NULLIF is often used to display a nonnull NULL marker as NULL. For example, undecided weights are coded as –1.00 in the product table. To make the output consistent with other tables, you can use NULLIF to display the –1 as NULL.

Adaptive Server Anywhere

```
select name, price, weight, nullif(weight, -1.00)
from product
```

name	price	weight	nullif(product.weight,-1.0)
cook & book	19.99	2.50	2.50
paper dolls	19.99	2.50	2.50
more paper dolls	19.99	2.50	2.50
tax time	49.99	2.50	2.50
memory tripler	119.99	-1.00	(NULL)
memory manager	19.99	-1.00	(NULL)
typing test	29.99	2.50	2.50
home poll kit	19.99	2.50	2.50
star systems	39.99	1.50	1.50
bugbane	49.00	1.00	1.00
memory8	400.00	-1.00	(NULL)
money master	29.00	5.80	5.80
teach yourself greek	49.99	2.50	2.50
mortgage minder	39.99	1.50	1.50
blood & guts	29.99	2.50	2.50
C++ for kids	39.99	2.50	2.50
bug stories	20.00	3.00	3.00
nt guru	20.00	3.00	3.00
how multi is media?	20.00	3.00	3.00
landlord logs	89.99	2.50	2.50
z_connector	149.00	2.20	2.20

[21 rows]

You can also rely on NULLIF to find two columns with the same value. In the following example, you're checking the employee table, comparing employee numbers to their boss's number. NULLIF identifies one employee who works for herself.

Adaptive Server Anywhere

```
select fname, empnum, bossnum, nullif ( empnum, bossnum )
from employee
```

```
fname                empnum    bossnum   nullif(employee.empnum,employ
=================    =======   =======   ============================
Hamid                123232345 223232366 123232345
laurna               223232366 443232366 223232366
ruby                 111223333 223232366 111223333
lauren               923457789 223232366 923457789
Bill                 222222221 443232366 222222221
Scorley              443232366 443232366 (NULL)
```

[6 rows]

You could wrap COALESCE or ISNULL around the NULLIF and get a more readable display.

Adaptive Server Anywhere

```
select fname, empnum, bossnum, coalesce (nullif ( empnum, bossnum ), 'the BOSS') as num
from employee
```

```
fname                empnum    bossnum   num
=================    =======   =======   =======
Hamid                123232345 223232366 123232345
laurna               223232366 443232366 223232366
ruby                 111223333 223232366 111223333
lauren               923457789 223232366 923457789
Bill                 222222221 443232366 222222221
Scorley              443232366 443232366 the BOSS
```

[6 rows]

Table 3–2 is a summary of current availability of these conditional expressions. Syntax is not included, since it is complex. Check your system manuals for details.

Table 3-2. Conditional Functions

ANSI	ASA	ASE	MS SQL Server	Oracle	Informix
NULLIF	NULLIF	NULLIF	NULLIF		
COALESCE	COALESCE	COALESCE	COALESCE		
	ISNULL	ISNULL	ISNULL	NVL	NVL

Point Functions

If your system doesn't offer an equivalent to DECODE or CASE, or there are awkward limitations, don't despair. You may be able to use point (also called characteristic) functions in much the same way. David Rozenshtein, Anatoly Abramovich, and Eugene Birger detail this method in *Optimizing Transact-SQL* (The Coriolis Group, 1997). Although the authors used Sybase Transact-SQL for examples, the techniques can be used with other RDBMSs. Of course, you'll need to modify code to work with syntax variants.

Basically, a point function tests a value in the SELECT clause to find whether it is true or false and takes action based on the result. Since the test is in the SELECT, not the WHERE, performance is usually not an issue. The point functions cause fewer traversals of the table than many other methods.

Getting CASE Effects from Functions and Column Values

Here's an example of using a function in the SELECT clause as a condition. In the employee table, the mstatus column holds 1 for single employees and 2 for married employees. You want to display the letter S or M rather than the number. Since mstatus contains the value 1 or 2, the contents of mstatus can function as the START value for SUBSTR. You provide a SIZE of 1. Here's the example. (Information on substring functions is given in "Locating Patterns" in Chapter 2.)

If mstatus is 1, the SUBSTR function displays the first letter in the string, S. If mstatus is 2, the function displays the second letter, M (Figure 3-1). In substring functions, most systems treat 0 and 1 the same: both mean "start from the first character." Transact-SQL does not. Instead, it interprets 0 as "don't start the substring" and 1 as "start from the first character." This can be important in using point functions (more about this in "Getting CASE Effects from Multiple Functions").

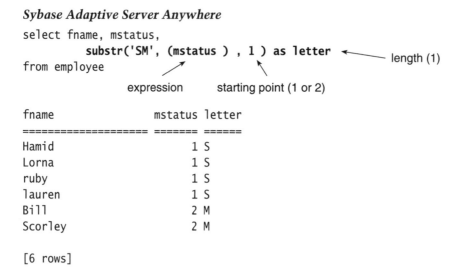

Sybase Adaptive Server Anywhere

```
select fname, mstatus,
          substr('SM', (mstatus ) , 1 ) as letter
from employee
```

Figure 3-1. Logic in SELECT

Getting CASE Effects from Multiple Functions

Here's a more complex example using character functions to do CASE/DECODE-like work in solving the customer.status translation problem introduced at the beginning of the chapter. The functions are specific to the system included on the CD, but the method works with any SQL dialect. (At the end of the section, there is an example of modifying this code to work on a different system.)

Since a number of functions are included, take a look at the steps the code goes through. (You'll find pointers to detailed function discussions in the text.)

1. Find out if an expression (1) exists in a column (customer.status) and where it starts (here the CHARINDEX function).

2. Use the expression location (0 if it doesn't exist, 1 if it does, for this one-character column) as the number-of-times argument and the translation ("up to 5000") as the value-to-replicate (REPEAT function).

3. Do the same thing for each status-translation pair, producing a translation column for each status value.

4. Concatenate all the translations into a single column.

5. Handle NULLs (here ISNULL).

Find Value in* status: *0 or 1 As you recall, CHARINDEX (aka LOCATE, POSITION, INSTR—see "Locating Patterns" in Chapter 2) returns a number representing where one string occurs inside another. The syntax is

```
CHARINDEX (expr1, expr2)
```

If expr1 is the number 2 and expr2 is the status column, a zero means that status does not contain 2. A 1 means that it is the first (and in this one-character column, only) character.

Adaptive Server Anywhere

```
select fname, status, charindex('2', status) as NUMBER
from customer
```

fname	status	NUMBER
===================	======	===========
geoff lowell	(NULL)	(NULL)
phillip	1	0
SAM	2	1
merit	1	0
Pete	2	1
LI-REN	3	0
ruby	2	1
felipe	3	0
kimiko	3	0
(NULL)	(NULL)	(NULL)
pete pete	2	1
lauren	3	0

[12 rows]

Use CHARINDEX 1/0 as REPEAT Argument Use the exists/doesn't exist 1/0 value you get from CHARINDEX to trigger another function. In this case, combine CHARINDEX with REPEAT, using CHARINDEX as the second argument (number of times) to REPEAT. REPEAT (called REPLICATE in Transact-SQL) displays an expression a specified number of times—in this case, either zero times or one time. SPACE is similar but works with spaces instead of characters. LPAD and RPAD are related functions. They allow you to pad an expression with leading or trailing spaces (the default) or any character you specify. Table 3–3 shows how these functions are distributed.

Table 3-3. REPLICATE/REPEAT/SPACE/PAD

ANSI	ASA	ASE	MS SQL Server	Oracle	Informix
	REPEAT (char_expr, number) REPLICATE (char_expr, number)	REPLICATE (char_expr, number)	REPLICATE (char_expr, number)		
	SPACE (number)	SPACE (number)	SPACE (number)		
				LPAD (expr, number [,expr]) RPAD (expr, number [, expr])	LPAD (expr, number [, expr]) RPAD (expr, number [, expr])

Adaptive Server Anywhere

```
select fname, status,
    repeat ('up to 2500', charindex('2', status) ) as Limit
from customer
```

```
fname                status Limit
==================== ====== ===========
geoff lowell         (NULL) (NULL)
phillip              1
SAM                  2      up to 2500
merit                1
Pete                 2      up to 2500
LI-REN               3
ruby                 2      up to 2500
felipe               3
kimiko               3
(NULL)               (NULL) (NULL)
pete pete            2      up to 2500
lauren               3

[12 rows]
```

When CHARINDEX finds a match for 2, REPEAT displays the string "up to 2500" one time. When CHARINDEX does not find a 2 match, REPEAT is not triggered.

Expand for All* status-*Translation Pairs But what about the other translations? Doing the same for each of them is the next logical step.

Adaptive Server Anywhere

```
select fname, status,
    repeat ('up to 5000', charindex('1', status) ) as Limit1,
    repeat ('up to 2500', charindex('2', status) ) as Limit2,
    repeat ('chk rpt', charindex('3', status) ) as Limit3
from customer
```

fname	status	Limit1	Limit2	Limit3
====================	======	==========	==========	==========
geoff lowell	[NULL]	[NULL]	[NULL]	[NULL]
phillip	1	up to 5000		
SAM	2		up to 2500	
merit	1	up to 5000		
Pete	2		up to 2500	
LI-REN	3			check rpt
ruby	2		up to 2500	
felipe	3		up to 2500	
kimiko	3			check rpt
[NULL]	[NULL]			
pete pete	2		up to 2500	
lauren	3			check rpt

```
[12 rows]
```

Combine Translation Result Columns However, you don't really want the
REPEAT results in three separate columns. To combine them into one, concat-
enate ("||" in most systems, "+" in Transact-SQL—see Table 2–1). Notice that
the three REPEAT phrases don't have to be the same size and that you retain
only one column heading.

Adaptive Server Anywhere

```
select fname, status,
    repeat('up to 5000',    charindex('1', status) ) ||
    repeat('up to 2500',    charindex('2', status) ) ||
    repeat('check rpt',    charindex('3', status) ) as Limit
from customer
```

```
fname                 status  Limit
==================== ====== ===============================
geoff lowell         [NULL] [NULL]
phillip              1      up to 5000
SAM                  2      up to 2500
merit                1      up to 5000
Pete                 2      up to 2500
LI-REN               3      check rpt
ruby                 2      up to 2500
felipe               3      up to 2500
kimiko               3      check rpt
[NULL]               [NULL] [NULL]
pete pete            2      up to 2500
lauren               3      check rpt

[12 rows]
```

Display Value for NULL   Only one thing is missing to make this code do everything CASE/DECODE can: NULL handling. In this final step in using point functions to translate, you wrap COALESCE (or ISNULL for Transact-SQL, NVL for Oracle and Informix) around the whole concatenated REPEAT expression (Figure 3–2).

Adaptive Server Anywhere

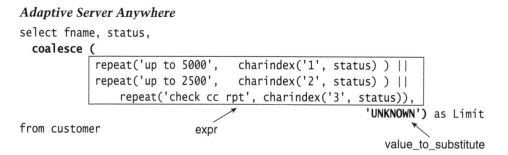

Figure 3-2. NULL in Point Function Translation

The output looks like this:

Adaptive Server Anywhere

fname	status	Limit
====================	======	=============================
geoff lowell	(NULL)	**UNKNOWN**
phillip	1	up to 5000
SAM	2	up to 2500
merit	1	up to 5000
Pete	2	up to 2500
LI-REN	3	check cc rpt
ruby	2	up to 2500
felipe	3	check cc rpt
kimiko	3	check cc rpt
(NULL)	(NULL)	**UNKNOWN**
pete pete	2	up to 2500
lauren	3	check cc rpt

[12 rows]

System Variation Just as an example of how you need to play around with these formulas when you move from system to system, here's a solution on Sybase Adaptive Server Enterprise. The code does not work on related Microsoft SQL Server or Adaptive Server Anywhere because of SUBSTRING differences. (See "Choosing a Subset" in Chapter 2 for more information.) However, you'll recognize the same logical structure you saw in the Adaptive Server Anywhere code.

This version uses SUBSTRING instead of REPEAT, concatenates with + rather than ||, and wraps ISNULL (not COALESCE) around the three substrings.

Sybase Adaptive Server Enterprise

```
select fname, status,
  isnull (
        substring('up to 5000',   charindex('1', status), 10) +
        substring('up to 2500',   charindex('2', status), 10) +
        substring('check cc rpt', charindex('3', status), 12)
          , 'UNKNOWN') as Limit
from customer
```

```
fname                status Limit
------------         ------ -----
geoff lowell         NULL   UNKNOWN
ruby                 2      up to 2500
phillip              1      up to 5000
felipe               3      check cc rpt
kimiko               3      check cc rpt
SAM                  2      up to 2500
NULL                 NULL   UNKNOWN
merit                1      up to 5000
pete pete            2      up to 2500
Pete                 2      up to 2500
lauren               3      check cc rpt
LI-REN               3      check cc rpt

(12 rows affected)
```

Point functions are homemade CASE/DECODE statements. They are flexible and have good performance. However, they can be very hard to read and understand and hence to maintain. If CASE/DECODE statements are available to you, go for them.

UNION

But wait, there's more! You can also use UNION to translate codes. This is not a good solution for a large data set, because the condition in the WHERE clause forces you to traverse the table numerous times, and the UNION itself generally involves creating temporary tables for the intermediate results. However, UNION statements are easy to put together and easy to read. (UNION's sister verbs, MINUS and INTERSECT, are described in "Locating Disconnected Rows" in Chapter 4.)

How UNION Works

UNION gets results from each separate query, then combines the results, and finally eliminates duplicates. In this case, since duplicates are not expected, you can skip the last step and improve performance by specifying UNION ALL (see "Sorting with DISTINCT and UNION" in Chapter 6 for more on this topic). The queries must have the same number of terms in the SELECT statement, with compatible datatypes. Figure 3–3 is a conceptual sketch. In the

Adaptive Server Anywhere

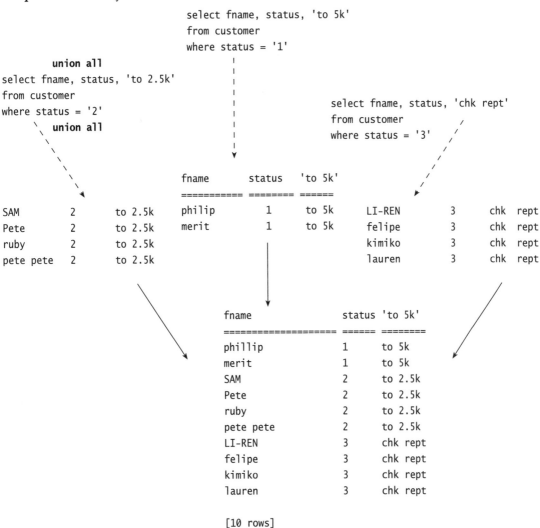

Figure 3-3. UNION Formation

output, UNION uses the first query column headings or display aliases only and honors no ORDER BY but the last (Figure 3–4). In fact, most systems will give an error message if ORDER BY appears before the last query in a UNION.

Check your manuals for details on column headings and ORDER BY variants. Some systems (such as ASA) require a SELECT list position number in the

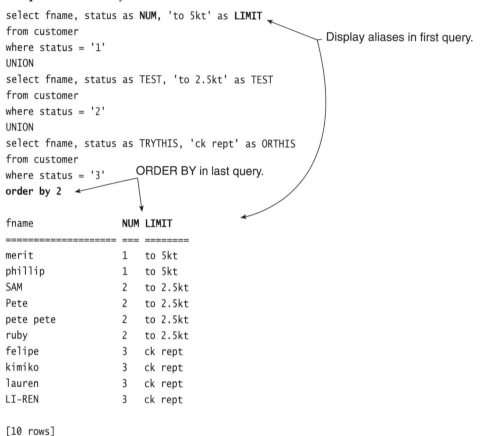

Adaptive Server Anywhere

```
select fname, status as NUM, 'to 5kt' as LIMIT
from customer
where status = '1'
UNION
select fname, status as TEST, 'to 2.5kt' as TEST
from customer
where status = '2'
UNION
select fname, status as TRYTHIS, 'ck rept' as ORTHIS
from customer
where status = '3'
order by 2
```

Display aliases in first query.

ORDER BY in last query.

```
fname                NUM LIMIT
==================== === ========
merit                1   to 5kt
phillip              1   to 5kt
SAM                  2   to 2.5kt
Pete                 2   to 2.5kt
pete pete            2   to 2.5kt
ruby                 2   to 2.5kt
felipe               3   ck rept
kimiko               3   ck rept
lauren               3   ck rept
LI-REN               3   ck rept

[10 rows]
```

Figure 3-4. UNION Rules

ORDER BY rather than a column heading or display alias (here 2, rather than NUM or status).

UNION and NULL

To include null status values, add one more query to the statement, with IS NULL in the WHERE clause. Some systems allow = NULL in addition to IS NULL.

Adaptive Server Anywhere

```
select fname, status as NUM, 'to 5k' as LIMIT
from customer
where status = '1'
        union all
select fname, status, 'to 2.5k'
from customer
where status = '2'
        union all
select fname, status, 'chk rept'
from customer
where status = '3'
        union all
select fname, status, 'UNKNOWN'
from customer
where status is null
```

```
fname                   NUM LIMIT
==================== === ========
phillip                 1   to 5k
merit                   1   to 5k
SAM                     2   to 2.5k
Pete                    2   to 2.5k
ruby                    2   to 2.5k
pete pete               2   to 2.5k
LI-REN                  3   chk rept
felipe                  3   chk rept
kimiko                  3   chk rept
lauren                  3   chk rept
geoff lowell           (NU UNKNOWN
(NULL)                 (NU UNKNOWN
[12 rows]
```

UNION Problems?

If participants in a UNION don't have matching columns, you can fiddle a little. For example, you can make three columns from one query work with two columns from another by adding a string to fill in for the missing expression (Figure 3–5). Here, you want to list customers and suppliers by city. There is no country column in customer (Figure 3–6), but you know they are all domestic, so you can add a string in the appropriate place. You can also add NULL handling

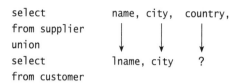

```
select          name, city, country,
from supplier
union
select          lname, city    ?
from customer
```

Figure 3–5. UNION Fixes

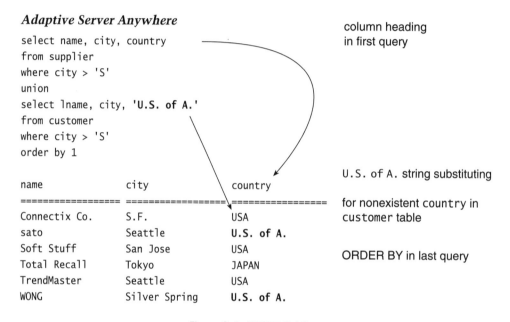

Adaptive Server Anywhere

```
select name, city, country
from supplier
where city > 'S'
union
select lname, city, 'U.S. of A.'
from customer
where city > 'S'
order by 1
```

column heading
in first query

U.S. of A. string substituting

for nonexistent country in
customer table

ORDER BY in last query

name	city	country
===	===	===
Connectix Co.	S.F.	USA
sato	Seattle	**U.S. of A.**
Soft Stuff	San Jose	USA
Total Recall	Tokyo	JAPAN
TrendMaster	Seattle	USA
WONG	Silver Spring	**U.S. of A.**

Figure 3–6. UNION Fiddles

as needed (see "Handling NULL" earlier in this chapter for a discussion of possibilities).

ORDER BY 1 means sort by the first expression in the the SELECT list.

Joins and Outer Joins

Sometimes you can solve the translation problem with a join or an outer join. For example, you can create a table to hold translation values.

Adaptive Server Anywhere

```
create table expand
(status char(1) not null,
limit varchar(15)  not null)

[table created]

create unique index exix on expand(status)

[index created]

insert into expand
values ('1', 'up to 5000')
insert into expand
values ('2', 'up to 2500')
insert into expand
values ('3', 'check cc rpt')

[3 rows]

select *
from expand

status limit
====== ===============
1      up to 5000
2      up to 2500
3      check cc rpt

[3 rows]
```

Then you can join the two tables and get a listing including status and its current meaning (limit). ASA supports two forms of join syntax. The ANSI version is on the left, with the keywords JOIN and ON. The older WHERE clause style is on the right. Because it is widely supported, it is used in most join examples in the book.

Adaptive Server Anywhere

```
select fname, c.status, e.limit          select fname, c.status, e.limit
from customer c join expand e            from customer c, expand e
on c.status = e.status                   where c.status = e.status
```

```
fname                status limit
==================== ====== ===============
phillip              1      up to 5000
merit                1      up to 5000
ruby                 2      up to 2500
SAM                  2      up to 2500
pete pete            2      up to 2500
Pete                 2      up to 2500
felipe               3      check cc rpt
kimiko               3      check cc rpt
lauren               3      check cc rpt
LI-REN               3      check cc rpt

[10 rows]
```

Joins and NULL Values

Using a table to hold definitions and then joining to it works fine. However, you don't get a listing for the null values—how could you, when they don't join anything? You might think IS NULL in the WHERE clause would help so that you'd get both joins and null values.

Adaptive Server Anywhere

```
select fname, c.status, e.limit
from customer c,  expand e
where c.status = e.status
   or c.status is null
order by c.status
```

```
fname                status  limit
==================== ======  ===============
geoff lowell         (NULL)  up to 5000
(NULL)               (NULL)  up to 5000
geoff lowell         (NULL)  up to 2500
(NULL)               (NULL)  up to 2500
geoff lowell         (NULL)  check cc rpt
(NULL)               (NULL)  check cc rpt
phillip              1       up to 5000
merit                1       up to 5000
```

```
SAM                      2      up to 2500
Pete                     2      up to 2500
ruby                     2      up to 2500
pete pete                2      up to 2500
LI-REN                   3      check cc rpt
felipe                   3      check cc rpt
kimiko                   3      check cc rpt
lauren                   3      check cc rpt

[16 rows]
```

In fact, since you don't specify how to join the rows with NULL status values, SQL decides to try every possible combination and shows the two names (Geoff and no-first-name) with limit 1, 2, and 3. Clearly, adding IS NULL to the WHERE clause of a join is not producing the results you want.

Outer Joins

An outer join is the answer. It allows you to see all the qualified rows from one table, whether or not there are joins, without creating a Cartesian product. An outer join can be left or right, depending on which table you want to show fully.

Outer Join Summary   Before looking at syntax or pursuing the details of constructing an outer join, let's digress briefly from customer and expand and consider just the results from joins of two tables that share some data but do not join on every column: customer and employee. There are six employees and 12 customers. Two employees are also customers. Compare the results of the following.

- "Regular" join of customer and employee on ID number
- Left outer join of customer and employee on ID number
- Right outer join of customer and employee on ID number

A plain vanilla join shows just two rows—names that occur in both tables.

Adaptive Server Anywhere

```
select c.fname as CName, e.fname as EName
from customer c, employee e
where c.custnum = e.empnum
```

CName	EName
====================	====================
ruby	ruby
lauren	lauren

[2 rows]

A left outer join shows all the customers (customer is the table on the left) and matching employees. Where there is no match, SQL supplies a NULL. There are 12 rows, one for each of the 12 customers.

Adaptive Server Anywhere

CName	EName
====================	====================
geoff lowell	(NULL)
phillip	(NULL)
SAM	(NULL)
merit	(NULL)
Pete	(NULL)
LI-REN	(NULL)
ruby	ruby
felipe	(NULL)
kimiko	(NULL)
(NULL)	(NULL)
pete pete	(NULL)
lauren	lauren

[12 rows]

A right outer join (employee is the table on the right) shows all six employees and the two matching customers. SQL adds NULL for missing values.

Adaptive Server Anywhere

CName	EName
====================	====================
(NULL)	Hamid
(NULL)	Lorna
ruby	ruby
lauren	lauren
(NULL)	Bill
(NULL)	Scorley

[6 rows]

Decoding with an Outer Join   Now let's apply the outer join to the customer-expand problem. The following left outer join shows

- all the values in the (left) customer table, whether or not they join rows in the expand table.
- joining values from the expand table, and NULL where there is no join.

ASA supports two ways to do the outer join, and they are shown side by side in the following example. On the left is the ANSI version, where you see the words LEFT OUTER JOIN in the FROM clause and joining columns in the ON clause. On the right is the Transact-SQL version. The *= in the WHERE clause represents a left outer join, because the * is on the left side of the equal sign.

Adaptive Server Anywhere

```
select fname, c.status, e.limit          select fname, c.status, e.limit
from customer c left outer join  expand e   from customer c,  expand e
on c.status = e.status                    where c.status *= e.status
```

The two versions of the query return the same results. Notice that two customers have no known status, but each has a result row. All values in the left table are accounted for.

Adaptive Server Anywhere

fname	status	limit
geoff lowell	(NULL)	(NULL)
phillip	1	up to 5000
SAM	2	up to 2500
merit	1	up to 5000
Pete	2	up to 2500
LI-REN	3	check cc rpt
ruby	2	up to 2500
felipe	3	check cc rpt
kimiko	3	check cc rpt
(NULL)	(NULL)	(NULL)
pete pete	2	up to 2500
lauren	3	check cc rpt

[12 rows]

Outer join syntax varies greatly from system to system. Depending on your SQL dialect, the outer join specification can be in the FROM clause, the WHERE clause, or the combination of FROM and ON clauses.

Figure 3–7 shows the same outer join as it is written for all the systems used in this book. Microsoft SQL Server and Adaptive Server Anywhere use two forms. Table 3–4 is a corresponding syntax table. Notice that Transact-SQL has the * in *= or =* on the side of the table you want to see in full, while Oracle puts the (+) after the name of the table that needs to be expanded. The syntax in Table 3–4 shows both left and right outer joins.

You can add null handling to this solution with the appropriate function (COALESCE or ISNULL with Adaptive Server Anywhere—Table 3–2 lists some variants).

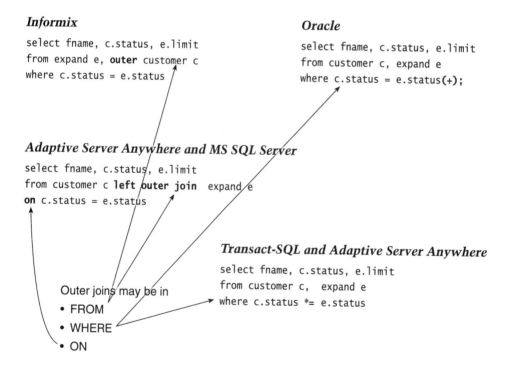

Informix

```
select fname, c.status, e.limit
from expand e, outer customer c
where c.status = e.status
```

Oracle

```
select fname, c.status, e.limit
from customer c, expand e
where c.status = e.status(+);
```

Adaptive Server Anywhere and MS SQL Server

```
select fname, c.status, e.limit
from customer c left outer join   expand e
on c.status = e.status
```

Transact-SQL and Adaptive Server Anywhere

```
select fname, c.status, e.limit
from customer c,   expand e
where c.status *= e.status
```

Outer joins may be in
• FROM
• WHERE
• ON

Figure 3–7. Outer Join Examples

Table 3-4. Outer Join Syntax

ANSI	ASA	ASE	MS SQL Server	Oracle	Informix
SELECT select_list FROM t1 LEFT OUTER JOIN t2 ON t1.col=t2.col	SELECT select_list FROM t1 LEFT OUTER JOIN t2 ON t1.col=t2.col SELECT select_list FROM t1, t2 WHERE t1.col*=t2.col	SELECT select_list FROM t1, t2 WHERE t1.col*=t2.col	SELECT select_list FROM t1 LEFT OUTER JOIN t2 ON t1.col=t2.col SELECT select_list FROM t1, t2 WHERE t1.col*=t2.col	SELECT select_list FROM t1, t2 WHERE t1.col=t2.col(+)	SELECT select_list FROM t1, OUTER t2 WHERE t1.col=t2.col
SELECT select_list FROM t1 RIGHT OUTER JOIN t2 ON t1.col=t2.col	SELECT select_list FROM t1 RIGHT OUTER JOIN t2 ON t1.col=t2.col SELECT select_list FROM t1, t2 WHERE t1.col=*t2.col	SELECT select_list FROM t1, t2 WHERE t1.col=*t2.col	SELECT select_list FROM t1 RIGHT OUTER JOIN t2 ON t1.col=t2.col SELECT select_list FROM t1, t2 WHERE t1.col=*t2.col	SELECT select_list FROM t1, t2 WHERE t1.col(+)=t2.col	SELECT select_list FROM t2, OUTER t1 WHERE t1.col=t2.col

Adaptive Server Anywhere

```
select fname, c.status, coalesce ( e.limit , 'Who knows?' )
from customer c left outer join expand e
on c.status = e.status
```

```
fname                    status coalesce(e.limit,'Who knows?'
====================     ====== =============================
geoff lowell             (NULL) Who knows?
phillip                  1      up to 5000
SAM                      2      up to 2500
merit                    1      up to 5000
Pete                     2      up to 2500
LI-REN                   3      check cc rpt
ruby                     2      up to 2500
felipe                   3      check cc rpt
kimiko                   3      check cc rpt
(NULL)                   (NULL) Who knows?
pete pete                2      up to 2500
lauren                   3      check cc rpt

[12 rows]
```

Subqueries

You might think that a subquery involving customer and expand would give the same display as a join of the two tables, but that's not quite true. A subquery can act only as a condition for the outer query—it cannot contribute additional columns to the results, as a join can.

Subqueries and Displays

A query like the following produces correct results, but the subquery provides no advantage over a plain WHERE clause with status = 1. There is no simple way to display expand.limit and customer.fname in the results.

Adaptive Server Anywhere

```
select fname, 'up to 5k'
from customer
where status =
    (select status
     from expand
     where limit = 'up to 5000')
```

```
fname                   'up to 5k'
==================== ==========
phillip                 up to 5k
merit                   up to 5k
```

```
[2 rows]
```

Embedded Correlated Subqueries

An expansion of the previous query, this solution has the worst performance of any "translation" method offered so far, and it works only in Transact-SQL and Adaptive Server Anywhere. It is presented here more as an opportunity to play with correlated subqueries than as a suggested approach. Each subquery

- uses the table (customer) with 4 different aliases (c, c1, c2, c3).
- joins each subquery back to to the main table (customer c) on the primary key, so that you are looking at each row just once.
- generates a string ("up to 5000") based on the subquery WHERE condition (c1.status = '1').

Adaptive Server Anywhere

```
select fname,
(select 'up to 5000' from customer c1 where c1.status = '1' and c1.custnum = c.custnum),
(select 'up to 2500' from customer c2 where c2.status = '2' and c2.custnum = c.custnum),
(select 'check rept' from customer c3 where c3.status = '3' and c3.custnum = c.custnum)
from customer c
```

fname	'up to 5000'	'up to 2500'	'check rept'
===	===	===	===
geoff lowell	(NULL)	(NULL)	(NULL)
phillip	up to 5000	(NULL)	(NULL)
SAM	(NULL)	up to 2500	(NULL)
merit	up to 5000	(NULL)	(NULL)
Pete	(NULL)	up to 2500	(NULL)
LI-REN	(NULL)	(NULL)	check rept
ruby	(NULL)	up to 2500	(NULL)
felipe	(NULL)	(NULL)	check rept
kimiko	(NULL)	(NULL)	check rept
(NULL)	(NULL)	(NULL)	(NULL)
pete pete	(NULL)	up to 2500	(NULL)
lauren	(NULL)	(NULL)	check rept

[12 rows]

As in other solutions, the results are more readable when you concatenate the three result columns into one (Table 2–1 lists concatenate functions).

Adaptive Server Anywhere

```
select fname,
(select 'up to 5000' from customer c1 where c1.status='1' and c1.custnum = c.custnum) ||
(select 'up to 2500' from customer c2 where c2.status='2' and c2.custnum = c.custnum) ||
(select 'check rept' from customer c3 where c3.status='3' and c3.custnum = c.custnum)
from customer c
```

fname	(select 'up to 5000' from cus
===	===
geoff lowell	(NULL)
phillip	up to 5000
SAM	up to 2500
merit	up to 5000
Pete	up to 2500
LI-REN	check rept
ruby	up to 2500
felipe	check rept

```
kimiko              check rept
(NULL)              (NULL)
pete pete           up to 2500
lauren              check rept
```

[12 rows]

Why is this query tagged a "poor performer?" There are a couple of reasons.

- As a triple self-join, it requires SQL to traverse the table at least four separate times—once for the outer table and once for each inner table.
- Because the subqueries are correlated, they force looping on individual rows, a potential problem in set-oriented relational databases.

Correlated and Noncorrelated Subqueries

Correlated versus noncorrelated subqueries are summarized in Figure 3–8. Both queries return the same results.

Adaptive Server Anywhere

```
select name
from product ←
where suplrnum =
( select suplrnum
  from supplier
  where supplier.state = 'WA' )
```

```
select name
from product
where exists
  (select *
  from supplier
  where product.suplrnum =
        supplier.suplrnum )
  and supplier.state = 'WA'
```

Subquery

- Can run independently
- Passes subquery results once to outer query
- Connects to outer query WHERE clause with corresponding inner query SELECT clause

Correlated subquery

- Needs information from outer query
- Passes subquery results once to outer query for each qualifying outer query row
- Connects to outer query through join in inner query WHERE clause

Figure 3-8. Correlated Subqueries

Adaptive Server Anywhere

```
name
====================
cook & book
home poll kit
star systems

[3 rows]
```

If a subquery like the one in Figure 3–8 can be expressed as either a correlated or a "plain" subquery, you'll probably get better performance from the vanilla version. However, there are many cases in which a correlated subquery is the best way to handle an issue.

TRANSLATE: Another Conditional Expression

There is a lot of variety in translation options. If you're using Oracle, play around with TRANSLATE (Table 3–5)—other systems don't support it. It is not the same as the ANSI TRANSLATE function, which has to do with internationalization and character sets (there's more about character sets in "Case" in Chapter 2).

The Oracle TRANSLATE function looks like this:

```
TRANSLATE ( string , if , then )
```

It's a good way to make numeric codes more readable as alphabetic codes. You can use it to display the marital status column in the employee table as S (single) or M (married) rather than 1 or 2. This is the same problem solved with point functions in "Getting CASE Effects from Functions and Column Values" in this chapter.

Table 3–5. Another Conditional Function

ANSI	SQL Anywhere	SAE	MS SQL Server	Oracle	Informix
				TRANSLATE	

Oracle

```
SQL> select fname, mstatus, translate (mstatus, '12', 'MS')
  2  from employee
  3  order by mstatus;

FNAME                   MSTATUS TRANSLATE(MSTATUS,'12','MS')
-------------------- --------- --------------------------------
Hamid                         1 M
Lorna                         1 M
ruby                          1 M
lauren                        1 M
Bill                          2 S
Scorley                       2 S

6 rows selected.
```

TRANSLATE does not do set translating—it works position by position. Translate the first item in the first list to the first item in the second, translate the second item in the first list to the second item in the second, and so on:

TRANSLATE 1 2 3 , M S O

You'll see how this works if you try to translate using 18 and 81. All 1s become 8s, all 8s become 1s. Order is not important—it doesn't matter that there is no 18 in the original ordnum. TRANSLATE handles 81 just fine.

Oracle

```
SQL> select ordnum, translate (ordnum, 18, 81)
  2    from ordermaster
  3    order by ordnum;

  ORDNUM TRANSLATE(ORDNUM,18,81)
--------- ----------------------------------------
      81 18
      85 15
      86 16
      87 17
      89 19
      90 90
      91 98
      92 92
      93 93
```

```
94 94
95 95
99 99
```

12 rows selected.

You can also use TRANSLATE to remove characters. Let's say you want to eliminate all alpha characters and spaces from product.version.

Oracle

```
SQL> select distinct version, translate (version, 'qSupera ', 'x')
  2  from product;

VERSION  TRANSLAT
-------- --------
1.1      1.1
10.1     10.1
10.1.01  10.1.01
10.1_6.5 10.1_6.5
2.2      2.2
6.5_a    6.5_
Super 6. 6.
```

8 rows selected.

The last row contains null values. The code translates all q's to x's and the following letters to nothing. The q is a dummy value, since you must have at least one element in the second list. Pick something that does not occur in the second set of characters. Without the q, the S would be translated to x.

Here's another example. You want to see just those versions that have alphabetic or special characters, excluding decimal points. You might begin by translating numbers and decimal points to 9. Six version number translations contain values other than 9.

Oracle

```
SQL> select prodnum, version,
  2  translate (version, '0123456789.', '99999999999')
  3  from product;
```

```
PRODNUM VERSION   TRANSLAT
--------- --------- --------
    2000 Super 6.  Super 99
    2047 10.1.01   9999999
    2049 10.1.01   9999999
    2050
    2111 6.5_a     999_a
    1084 10.1_6.5  9999_999
    1099
    1105 Super 6.  Super 99
    1110 Super 6.  Super 99
    2113
    1794 6.5_a     999_a
    1083 1.1       999
    1104
    1107
    1108
    1109 1.1       999
    1255 2.2       999
    1357 2.2       999
    1457 10.1      9999
    2110 1.1       999
    1106 1.1       999

21 rows selected.
```

Then move the TRANSLATE to the WHERE clause, and compare its results to a string of 9s of the same size. (See Table 3–3 for more information on LPAD/RPAD.) The results show only those product numbers that contain characters other than numbers and the decimal point.

Oracle

```
SQL> select prodnum, version
  2  from product
  3  where translate (version, '0123456789.', '99999999999') <>
  4     rpad('9', length(version), '9');
```

```
PRODNUM  VERSION
-------- --------
    2000 Super 6.
    2111 6.5_a
    1084 10.1_6.5
    1105 Super 6.
    1110 Super 6.
    1794 6.5_a

6 rows selected.
```

Summary

This chapter presents a number of ways to translate one value into another.

- CASE and DECODE have recently become widely available, and they allow the SQL programmer to pose complex conditional questions. Because the logic is in the SELECT clause, not the WHERE clause, performance is usually good.
- COALESCE (aka NVL or ISNULL on some systems) and NULLIF are special, very useful cases of CASE/DECODE. Designed to handle NULL, they have many practical applications.
- Point (or characteristic) functions give you the capability to do CASE/DECODE work if your system or version doesn't support CASE/DECODE. As CASE becomes more generally available, you won't use point functions much. The logic and techniques are interesting, and you may find examples in code written before your system had CASE.
- UNION is a standard SQL command that is widely supported. Here it introduces another way to translate one value to another. Because the condition is in the WHERE clause and the tables are traversed once for each UNION clause, performance is not as good as with CASE/DECODE or point functions. However, the code is easy to read and easy to write.
- Joins and outer joins can also solve the translation problem and may be the most straightforward approach. There is a great deal of variety in outer join syntax. Be cautious when porting from one system to another.
- Subqueries are a little different from joins and present some problems for translation. The example of embedded subqueries in the SELECT clause is interesting but probably the worst performer in the batch—and hard to read, too.
- Finally, Oracle offers a function called TRANSLATE. Not as flexible as Oracle's DECODE, it offers some similar capabilities.

Chapter 4

Managing Multiples

In This Chapter

- Capturing Duplicates
- Finding Near-Duplicates
- Locating Disconnected Rows
- Counting Items Based on Characteristics
- Figuring Distribution

What's the Issue with Multiples?

Multiples are dirty data writ large. Because relational theory requires that data be stored as a "heap," with no enduring or guaranteed order, you find rows by describing them. If two or more rows have identical data in every column, you cannot distinguish them. In essence, you are wasting space for no purpose. Rows with almost the same information are more dangerous—before long, they will hold slightly different versions of reality. Which is right? Is *any* one right?

Master rows that have no detail rows and detail rows that have no master rows may be errors. That is, there's a chance that the master row was added or deleted by mistake or the detail rows were added incorrectly. It's a good idea to check for these cases. The unmatched master row may be allowed by your business rules, but the unmatched detail row is always trouble. With the ANSI FOREIGN KEY . . . REFERENCES clause, you can prevent lost details.

Products with multiple versions are still the same product, in some way, and may need to be counted as such. If your database was not designed with this capability, there are ways you can work around it. Finally, it's important to be able to look at distribution. Are any products included in every order? Are there common combinations of products?

Many of the solutions in this chapter involve interesting elements: self joins, outer joins, unequal joins, GROUP BY.

Capturing Duplicates

Ah, the inherited database! Once you are familiar with your business model, take a close look at the data. If, as is often the case, your database was put together without indexes or other primary key protections, you may have duplicate rows. This section covers two ways to deal with duplicates: creating a holding table and using a built-in function such as ROWID. Either way, you need to find those duplicate rows, remove the extra copies, and make sure you don't get more copies of this or any other data.

Duplicates and a Holding Table

The holding table gives you a place to store a single copy of each row. Here are the steps to follow.

0. Back up the database, if you are dealing with real data. (In practice mode, use this step to create some dirty data by dropping the unique index and adding some copies of existing rows.)

1. Locate duplicate data with GROUP BY, COUNT, and HAVING.

2. Store a *single* copy of each duplicate set in a holding table.

3. Using a join between the original and holding tables, delete *all* duplicates from the original table.

4. Add a unique index (at least!) to the original table to prevent more dirt. *Do not skip this step!*

5. Insert the data stored in the holding table back into the original table.

0. Prepare: Drop the Index, Add Duplicate Data   In real life, start by backing up your data according to the customs of your system. To follow along with this example, you'll need to drop the existing unique index and add duplicate rows to the ordermaster table.

Adaptive Server Anywhere

```
drop index ordix

[index dropped]

insert into ordermaster
```

```
select *
from ordermaster
where ordnum in (81, 91, 94)


[3 rows inserted]

insert into ordermaster
select *
from ordermaster
where ordnum in (81, 91)


[4 rows inserted]
```

These three commands should give you two copies for order 94 and four copies each for orders 81 and 91. To make sure that this is what you have, run a SELECT. (The orderdate format is simplified in this section, dropping seconds and AM/PM notation. You can change your format to match, or leave it as is. See "Notes on Environment and Display" in Appendix B).

Adaptive Server Anywhere

```
select *
from ordermaster
order by ordnum
```

ordnum	custnum	orderdate	creditcard	empnum
81	223456789	1999-01-02 02:30	1222222232224222	123232345
81	223456789	1999-01-02 02:30	1222222232224222	123232345
81	223456789	1999-01-02 02:30	1222222232224222	123232345
81	223456789	1999-01-02 02:30	1222222232224222	123232345
85	111334444	1999-01-02 00:00	7777 7777 7777 7777	123232345
86	777777779	1999-01-02 00:00	7777 7777 6663	111223333
87	111333333	1999-01-02 00:00	00001111222233334444	111223333
89	111222222	1999-01-02 00:00	1234333331114123	923457789
90	111444444	1999-01-02 00:00	111112111121111	923457789
91	111223333	1999-01-02 00:00	1111222233334444	923457789
91	111223333	1999-01-02 00:00	1111222233334444	923457789
91	111223333	1999-01-02 00:00	1111222233334444	923457789
91	111223333	1999-01-02 00:00	1111222233334444	923457789
92	777777778	1999-01-02 00:00	777766661234X	222222221
93	111334444	1999-01-05 14:30	X7777 7777	222222221

```
94 777777778 1999-01-02 00:00  777766661234X         222222221
94 777777778 1999-01-02 00:00  777766661234X         222222221
95 923456789 1999-01-03 00:00  3131 7777 7777 7777   443232366
99 776677778 1999-01-02 00:00  1222222232224222      923457789
```

[19 rows]

Now we're set: we have ugly duplicate data. The ordermaster table has grown from 12 to 19 rows.

1. Find Duplicates To find duplicates, group by all columns in the row. Use HAVING to locate those groups that contain more than one copy.

Adaptive Server Anywhere

```
select ordnum, custnum, orderdate, creditcard, empnum, count(*)
from ordermaster
group by ordnum, custnum, orderdate, creditcard, empnum
having count(*) >1
```

ordnum	custnum	orderdate	creditcard	empnum	count(*)
81	223456789	Jan 02 1999 02:30	1222222232224222	123232345	4
91	111223333	Jan 02 1999 00:00	1111222233334444	923457789	4
94	777777778	Jan 02 1999 00:00	777766661234X	222222221	2

[3 rows]

GROUP BY syntax varies quite a bit from system to system. ANSI requires that everything in the SELECT list be either a group (and appear in the GROUP BY clause) or an aggregate value. If you stick to these rules, you shouldn't have any problems. Since the row copies are identical, you could display and GROUP BY ordnum alone in the first step. However, you'll be grouping by multiple columns in step 2, so you might as well do it here.

HAVING is a WHERE clause for group results. Unlike WHERE, it can use aggregate functions. See "HAVING" at the end of this chapter for reasons why you should not confuse the two clauses.

2. Store a single copy in a holding table Create a holding table, and insert a single copy of each duplicate row into it. In systems that support creating and filling a table based on another table (Transact-SQL SELECT INTO, Oracle

CREATE TABLE AS), you can do this in one step instead of two. If you're not using ASA, you may need to modify the datatypes in the CREATE TABLE statement (see "Datatype Comparison" in Appendix B for some ideas).

Adaptive Server Anywhere

```
create table holdem
(
ordnum      int        not null,
custnum     char(9)    not null,
orderdate   timestamp  not null,
creditcard  varchar(20) not null,
empnum      char(9)    not null
)

[table created]

insert into holdem
    select ordnum, custnum, orderdate, creditcard, empnum
    from ordermaster
    group by ordnum, custnum, orderdate, creditcard, empnum
    having count(*) >1

[3 rows inserted]
```

Check your results with a SELECT. You should have one copy of each duplicate row.

Adaptive Server Anywhere

```
select *
from holdem
```

ordnum	custnum	orderdate	creditcard	empnum
81	223456789	Jan 02 1999 02:30	1222222232224222	123232345
91	111223333	Jan 02 1999 00:00	1111222233334444	923457789
94	777777778	Jan 02 1999 00:00	777766661234X	222222221

```
[3 rows]
```

3. Delete Duplicate Rows From the Original Table Now that you have saved a single copy of each set of duplicate rows in the holding table, you can remove all the original duplicate rows from ordermaster.

Adaptive Server Anywhere

```
delete from ordermaster
where ordnum in
    (select ordnum
     from holdem)
```

[10 rows deleted]

A query shows that you have removed all copies of 81, 91, and 94.

Adaptive Server Anywhere

```
select *
from ordermaster
order by ordnum
```

ordnum	custnum	orderdate	creditcard	empnum
85	111334444	Jan 02 1999 00:00	7777 7777 7777 7777	123232345
86	777777779	Jan 02 1999 00:00	7777 7777 6663	111223333
87	111333333	Jan 02 1999 00:00	00001111222233334444	111223333
89	111222222	Jan 02 1999 00:00	1234333331114123	923457789
90	111444444	Jan 02 1999 00:00	111112111121111	923457789
92	777777778	Jan 02 1999 00:00	777766661234X	222222221
93	111334444	Jan 05 1999 14:30	X7777 7777	222222221
95	923456789	Jan 03 1999 00:00	3131 7777 7777 7777	443232366
99	776677778	Jan 02 1999 00:00	1222222232224222	923457789

[9 rows]

4. Create a Unique Index on the Original Table Your indexing options may vary. You probably have a CREATE INDEX command and an ALTER TABLE command.

The important point is to create a unique index to prevent users from inserting duplicate rows. Here, ordnum should be distinct for each row, while other values (custnum, orderdate) have no such logical requirement—ordnum is the best choice for the index.

For CREATE INDEX, the code looks something like this:

Adaptive Server Anywhere
```
create unique index ordix
on ordermaster(ordnum)
```

```
[index created]
```

If you use ALTER TABLE, the command is more complex. Check your syntax to make sure you use the correct option to ensure uniqueness, either PRIMARY KEY or UNIQUE.

Adaptive Server Anywhere
```
alter table ordermaster
add constraint ordix unique(ordnum)
```

```
[unique constraint created]
```

5. Insert the Holding Table Rows into the Original Table The original table now has *no* copies of the duplicate rows. The holding table has *one* copy of each set. By inserting the contents of the holding table into the original table, you're restoring the table to its proper shape. The unique index will prevent any rows with duplicate primary keys—you'll get an error message if you accidentally include a duplicate in the INSERT.

Adaptive Server Anywhere
```
insert into ordermaster
   select *
   from holdem
```

```
[3 rows]
```

```
select *
from ordermaster
```

ordnum	custnum	orderdate	creditcard	empnum
81	223456789	Jan 02 1999 02:30	1222222232224222	123232345
85	111334444	Jan 02 1999 00:00	7777 7777 7777 7777	123232345
86	777777779	Jan 02 1999 00:00	7777 7777 6663	111223333

```
87 111333333 Jan 02 1999 00:00 00001111222233334444 111223333
89 111222222 Jan 02 1999 00:00 1234333331114123        923457789
90 111444444 Jan 02 1999 00:00 111112111121111         923457789
91 111223333 Jan 02 1999 00:00 1111222233334444        923457789
92 777777778 Jan 02 1999 00:00 777766661234X           222222221
93 111334444 Jan 05 1999 14:30 X7777 7777              222222221
94 777777778 Jan 02 1999 00:00 777766661234X           222222221
95 923456789 Jan 03 1999 00:00 3131 7777 7777 7777     443232366
99 776677778 Jan 02 1999 00:00 1222222232224222        923457789
```

[12 rows]

Of course, few tables in real life have only five columns and twelve rows, nor are duplicates so obvious. You'll have to modify these steps, taking your data, your database system, and your business needs into consideration.

Using ROWID to Remove Duplicates

If your system supports a unique internal number for each row (such as Oracle's ROWID), you can use this feature to remove duplicate rows. (To follow along, if you have Oracle, remove the index and add the duplicate rows, as in step 0 of the earlier procedure. When you're done, be sure to add the index.)

Here, a correlated subquery using the same table for the outer and inner query compares rows that have identical primary keys (ordnum). (There's more about nested queries in "Subqueries" at the end of Chapter 3. There is also information on joining a table to itself in "Self-Joins" in this section.)

Oracle automatically generates a virtual column called rowid for each row. You can retrieve the value by including rowid in your SELECT list, using it in conjunction with ordnum to remove all but the high rowid in each set. To see how this works, look at the ordnum and rowid values after you insert duplicate rows.

Oracle
```
SQL> select ordnum, rowid
  2  from ordermaster
  3  order by ordnum;
```

```
  ORDNUM ROWID
--------- ------------------
       81 AAAAqsAABAAAErtAAA
       81 AAAAqsAABAAAErtAAD
       81 AAAAqsAABAAAErtAAL
       81 AAAAqsAABAAAErtAAF
       85 AAAAqsAABAAAErtAAM
       86 AAAAqsAABAAAErtAAN
       87 AAAAqsAABAAAErtAAO
       89 AAAAqsAABAAAErtAAP
       90 AAAAqsAABAAAErtAAQ
       91 AAAAqsAABAAAErtAAB
       91 AAAAqsAABAAAErtAAG
       91 AAAAqsAABAAAErtAAR
       91 AAAAqsAABAAAErtAAE
       92 AAAAqsAABAAAErtAAS
       93 AAAAqsAABAAAErtAAT
       94 AAAAqsAABAAAErtAAC
       94 AAAAqsAABAAAErtAAU
       95 AAAAqsAABAAAErtAAV
       99 AAAAqsAABAAAErtAAW

19 rows selected.
```

Now remove all but the low rowid value for each duplicated ordnum.

Oracle

```
SQL> delete from ordermaster om
  2  where om.rowid >
  3      (select min (im.rowid)
  4       from ordermaster im
  5       where om.ordnum = im.ordnum);

7 rows deleted
```

This DELETE uses a correlated subquery to compare a table to itself. The outer DELETE passes an ordnum to the inner query, which finds a matching ordnum value row. It then compares the rowids for that ordnum in the inner and outer tables and removes the outer row if it has a rowid greater than the rowid of the corresponding inner row. If there is only one copy of the ordnum, the outer rowid and the inner rowid values are exactly the same. If there are multiple copies of the ordnum, only the one with the low rowid remains. Correlated subqueries are very useful for this kind of row-by-row comparison.

After you run the DELETE, the table looks like this:

Oracle

```
SQL> select ordnum, rowid
  2  from ordermaster
  3  order by ordnum;

   ORDNUM ROWID
---------- -------------------
       81 AAAAqsAABAAAErtAAA
       85 AAAAqsAABAAAErtAAM
       86 AAAAqsAABAAAErtAAN
       87 AAAAqsAABAAAErtAAO
       89 AAAAqsAABAAAErtAAP
       90 AAAAqsAABAAAErtAAQ
       91 AAAAqsAABAAAErtAAB
       92 AAAAqsAABAAAErtAAS
       93 AAAAqsAABAAAErtAAT
       94 AAAAqsAABAAAErtAAC
       95 AAAAqsAABAAAErtAAV
       99 AAAAqsAABAAAErtAAW

12 rows selected.
```

You can see that duplicate ordnum 81, 91, and 94 are gone. Only the row with the lowest ROWID value in each case remains. Recreate the unique index or constraint to protect the data (step 4 of the procedure).

Informix also supports a ROWID, but you have to explicitly add it to your table, and it is not recommended as an access method. The primary key is preferred.

Finding Near-Duplicates

Near-duplicates are similar to duplicates, but not every column is the same. In fact, the problem may be as isolated as multiple different spellings of the same name, which spark different identification numbers, which come to be associated with different addresses—when in fact, it's just one customer. In this case, you start out by doing an unequal self-join to find out how many near-matches there are. Then human intervention is required. Which of the similar names is correct? Once you've decided, you remove or edit the incorrect versions. (See "Sounds Like . . ." in Chapter 2 for details on comparing sounds with SOUNDEX. Because of the differences in the function, your system may return different results than the ones you see here.)

Self-Joins

A self-join is a way of comparing data with itself. There are three conditions for a useful self-join (Figure 4–1).

If your system supports ANSI join syntax, you can write the query like this, using the JOIN or INNER JOIN keyword in the FROM clause and adding an ON clause for the joining columns:

Adaptive Server Anywhere

```
select c1.fname,c2.fname
from customer c1 join customer c2
on soundex(c1.fname) = soundex(c2.fname)
    and c1.custnum <> c2.custnum
```

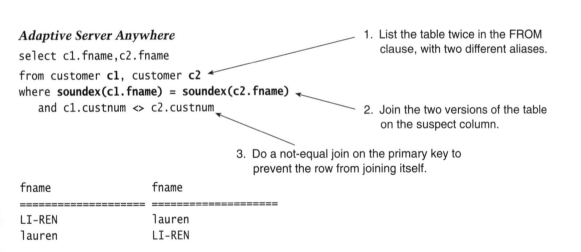

Figure 4-1. Self-Joins

In the rest of the chapter, you'll see the older WHERE clause join form, since it works with all systems used in the book; the ANSI version is less widely supported at present.

You've found names with similar sounds, but you're seeing multiple copies of each match (Lauren/LI-REN and LI-REN/Lauren). Here's where you can change the not-equal join to a less-than or greater-than join to simplify the results.

Adaptive Server Anywhere

```
select c1.fname, c2.fname
from customer c1, customer c2
where soundex (c1.fname) = soundex (c2.fname)
    and c1.custnum < c2.custnum
```

fname	fname
===================	===================
lauren	LI-REN

[1 row]

The not-equal join showed pairs of sound-alike names in every possible order. The less-than join displays names in one order only, based on custnum.

On Transact-SQL systems, the dash in Li-ren causes the SOUNDEX values to be different. Results look like this:

Transact -SQL

fname	fname
Pete	pete pete

(1 row(s) affected)

If your system shows surprising results, experiment with SOUNDEX, and make sure you understand its implementation in your system.

Unequal Joins

Back to the unequal (less-than or greater-than) join. Why does the unequal join work in this situation? How does it coax out a single copy of each pair? Let's start with a simple set of data. The testjoin table looks like this:

Adaptive Server Anywhere

```
create table testjoin
(
num int            not null,
name varchar(5)    not null
)

[table created]
```

The num field is the unique identifier (primary key). To prevent duplicates, create a unique index. Then add three rows of data.

Adaptive Server Anywhere

```
create index tjix on testjoin(num)

[index created]

insert into testjoin
values (1, 'one')
insert into testjoin
values (2, 'two')
insert into testjoin
values (3, 'one')

[3 rows]

select *
from testjoin

        num name
=========== =====
          1 one
          2 two
          3 one

[3 rows]
```

A cartesian product (no join specified) produces 9 rows (3 * 3).

Adaptive Server Anywhere

```
select t1.name, t2.name, t1.num, t2.num
from testjoin t1, testjoin t2
```

name	name	num	num
=====	=====	===========	===========
one	one	1	1
one	two	1	2
one	one	1	3
two	one	2	1
two	two	2	2
two	one	2	3
one	one	3	1
one	two	3	2
one	one	3	3

```
[9 rows]
```

An equal join on `name` produces five rows—each of the three rows joining to itself, plus one-1 and one-3 joining to each other in both directions.

Adaptive Server Anywhere

```
select t1.name, t2.name, t1.num, t2.num
from testjoin t1, testjoin t2
where t1.name = t2.name
```

name	name	num	num
=====	=====	===========	===========
one	one	1	1
one	one	1	3
two	two	2	2
one	one	3	1
one	one	3	3

```
[5 rows]
```

What we're looking for is matching names with different numbers. Adding a not-equal join on num finds the pair we want, but we get two versions:

Adaptive Server Anywhere
```
select t1.name, t2.name, t1.num, t2.num
from testjoin t1, testjoin t2
where t1.name = t2.name
    and t1.num <> t2.num
```

```
name   name          num          num
=====  =====  ===========  ===========
one    one              1            3
one    one              3            1

[2 rows]
```

Changing the not-equal (<>) join to a less-than join (or a greater-than join) results in one row:

Adaptive Server Anywhere
```
select t1.name, t2.name, t1.num, t2.num
from testjoin t1, testjoin t2
where t1.name = t2.name
    and t1.num < t2.num
```

```
name   name          num          num
=====  =====  ===========  ===========
one    one              1            3

[1 row]
```

To summarize the different ways you can compare columns from identical tables, this time displaying just one column from each table, see Figure 4–2.

n1	n2
==========	==========
1	1
1	2
1	3
2	1
2	2
2	3
3	1
3	2
3	3

Cartesian product: all possible
combinations (3 * 3 = 9)

n1	n2
==========	==========
1	1
2	2
3	3

Equal join: matches only (3)

n1	n2
==========	==========
2	1
3	1
3	2

Less-than (<) or greater-than
(>) join: ordered nonmatches

n1	n2
==========	==========
1	1
2	1
2	2
3	1
3	2
3	3

Less-than or equal (<=):
both sets

Figure 4-2. Comparing Joins

Using SOUNDEX as one term in a self-join gives this query and result:

Adaptive Server Anywhere

```
select c1.fname, c2.fname, c1.custnum, c2.custnum
from customer c1, customer c2
where soundex(c1.fname) = soundex(c2.fname)
    and c1.custnum < c2.custnum
```

fname	fname	custnum	custnum
====================	====================	=========	=========
lauren	LI-REN	923457789	999456789

[1 row]

But don't forget precedence! If you decide to look for people with near-matches
in *either* the first name or the second, you may be tempted to write code like
this:

Adaptive Server Anywhere

```
select c1.fname, c2.fname, c1.lname, c2.lname
from customer c1, customer c2
where  c1.custnum > c2.custnum and
   soundex(c1.fname) = soundex(c2.fname) or soundex(c1.lname) = soundex(c2.lname)
```

However, the results are surprising—you get 15 rows, a lot more than you expect.

Adaptive Server Anywhere

fname	fname	lname	lname
geoff lowell	geoff lowell	McBaird	McBaird
geoff lowell	merit	McBaird	mokoperto
phillip	phillip	aziz	aziz
SAM	SAM	khandasamy	khandasamy
merit	geoff lowell	mokoperto	McBaird
merit	merit	mokoperto	mokoperto
Pete	Pete	Peters	Peters
LI-REN	LI-REN	WONG	WONG
LI-REN	lauren	WONG	Menendez
ruby	ruby	archer	archer
felipe	felipe	le blanc	le blanc
kimiko	kimiko	sato	sato
(NULL)	(NULL)	deathmask-z	deathmask-z
pete pete	pete pete	rs	rs
lauren	lauren	Menendez	Menendez

[15 rows]

This is because the AND is processed before the OR. See Figure 4–3 for an operator precedence chart. That is, the AND clause is processed first, finding customers with alike-sounding first names *and* nonmatching customer numbers. This produces the one row you expect (for this example, the clause bracketed with /* and */ is treated as a comment and not executed).

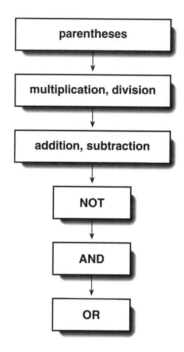

Figure 4-3. Precedence Hierarchy

Adaptive Server Anywhere

```
select c1.fname, c2.fname, c1.lname, c2.lname
from customer c1, customer c2
where c1.custnum > c2.custnum
    and soundex (c1.fname) = soundex (c2.fname)
  /*or soundex (c1.lname) = soundex (c2.lname)*/
```

fname	fname	lname	lname
===================	====================	====================	==================
LI-REN	lauren	WONG	Menendez

[1 row]

Then the OR clause is processed, looking for matching last names. Because there is no condition preventing self-matches, a lot more rows are returned.

Adaptive Server Anywhere

```
select c1.fname, c2.fname, c1.lname, c2.lname
from customer c1, customer c2
where  /* c1.custnum > c2.custnum
    and soundex(c1.fname) = soundex(c2.fname)
    or */ soundex(c1.lname) = soundex(c2.lname)
```

fname	fname	lname	lname
===================	====================	====================	====================
geoff lowell	geoff lowell	McBaird	McBaird
geoff lowell	merit	McBaird	mokoperto
phillip	phillip	aziz	aziz
SAM	SAM	khandasamy	khandasamy
merit	geoff lowell	mokoperto	McBaird
merit	merit	mokoperto	mokoperto
Pete	Pete	Peters	Peters
LI-REN	LI-REN	WONG	WONG
ruby	ruby	archer	archer
felipe	felipe	le blanc	le blanc
kimiko	kimiko	sato	sato
(NULL)	(NULL)	deathmask-z	deathmask-z
pete pete	pete pete	rs	rs
lauren	lauren	Menendez	Menendez

[14 rows]

What you are looking for is customers whose first or last name sounds like the first or last name of another customer—and you want to eliminate self-matches in both cases. In fact, you want the custnum condition to apply to both fname and lname. Throw in some parentheses, and you'll get what you expect.

Adaptive Server Anywhere

```
select c1.fname, c2.fname, c1.lname, c2.lname
from customer c1, customer c2
where  c1.custnum > c2.custnum and
  (
    soundex(c1.fname) = soundex(c2.fname)
    or soundex(c1.lname) = soundex(c2.lname)
  )
```

fname	fname	lname	lname
===================	===================	===================	===================
merit	geoff lowell	mokoperto	McBaird
LI-REN	lauren	WONG	Menendez

[2 rows]

Merit Mokoperto and Geoff McBaird have the same SOUNDEX value for last name. Lauren Menendez and Li-ren Wong match on the first name but not the last. The parentheses ensure that you get the answer you want.

SIMILAR

Adaptive Server Anywhere provides another function to help you work with almost-the-same names (it is called SIMILAR). It returns an integer (0–100) showing the percentage of matched characters (not matched sounds) in two strings. The syntax is

```
SIMILAR( string-expr1, string-expr2 )
```

Here's an example, drawn from the employee table.

Adaptive Server Anywhere
```
select e1.fname, e2.fname
from employee e1, employee e2
where e1.empnum < e2.empnum and
     similar (e1.fname, e2.fname) between 65 and 100
```

fname	fname
===================	===================
laurna	lauren

[1 row]

Locating Disconnected Rows

It's easy to find the rows that match—the joins—but how do you list those that don't? These rows may become lost or invisible, and their very existence may indicate an error in the way data was entered or protected.

In this section are three methods for locating and deleting disconnected rows:

- Outer join
- NOT IN subquery
- MINUS

Here's a listing of products that have sold: their product numbers show up in both the product and orderdetail tables.

Adaptive Server Anywhere

```
select distinct p.prodnum as Prod, o.prodnum as OrderedProd
from product p, orderdetail o
where p.prodnum = o.prodnum
order by p.prodnum
```

```
       Prod OrderedProd
=========== ===========
       1083        1083
       1099        1099
       1105        1105
       1106        1106
       1107        1107
       1108        1108
       1255        1255
       1357        1357
       1794        1794
       2000        2000
       2047        2047
       2050        2050
       2110        2110
       2111        2111
       2113        2113

[15 rows]
```

How do you find the other rows—the products that haven't sold? You certainly want to know what they are: you may want to change your marketing plan or call someone on the carpet or even drop a product, depending on how badly it has sold.

This section deals with unmatched master rows. Information on dealing with unmatched detail ("orphan") rows appears in "Checking Detail Against Master" in this chapter.

Using Outer Joins

If you use an outer join (see "Joins and Outer Joins" in Chapter 3) to list all products in the product table and only those that join (have been sold) in the orderdetail table, you get different results. The null markers highlight products that have not sold.

Adaptive Server Anywhere

```
select distinct p.prodnum as Prod, o.prodnum as OrderedProd
from product p left outer join orderdetail o
on p.prodnum = o.prodnum
order by p.prodnum
```

Prod	OrderedProd
======	======
1083	1083
1084	(NULL)
1099	1099
1104	(NULL)
1105	1105
1106	1106
1107	1107
1108	1108
1109	(NULL)
1110	(NULL)
1255	1255
1357	1357
1457	(NULL)
1794	1794
2000	2000
2047	2047
2049	(NULL)

```
2050        2050
2110        2110
2111        2111
2113        2113
```

[21 rows]

From the results, you can see that products numbered 1084, 1104, 1109, 1110, 1457, and 2049 have no sales.

Be sure to check your implementation's manual for outer join syntax—it's an important area with a lot of variation in notation. Figure 3–7 shows examples and Table 3–4 is a syntax table. The code samples in Figure 4–4 show the same outer join in four forms.

Outer Joins with IS NULL and IN Subquery   To see only the master rows that have no detail rows, check your system to see if it permits or returns meaningful results on an outer join query with a condition on the null values returned by the outer join.

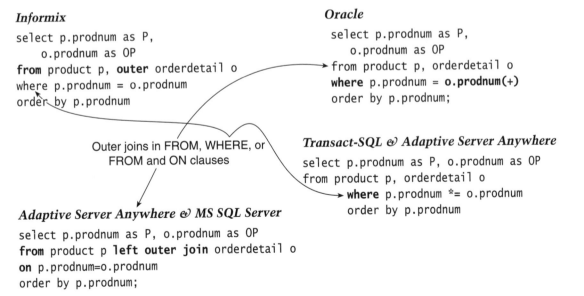

Informix
```
select p.prodnum as P,
    o.prodnum as OP
from product p, outer orderdetail o
where p.prodnum = o.prodnum
order by p.prodnum
```

Oracle
```
select p.prodnum as P,
    o.prodnum as OP
from product p, orderdetail o
where p.prodnum = o.prodnum(+)
order by p.prodnum;
```

Outer joins in FROM, WHERE, or
FROM and ON clauses

Transact-SQL & Adaptive Server Anywhere
```
select p.prodnum as P, o.prodnum as OP
from product p, orderdetail o
where p.prodnum *= o.prodnum
order by p.prodnum
```

Adaptive Server Anywhere & MS SQL Server
```
select p.prodnum as P, o.prodnum as OP
from product p left outer join orderdetail o
on p.prodnum=o.prodnum
order by p.prodnum;
```

Figure 4-4. Outer Join Examples

Adaptive Server Anywhere

```
select p.prodnum as Prod, o.prodnum as OrderedProd
from product p left outer join orderdetail o
on p.prodnum = o.prodnum
where o.prodnum is null
order by p.prodnum
```

```
         Prod OrderedProd
    =========== ===========
         1084      (NULL)
         1104      (NULL)
         1109      (NULL)
         1110      (NULL)
         1457      (NULL)
         2049      (NULL)
```

[6 rows]

Assuming that this technique works and you want to get rid of these no-sales products, you can use an IN subquery to remove nonmatching rows. To follow along with this example, do a BEGIN TRAN before you delete data and a ROLLBACK after you finish to restore the data, or be prepared to reload some rows in the product table.

Adaptive Server Anywhere

```
begin tran
```

[command completed]

```
delete from product
 where prodnum in
 (select p.prodnum
 from product p left outer join orderdetail o
 on p.prodnum = o.prodnum
 where o.prodnum is null)
```

[6 rows]

```
rollback
```

[command completed]

Transaction syntax is not the same everywhere. Some systems require ROLLBACK WORK or ROLLBACK TRAN. If you're using Oracle SQL Plus, you can type ROLLBACK after any data modification statement, restoring everything to the last COMMIT. You'll find information on transaction commands in "Experimenting and Transaction Management" in Appendix A.

Outer Joins with IS NULL and Join   For systems that allow multiple tables in the DELETE FROM clause and the IS NULL use we've looked at, you can do a DELETE based on the outer join NULL results.

Adaptive Server Anywhere
```
begin tran

[command completed]

delete product
 from product p left outer join  orderdetail o
 on p. prodnum = o.prodnum
where o.prodnum is null

[6 rows]

rollback

[command completed]
```

However, multiple tables in the DELETE FROM clause is not ANSI standard (it's a Transact-SQL variant), and not every system supports this use of IS NULL in an outer join. A works-everywhere method to remove nonmatching rows is to insert them into a holding table. Then do your deletion based on a join.

Outer Joins with a Holding Table   Create a table to hold prodnum from both tables. Add a unique index to make sure you don't get any duplicates.

Adaptive Server Anywhere
```
create table dumpem
(
prodnum      int          not null,
oprodnum     int
)
```

```
[table created]

create unique index dumpix on dumpem(prodnum)

[index created]

insert into dumpem
select p.prodnum, o.prodnum
from product p  left outer join orderdetail o
on p.prodnum=o.prodnum
where o.prodnum is null

[6 rows]
```

Do a SELECT from dumpem to check the data. It should contain the same six rows you found earlier. Now remove the rows from product.

Adaptive Server Anywhere
begin tran

```
delete product
where prodnum in
(select prodnum from dumpem)
```

Check the contents of product to make sure that the rows were removed.

Adaptive Server Anywhere
```
select prodnum
from product
order by prodnum

     prodnum
===========
       1083
       1099
       1105
       1106
       1107
       1108
```

```
              1255
              1357
              1794
              2000
              2047
              2050
              2110
              2111
              2113
```

[15 rows]

Now restore the deletion with a ROLLBACK and check the data again.

Adaptive Server Anywhere
```
rollback

select prodnum
from product
order by prodnum

      prodnum
===========
         1083
         1084
         1099
         1104
         1105
         1106
         1107
         1108
         1109
         1110
         1255
         1357
         1457
         1794
         2000
         2047
         2049
         2050
```

```
        2110
        2111
        2113
```

[21 rows]

Using NOT IN Subqueries

Another way to find master rows without matching detail rows is with a NOT IN subquery. The subquery (or inner query) finds products that have sold. The outer query locates all products that are not in the list produced by the inner query.

Adaptive Server Anywhere

```
select p.prodnum
from product p
where p.prodnum not in
    (select prodnum
    from orderdetail)
order by p.prodnum
```

```
    prodnum
===========
       1084
       1104
       1109
       1110
       1457
       2049
```

[6 rows]

You can then remove the disconnected rows with a related subquery. Again, for this example, bracket the DELETE with a BEGIN TRAN and a ROLLBACK (depending on the customs of your system) or plan to reload the rows you remove.

Adaptive Server Anywhere
begin tran

[command completed]

```
delete product
where prodnum not in
    (select prodnum
    from orderdetail)
```

[6 rows]

```
select count(*) from product
```

```
    count(*)
===========
         15
```

[1 row]

```
rollback
```

[command completed]

```
select count(*) from product
```

```
    count(*)
===========
         21
```

[1 row]

This method is highly portable. It relies on no special tricks in the DELETE FROM clause, puts no strains on outer joins and IS NULL, and avoids the problem of outer join syntax variants. However, NOT IN can be a performance hog, as noted in "Negating with NOT" in Chapter 6.

Using MINUS

If your system supports the MINUS operation, you can use it to find disconnected rows. MINUS "subtracts" rows in the second query from those in the
first. However, MINUS is not widely supported at present. Here's how it looks
on Oracle:

> ### Oracle
>
> ```
> SQL> select prodnum from product
>   2  minus
>   3  select prodnum from orderdetail
>   4  order by prodnum;
>
>    PRODNUM
> ---------
>       1084
>       1104
>       1109
>       1110
>       1457
>       2049
>
> 6 rows selected.
> ```

If you reverse the two MINUS queries, subtracting product from orderdetail,
this is what you see:

> ### Oracle
>
> ```
> SQL> select prodnum from orderdetail
>   2  minus
>   3  select prodnum from product
>   4  order by prodnum;
>
> no rows selected
> ```

There are no products in orderdetail that don't appear in product.

Comparing MINUS, INTERSECT, and UNION   As you probably guessed from
looking at the preceding code, MINUS is related to UNION. In fact, there are
three sister set operations (Figure 4–5).

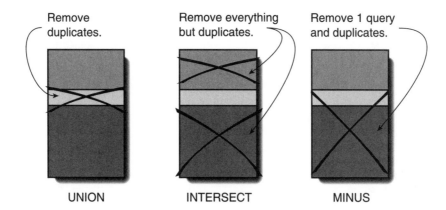

Remove duplicates.

Remove everything but duplicates.

Remove 1 query and duplicates.

UNION   INTERSECT   MINUS

Figure 4-5. UNION, INTERSECT, and MINUS

- UNION returns results from sets of queries. By default, it removes duplicate rows, so you see all unique rows and one copy (not two) of duplicates (see "UNION" in Chapter 3 for details).
- INTERSECT returns common results—that is, only the duplicates—from sets of queries.
- MINUS shows the rows from the first query less any copies from the second. You get different results when you change the order of queries.

Looking at Results To satisfy the curious, here is code for UNION and INTERSECT. Note that in these two cases, the order of the tables in the query makes no difference.

A UNION query of the two tables finds 22 rows. This includes the 21 prodnums in the product table plus one prodnum (1199) that appears only in the orderdetail table.

Oracle

```
SQL> select prodnum from product
  2  union
  3  select prodnum from orderdetail
  4  order by prodnum;
```

```
    PRODNUM
---------
      1083
      1084
      1099
      1104
      1105
      1106
      1107
      1108
      1109
      1110
      1199
      1255
      1357
      1457
      1794
      2000
      2047
      2049
      2050
      2110
      2111
      2113

22 rows selected.
```

INTERSECT finds the 15 prodnums that appear in both product and orderdetail.

Oracle

```
SQL> select prodnum from orderdetail
  2  intersect
  3  select prodnum from product
  4  order by prodnum;
```

```
     PRODNUM
     ---------
        1083
        1099
        1105
        1106
        1107
        1108
        1255
        1357
        1794
        2000
        2047
        2050
        2110
        2111
        2113

15 rows selected.
```

How is INTERSECT different from a join? It returns only one copy of each match. A join returns 32 rows, one for each row in orderdetail, except the orphan 1199.

Counting Items Based on Characteristics

How do you group items by some subset of their identity? The question is the answer: use GROUP BY and whatever functions you need to tease out the relevant feature.

Grouping By a Subset

Imagine that you want to divide customers up alphabetically, giving each of your support people a group of customers having the same initial letter. You can use string functions with GROUP BY to see if the customers are equally distributed. (Take a look at "Choosing a Subset" in Chapter 2 if you're not familiar with SUBSTR.)

Adaptive Server Anywhere

```
select substr (lname, 1,1), count(*)
from customer
group by substr (lname, 1,1)
```

substr(customer.lname,1,1)	count(*)
M	3
a	2
k	1
P	1
W	1
l	1
s	1
d	1
	1

[**9** rows]

In the customer table, names are in mixed case. The Adaptive Server Anywhere used in the example has a case-insensitive sort order—McBaird, Menendez, and mokoperto all fall in the M group. A system using a case-sensitive sort order shows ten groups rather than nine, because it recognizes M and m as different.

Oracle

```
SQL> select substr (lname, 1,1), count(*)
  2  from customer
  3  group by substr (lname, 1,1);
```

S	COUNT(*)
	1
M	2
P	1
W	1
a	2
d	1
k	1
l	1
m	1
s	1

10 rows selected.

You can make case irrelevant with the UPPER or LOWER function. (See "Case" in Chapter 2 for details on these functions and for background information on sorting.)

Oracle

```
SQL> select substr (upper (lname), 1,1), count(*)
  2  from customer
  3  group by substr (upper (lname), 1,1);


S   COUNT(*)
-   ---------
           1
A          2
D          1
K          1
L          1
M          3
P          1
S          1
W          1


9 rows selected.
```

ANSI and most SQL dialects require an exact match between the GROUP BY expression and the SELECT clause expression—and forbid any entries in the SELECT list other than the GROUP BY and aggregate expressions. This non-matching variant produces an error message:

Adaptive Server Anywhere

```
select substr (upper (lname), 1,1), count(*)
from customer
group by substr (lname, 1,1)


Error. Function or column reference to 'lname in the select list
must also appear in the group by.
```

Systems that allow nonidentical expressions may produce hard-to-understand results, with multiple entries for each letter.

Locating the Critical Element

Here's a more complicated example. Most products have a version, and you want to know how many instances you have of each. A query with DISTINCT is a good place to start.

Adaptive Server Anywhere
```
select distinct version
from product

version
========
Super 6.
10.1.01
(NULL)
6.5_a
10.1_6.5
1.2
1.1
2.2
10.1
1.3

[10 rows]
```

But these results are not adequate. What you want to do is see how many 1s, 10s, 2's, and 6s you have, without all the release information clutter that comes after the decimal point. You can use the same SUBSTRING-GROUP BY technique, with the addition of a function that finds one string inside another. In SQL Anywhere it is LOCATE or CHARINDEX (notice that the syntax of these two commands is not the same: in LOCATE the expression to be searched comes first; in CHARINDEX it is second). Other names for similar functions in different implementations are POSITION and INSTR. (Check "Locating Patterns" in Chapter 2 for a more complete description.)

A first attempt is something like this: a two-character substring of version starting two characters (–2) before the dot (.).

Adaptive Server Anywhere

```
select version, (substr (version, locate (version, '.' ) -2, 2 ))
from product

version  substr(product.version,locate
======== ==============================
Super 6.  6
10.1.01  10
10.1.01  10
(NULL)   (NULL)
6.5_a    6.
10.1_6.5 10
(NULL)   (NULL)
Super 6.  6
Super 6.  6
(NULL)   (NULL)
6.5_a    6.
1.2      1.
(NULL)   (NULL)
(NULL)   (NULL)
(NULL)   (NULL)
1.1      1.
2.2      2.
2.2      2.
10.1     10
1.3      1.
1.1      1.

[21 rows]
```

When you add the GROUP BY, you can assign a column alias in the SELECT clause to cut down on the size of the GROUP BY clause.

Adaptive Server Anywhere
```
select substring (version, ( charindex('.', version ) -2) , 2 ) as V, count(*)
from product
group by V
```

```
V      count(*)
==  ===========
 6          3
10          4
(N          6
6.          2
1.          4
2.          2
```

[6 rows]

The only problem with the results is the trailing decimal points, which prevent the two 6 tallies from being counted together. You can get rid of the points with a function that converts to an integer, such as CEILING (see the next subsection).

Adaptive Server Anywhere
```
select ceiling( substring (version, ( charindex('.', version ) -2) , 2 )) as V, count(*)
from product
group by V
```

```
                          V    count(*)
==============================  ===========
                          6          5
                         10          4
                     (NULL)          6
                          1          4
                          2          2
```

[5 rows]

Approximating with ROUND, TRUNCATE, CEILING, and FLOOR These four functions provide ways of approximating numbers. Not all systems support all four functions, and there are minor differences in spelling. For syntax summaries, see Table 4–1. Be sure to consult your system manuals for details.

- ROUND finds the next highest or lowest number at the specified precision.
- TRUNCATE chops the number at the specified precision.
- CEILING finds the lowest whole number greater than or equal to the expression.
- FLOOR finds the whole number less than or equal to the expression.

Here is an example showing the differences in these four functions.

Adaptive Server Anywhere
```
select distinct price, ceiling(price) as Ceiling, floor(price) as Floor,
    round (price, 1) as Round, truncnum(price,1) as Trunc
from product
where price < 50.00
order by price
```

price	Ceiling	Floor	Round	Trunc
19.99	20	19	20.00	19.90
20.00	20	20	20.00	20.00
29.00	29	29	29.00	29.00
29.99	30	29	30.00	29.90
39.99	40	39	40.00	39.90
49.00	49	49	49.00	49.00
49.99	50	49	50.00	49.90

[7 rows]

Table 4-1. TRUNCATE, ROUND, CEILING, and FLOOR

ANSI	ASA	ASE	MS SQL Server	Oracle	Informix
	ROUND (num_expr, int)	ROUND (num_expr, int)	ROUND (num_expr, int)	ROUND (num_expr, int)	ROUND (num_expr, int)
	TRUNCATE (num_expr, int) TRUNCNUM (num_expr, int)			TRUNC (num_expr, int)	TRUNC (num_expr, int)
	CEILING (num_expr)	CEILING (num_expr)	CEILING (num_expr)	CEIL (num_expr)	
	FLOOR (num_expr)	FLOOR (num_expr)	FLOOR (num_expr)	FLOOR (num_expr)	

Locating and Trimming Another approach works with SQL dialects that allow you to specify a trim character. (See "Space" in Chapter 2 for more on TRIM functions.)

Oracle

```
SQL>  select rtrim ( substr(version, instr(version, '.' ) -2, 2), '.'), count(*)
  2    from product
  3    group by  rtrim ( substr(version, instr(version, '.' ) -2, 2), '.');

RT   COUNT(*)
--   --------
  6         3
  1         4
 10         4
  2         2
  6         2
            6

6 rows selected.
```

Here, Oracle displays a blank for NULL. There are six rows with NULL versions, just as in the ASA results. To display a value for the NULL, see "Following Conventions" in Chapter 1 for SQL Plus SET commands or "Handling NULL" in Chapter 3 for a function.

Although the decimal points after the numbers are gone, there are now two groups with 6. To make both reside in the same group, add LTRIM to remove the leading space.

Oracle

```
SQL> select ltrim (  rtrim ( substr(version, instr(version, '.' ) -2, 2), '.')),
  2   count(*)
  3   from product
  4   group by  ltrim (  rtrim ( substr(version, instr(version, '.' ) -2, 2), '.'));

LT   COUNT(*)
--   --------
 1         4
10         4
 2         2
 6         5
           6

5 rows selected.
```

The points to remember here are as follows:

- Find the version divider (here, the first dot).
- Use SUBSTRING to include only values before the version divider.
- Cluster the values with GROUP BY.

Groups and Outer Joins

One minor wrinkle is worth looking at: combining GROUP BY and outer joins. Let's say you want to see customers and their orders. You could do a query like this, with GROUP BY and COUNT:

Adaptive Server Anywhere

```
select c.custnum, count( ordnum)
from ordermaster om, customer c
where om.custnum = c.custnum
group by c.custnum
order by count( ordnum )
```

```
custnum    count(om.ordnum)
========= ================
111222222                 1
111223333                 1
111333333                 1
111444444                 1
223456789                 1
776677778                 1
111334444                 2
777777778                 2
```

```
[8 rows]
```

However, this gives you no information on customers who haven't bought anything. An outer join is the answer (for details, consult "Joins and Outer Joins" in Chapter 3 or Figure 4–4). An outer join shows all the customers, no matter what their status. Here, nonbuying customers have a COUNT of zero. This example uses the ANSI syntax.

Adaptive Server Anywhere

```
select c.custnum, count( ordnum)
from ordermaster om right outer join customer c
on om.custnum = c.custnum
group by c.custnum
order by count( ordnum)
```

```
custnum    count(om.ordnum)
=========  ================
776667778                 0
777777777                 0
923457789                 0
999456789                 0
111222222                 1
111223333                 1
111333333                 1
111444444                 1
223456789                 1
776677778                 1
111334444                 2
777777778                 2

[12 rows]
```

Figuring Distribution

This question comes up pretty frequently on Internet news groups: What products have been sold by all stores? What employees belong to all groups? Using the MegaSysDataProNet Co database, an equivalent question is "Do any suppliers appear in *all* orders?"

To answer this question you have to ask two others:

1.   How many orders are there?

2.   Do any suppliers have that number of different orders?

Checking Detail Against Master

To get the number of orders, check `ordermaster` or `orderdetail`.

Adaptive Server Anywhere
```
select count(ordnum)
from ordermaster

count(ordnum)
=============
           12

[1 row]

select count(ordnum)
from orderdetail

count(ordnum)
=============
           33

[1 row]
```

It's obvious why the two tables return different results. The master (or parent) table ordermaster has one row for each order, while the detail (child) table orderdetail has a row for each line in the order—possibly many entries for each ordermaster value. To get the same results from both tables, try a DISTINCT in the orderdetail COUNT.

Adaptive Server Anywhere
```
select count (distinct ordnum)
from orderdetail

count(distinc
=============
           13

[1 row]
```

When used with aggregates such as COUNT, DISTINCT goes inside the parentheses. It does not need to be the first element in the SELECT clause.

Unfortunately, there is a discrepancy between the orders in ordermaster and orderdetail. An outer join is an easy way to compare items in a small data set. It shows that orderdetail has an orphan row. That is, there is a detail (child)

row for order 84 in orderdetail with no matching master (parent) order in the
ordermaster table.

Adaptive Server Anywhere

```
select distinct om.ordnum as Master, od.ordnum as Detail
from ordermaster om right outer join orderdetail od
on om.ordnum = od.ordnum
order by om.ordnum
```

```
          Master      Detail
        =========== ===========
          (NULL)          84
              81          81
              85          85
              86          86
              87          87
              89          89
              90          90
              91          91
              92          92
              93          93
              94          94
              95          95
              99          99
```

```
[13 rows]
```

Let's assume that some searches showed that there should be an order 84 in
the ordermaster table. To follow along, enter the order.

Adaptive Server Anywhere

```
insert into ordermaster
select 84,custnum,orderdate, creditcard, empnum
from ordermaster where ordnum = 85
```

```
[1 row inserted]
```

In real life, you'd be more likely to find that the detail row is an error and
decide to remove it. Use the techniques covered in "Locating Disconnected
Rows" in Chapter 4.

Using FOREIGN KEY REFERENCES To prevent such errors (detail rows without master rows) in the future, use ALTER TABLE to add a FOREIGN KEY REFERENCES statement (check your system manuals for details). It will check orderdetail.ordnum values against ordermaster.ordnum values on INSERT. Values that don't exist in the master table are not allowed in the detail table.

You may have to begin by adding a primary key constraint to the column you want to reference in the master table (ordermaster). FOREIGN KEY needs to work against a guaranteed unique column. Some systems accept only PRIMARY KEY columns as the referenced columns. Others allow any unique index.

Adaptive Server Anywhere

```
alter table ordermaster
add primary key(ordnum)
```

[primary key added]

Next, add the foreign key constraint to the detail table.

Adaptive Server Anywhere

```
alter table orderdetail
add foreign key(ordnum)
references ordermaster(ordnum)
```

[references added]

Some systems provide a CASCADE clause in CREATE and ALTER TABLE that goes into effect on DELETE or UPDATE, removing or changing detail rows in synch with the master row.

Making the Query Dynamic Back to the original problem: Do any suppliers appear in all orders? To test the data again, try a query that lists the suppliers and the number of orders each has.

Adaptive Server Anywhere

```
select suplrnum, count( distinct ordnum)
from product p, orderdetail o
where p.prodnum = o.prodnum
group by suplrnum
order by count(distinct ordnum)
```

```
suplrnum count(distinct o.ordnum)
======== =========================
     222                         1
     111                         2
     333                         3
     777                         3
     555                         4
     666                         5
     444                        13
```

[7 rows]

This indicates that there is one supplier (444) with products in 13 different orders. An earlier query showed that there was a total of 13 orders. To make the query fully dynamic, all you have to do is add a HAVING clause. The HAVING subquery finds the current number of different orders. Then it looks for the group from the outer query with that number of distinct orders.

Adaptive Server Anywhere
```
select suplrnum, count(distinct ordnum)
from orderdetail   o, product p
where o.prodnum = p.prodnum
group by suplrnum
having count(distinct ordnum) =
  ( select count(distinct ordnum) from orderdetail )
```

```
suplrnum count(distinct o.ordnum)
======== =========================
     444                        13
```

[1 row]

Two Products Together?

Here's a similar problem. What combinations of two products occur in orders multiple times (maybe you should package them together)?

• Use a self-join to find products that occur together.
• Add a HAVING clause to pinpoint those that do it more than once.

Adaptive Server Anywhere

```
select a.prodnum, b.prodnum,  count(*)
from orderdetail a, orderdetail b
where a.ordnum = b.ordnum and b.prodnum > a.prodnum
group by a.prodnum, b.prodnum
having count(*) > 1
```

prodnum	prodnum	count(*)
1099	2050	2
1083	1105	3
1083	2000	2
1083	1108	2
1105	2000	2

[5 rows]

According to the report, products 1099 and 2050 occur together two times, products 1083 and 1105 three times, and so on. Let's check the data to see if the results are correct.

Adaptive Server Anywhere

```
select *
from orderdetail
where prodnum in (1083, 1099, 1105, 1108, 2000, 2050)
order by ordnum
```

ordnum	prodnum	unit	shipdate
81	2050	5	Jan 01 1999
84	1099	1	(NULL)
84	2050	1	Jan 05 1999
85	2050	25	Jan 05 1999
86	1083	7	Jan 05 1999
86	1105	20	Jan 05 1999
86	2000	2	(NULL)
87	1083	1	(NULL)
87	1105	20	Jan 05 1999
87	2000	20	Jan 05 1999
89	1099	1	Jan 04 1999
89	2050	2	Jan 04 1999

```
92      2050    3333 (NULL)
93      1105       1 (NULL)
93      2050       5 Jan 05 1999
94      1083       5 Jan 05 1999
94      1108       1 (NULL)
95      1083       2 Jan 05 1999
95      1105       1 (NULL)
95      1108       1 (NULL)
99      2050    2222 (NULL)
```

[21 rows]

From these results, it is clear that the combination of products 1083 and 1105 happens in three orders: 86, 87, and 95. The combination of 1083 and 1108 is found in orders 94 and 95.

Restore ordermaster

For consistency, remove the row you added for ordermaster. You'll have to alter the table first, and remove the FOREIGN KEY and REFERENCES constraints. If you're using a different system, check your manuals. ALTER TABLE can vary. When you remove a primary key in ASA, references from other tables are also removed. Make sure you do not have multiple connections to ASA (through Interactive SQL or Sybase Central) when you run the command.

Adaptive Server Anywhere
```
alter table ordermaster
drop primary key
```

[primary key dropped]

```
delete from ordermaster
where ordnum = 84
```

[1 row deleted]

HAVING

HAVING is a WHERE clause for groups, but it can do some things WHERE cannot, such as include aggregates in its conditions. Remember that WHERE screens rows first, then GROUP BY does its job, and finally HAVING is applied.

Don't make HAVING take the place of WHERE—it could get expensive to wait to the end to eliminate rows you don't want. Use HAVING for its real purpose: to limit groups in the results. For example, this query finds the number of customers in each state:

Adaptive Server Anywhere

```
select state, count(*)
from customer
group by state
```

```
state    count(*)
=====  ===========
CA           2
MA           4
NY           3
MD           1
WA           1
TX           1
```

```
[6 rows]
```

To see just those states with more than one customer, use HAVING.

Adaptive Server Anywhere

```
select state, count(*)
from customer
group by state
having count(*) > 1
```

```
state    count(*)
=====  ===========
CA           2
MA           4
NY           3
```

```
[3 rows]
```

Putting the qualification in the WHERE clause won't work for the following reasons.

- Aggregates are illegal in WHERE, unless they are in subqueries.
- The qualification applies to the GROUP BY result, which is not available when the WHERE is evaluated.

Adaptive Server Anywhere

```
select state, count(*)
from customer
where count(*) > 1
group by state

Error: Invalid expression near 'count(*)'.
```

Use WHERE to eliminate rows you don't want to be considered in your final groups. Here, customers with status equal to 3 are not included in the first results and hence do not make it into groups.

Adaptive Server Anywhere

```
select state, count(*)
from customer
where status <> 3
group by state
```

state	count(*)
=====	===========
MA	2
NY	2
CA	1
TX	1

[4 rows]

Combining the WHERE and HAVING, you find states that contain two or more customers with a status of 1 or 2.

Adaptive Server Anywhere

```
select state, count(*)
from customer
where status <> 3
group by state
having count(*) >1

state    count(*)
=====  ===========
MA             2
NY             2

[2 rows]
```

"Choosing Between HAVING and WHERE" in Chapter 6 has more information on this topic.

Summary

This chapter covers some issues involving multiples. In the process, it presents code with unequal joins, outer joins, self-joins, groups, and subqueries. It also discusses ways to prevent problems associated with duplicates, near-duplicates, and disconnected rows.

- There are several ways to find and remove duplicate rows. GROUP BY and HAVING help locate extras, which you can store in a holding table. Alternatively, you can use a row identifier if your system supports that feature. It is important to prevent new problems by adding a unique index, or a UNIQUE/PRIMARY KEY constraint, after you clean up your duplicate tables.
- Finding near-duplicates is a related skill. The example features unequal joins, self-joins, and the SOUNDEX function to pair names that sound alike and display them in one order.
- "Locating Disconnected Rows" focuses on master rows with no details, using outer joins as a way to find them. It also discusses IS NULL with joins and subqueries as methods for deleting these rows. Another solution involves a holding table. Some systems support MINUS for finding the difference between two tables, and there is a brief review of UNION, INTERSECT, and MINUS.

- The section on counting items reprises some of the functions from Chapter 2, such as SUBSTRING and LOCATE, used with GROUP BY, to categorize items based on some subset of their characteristics.
- How to find items that appear in every order, or products that often sell together, is a common question. Here, you use DISTINCT with aggregates, HAVING, and GROUP BY to figure distribution. You also consider the problem or orphans—detail rows with no master—and investigate using the REFERENCES constraint to prevent them.

Chapter 5

Navigating Numbers

In This Chapter

- Comparing Autonumbering Systems
- Locating the High Value
- Creating Row Numbers
- Finding the Top *N*: Six Approaches
- Picking Every *N*th
- Generating a Running Total

What's in a Number?

Most systems provide a way to create automatic unique sequential numbers for an identifier column (say a customer or part number) on insert. The mechanisms vary a great deal, from default to column property to database object to datatype. Since these numbers are so useful, the difference presents some special problems for porting from one system to another. The chapter begins with examples of setting up autonumbering for each of the test systems.

Next you'll find an assortment of answers to frequently asked questions, grouped together because they use similar techniques (self-joins, GROUP BY, and aggregates) and all have to do with numbers. In many cases, you'll see alternatives to the core technique—multiple ways to solve the same problem. Performance can vary greatly among these approaches, depending on how your system optimizes queries, the amount of data you have, and the indexes on your tables, so there are no guarantees! However, all the different methods are interesting. Working through them and trying some variants of your own is sure to give you new ideas. As always, do some testing before you decide how to tackle a particular problem, and keep checking as your application grows and changes. The self-join/GROUP BY/aggregate techniques are arranged by difficulty; each one builds on earlier solutions.

Comparing Autonumbering Systems

Most systems provide a way to generate unique numbers as data is inserted. For example, you want each new customer or part you enter to have a different numeric identifier, and you want it to happen automatically on INSERT. This is numbering on input; it is not the same as numbering output rows, described in "Creating Row Numbers" later in the chapter.

The approaches to this problem vary greatly. The following sections give examples for ASA, Microsoft SQL Server, Sybase Adaptive Server Enterprise, Oracle, and Informix. You'll find a summary in Table 5–1.

ASA: Default

On ASA, you define autonumbering as a default in the CREATE TABLE statement. The column must be integer or exact numeric datatype, and performance is best if the column is defined as PRIMARY KEY or is the first column of an index. This allows the system to find the high value without searching the entire table. (There is more on indexes in Chapter 6.)

Adaptive Server Anywhere

```
create table testseq
(num int not null default autoincrement,
name varchar(10) not null)

[table created]
```

Table 5–1. Sequences

ANSI	ASA	ASE	MS SQL Server	Oracle	Informix
	DEFAULT AUTOINCRE- MENT in CREATE TABLE (also implemented as IDENTITY)	IDENTITY column property in CREATE TABLE	IDENTITY column property in CREATE TABLE	CREATE SEQUENCE seq, then INSERT seq.nextval	SERIAL datatype in CREATE TABLE INSERT 0 for SERIAL to get next number

When you INSERT rows, give a value for the name column, but none for num:

Adaptive Server Anywhere

```
insert into testseq (name)
values ('Amir')

insert into testseq (name)
values ('Marge')

insert into testseq (name)
values ('Tri')

[3 rows]
```

A SELECT shows sequential numbers in the num column:

Adaptive Server Anywhere

```
select *
from testseq

        num name
=========== ==========
          1 Amir
          2 Marge
          3 Tri

[3 rows]
```

Transact-SQL: Column Property

In Transact-SQL, the autonumbering feature is a column property rather than a default. MS SQL Server and Sybase ASE have the same approach but show some differences.

Microsoft SQL Server: IDENTITY (start, increment)   IDENTITY can take start and increment values (here it is set to start at 1 and increment by 1).

MS SQL Server

```
create table testseq
(num int not null identity (1,1),
name varchar(10) not null)

The command(s) completed successfully.
```

INSERT just as in ASA, and when you look at the rows, you see the automatically inserted numbers.

MS SQL Server

```
insert into testseq (name)
values ('Amir')
....

select *
from testseq

num         name
----------- ----------
1           Amir
2           Marge
3           Tri

(3 row(s) affected)
```

Sybase Adaptive Server Enterprise: IDENTITY ASE requires IDENTITY columns to be NUMERIC datatype with a scale (number of digits to the right of the decimal point) of 0. IDENTITY takes the place of the NULL/NOT NULL status.

Adaptive Server Enterprise

```
create table testseq
(num numeric(4,0) identity,
name varchar(10) not null)

[table created]
```

Here's what you see after adding three rows and running a SELECT * on the table:

Adaptive Server Enterprise

```
num    name
------ ----
     1 Amir
     2 Marge
     3 Tri

(3 rows affected)
```

Oracle: CREATE SEQUENCE

Oracle requires that you create a sequence as a separate object and then use it in the INSERT. The sequence has no role in the CREATE TABLE statement.

Oracle
```
SQL> create sequence newseq;

Sequence created.

SQL>  create table testseq
  2  (num number not null,
  3  name varchar2(10) not null);

Table created.
```

The sequence you create can have any name, but you must use nextval with it in the INSERT to generate unique values.

Oracle
```
SQL>  insert into testseq
  2  values ( newseq.nextval,  'Amir');

1 row created.
```

Use the same code for two more inserts, changing the value in the name column so that you get rows for Marge and Tri. When you check the table, you'll find auto numbers in place.

Oracle
```
SQL> select *
  2  from testseq;

      NUM NAME
--------- ----------
        1 Amir
        2 Marge
        3 Tri

3 rows selected.
```

Informix: SERIAL Datatype

Informix handles sequential numbers in the CREATE TABLE statement with a special SERIAL datatype. Specifying 0 for the SERIAL column during INSERT makes Informix assign the next sequential number.

Informix
```
create table testseq
(num serial not null,
name varchar(10) not null)

Table created.

insert into testseq
values ( 0, 'Amir')
insert into testseq
values ( 0, 'Marge')
insert into testseq
values ( 0, 'Tri')

select *
from testseq
        num name
          1 Amir
          2 Marge
          3 Tri


[3 rows]
```

Associated Issues

With this much variation in autonumbering, be prepared to do some work when you move from system to system. Check your documentation for information on these areas:

- Specifying datatypes and other column properties (null/not null, for example)
- Setting the start number and increment value
- Relating to table constraints and indexes
- Locating the current highest number

- Creating ranges or maximums
- Dealing with DELETEs and UPDATEs (reuse the number or leave a gap?)
- Overriding autonumbering

Most SQL engines have a rich set of tools to manage the sequential numbers.

Locating the High Value

Which supplier has the largest number of products? Here are three methods for finding out.

- You can start by grouping on `supplier.name` and counting the products per group, then adding a HAVING clause to limit results.
- If that isn't allowed in your system, check to see if the FROM subquery is supported.
- Finally, some systems have built-in output row counters (ROWCOUNT, FIRST, TOP) that limit the number of rows returned.

GROUP BY, COUNT, HAVING MAX(COUNT)

Although the GROUP BY and COUNT are standard, HAVING shows some variations among systems in what is and is not allowed.

Adaptive Server Anywhere

```
select suplrnum, count(prodnum)
from product
group by suplrnum
```

```
suplrnum count(product.prodnum)
======== =====================
     555                      3
     666                      6
     444                      4
     333                      3
     222                      1
     777                      3
     111                      1

[7 rows]
```

An ORDER BY puts the data in the correct order.

Adaptive Server Anywhere

```
select suplrnum, count(prodnum)
from product
group by suplrnum
order by count(prodnum)
```

```
suplrnum count(product.prodnum)
======== ======================
     111                       1
     222                       1
     333                       3
     555                       3
     777                       3
     444                       4
     666                       6
```

```
[7 rows]
```

If your system allows nested aggregates (many don't, including Adaptive Server Anywhere; the following example runs on Sybase ASE) you can add a HAVING clause to find the MAX COUNT.

Adaptive Server Enterprise

```
select suplrnum, count(prodnum)
from product
group by suplrnum
having count (prodnum ) = max (count (prodnum ) )
```

```
suplrnum
--------- ----------
666        6
```

```
(1 row affected)
```

When nested aggregates are illegal, you get an answer like this:

Oracle

```
SQL> select suplrnum, count(prodnum)
  2  from product
  3  group by suplrnum
  4  having count (prodnum ) = max (count (prodnum ) );

ERROR at line 4:
ORA-00935: group function is nested too deeply
```

FROM Subquery

Here's another way to find the supplier with the largest number of products.

Although ASA doesn't allow nested aggregates in the HAVING clause, it does allow this more complex query (Figure 5–1). You calculate the COUNT values and assign a display alias (HiNum) in a FROM clause subquery (technically, it's a nested table expression, not a subquery). Then you figure the MAX of HiNum in the outer query. The ANSI standard supports this syntax, so it'll probably become more widely available as time goes on.

You can run the Oracle version of this with or without the table alias (the p that represents the inner SELECT as a table).

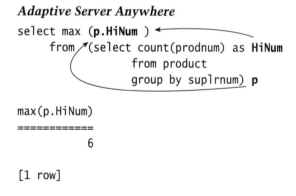

Adaptive Server Anywhere

```
select max (p.HiNum ) ←
     from (select count(prodnum) as HiNum
                from product
                group by suplrnum) p

max(p.HiNum)
============
           6

[1 row]
```

Figure 5-1. FROM Subquery

Oracle

```
SQL> select max (HiNum)
   2   from   (select count(prodnum) as HiNum
   3            from product
   4            group by suplrnum);


MAX(HINUM)
----------
         6


1 row selected.
```

The FROM subquery handles the nested aggregate neatly, returning the highest COUNT value. However, it does not display the suplrnum associated with the largest number of products. Applying the FROM nesting technique to the HAVING clause produces a complete result.

Adaptive Server Anywhere

```
select supplier.suplrnum, supplier.name, count(*)
from supplier, product
where supplier.suplrnum = product.suplrnum
group by supplier.suplrnum,  supplier.name
having count(*) =
        ( select max (p.HiNum)
         from  ( select count(*) as HiNum
                 from product
                 group by suplrnum ) p
        )


suplrnum name                      count(*)
======== ==================== ===========
     666 Above Average Arts            6


[1 row]
```

Thanks to John Viescas, who reviewed the manuscript, for this elegant solution.

Row Counts of Various Sorts

If restrictions on nesting aggregates apply to your system or the FROM sub-query doesn't work, check out the performance issues with setting a limit on the number of rows returned (SET ROWCOUNT *N* in Transact-SQL and Adaptive Server Anywhere, for example) and ordering results in descending order.

SET ROWCOUNT

Two problems are possible with SET ROWCOUNT.

1. You forget to turn the ROWCOUNT (or equivalent) off and get odd results on other queries. This is not an issue when you activate the counter for each query rather than for each session.

2. You may get poorer performance than you expect if some part of the query (such as an ORDER BY) forces you to bring back all the results before picking up the top *N*. An index on the column you want could prevent this—the SQL engine could go right to the top *N* values.

   Adaptive Server Anywhere
   ```
   set rowcount 1
   ```

   [command executed]

   ```
   select suplrnum, count(prodnum)
   from product
   group by suplrnum
   order by count(prodnum) desc
   ```

   ```
   suplrnum count(prodnum)
   ======== ==============
        666              6
   ```

   [1 row]

Turn ROWCOUNT off like this:

   Adaptive Server Anywhere
   ```
   set rowcount 0
   ```

   [command executed]

Select FIRST   Informix offers the keyword FIRST. Use it in the SELECT clause on a query-by-query basis to specify the maximum number of rows to return.

Informix
```
select first 1 suplrnum, count(prodnum) as num
from product
group by suplrnum
```

```
suplrnum num
-------- ---
666        6
```

```
1 row(s) retrieved.
```

Select TOP   Microsoft SQL Server 7 supports both ROWCOUNT and TOP (similar to Informix's FIRST). When you use TOP or FIRST with an ORDER BY, rows are returned in the order you specify but never more rows than indicated in the TOP or FIRST clause.

MS SQL Server 7
```
select top 5 suplrnum, count(prodnum) as num
from product
group by suplrnum
order by num desc
```

```
suplrnum num
-------- -----------
666      6
444      4
333      3
555      3
777      3
```

```
(5 row(s) affected)
```

SQL Server's TOP has an additional feature that allows you to specify a percentage of the output (rather than an absolute number of rows) by adding the keyword PERCENT after the number.

Table 5-2. Counting Rows

ANSI	ASA	ASE	MS SQL Server	Oracle	Informix
	ROWCOUNT	ROWCOUNT	ROWCOUNT TOP		FIRST

MS SQL Server 7

```
select top 25 percent suplrnum, count(prodnum) as num
from product
group by suplrnum
order by num desc


suplrnum num
-------- -----------
666      6
444      4


(2 row(s) affected)
```

Check your manuals for details on the commands listed in Table 5–2.

Creating Row Numbers

You number output rows in two ways:

- With a built-in capability, as in Oracle ROWNUM, or ASA's NUMBER(*)
- By creating the numbers on the fly

Either way you do it, remember that the numbers apply only to a particular result set. They do not imply any constant internal number.

System Numbers

Here are two examples of system-provided output numbering methods (summarized in Table 5–3):

- Oracle provides ROWNUM, an Oracle pseudo column you can include in SELECT statements.
- Adaptive Server Anywhere has a similar feature, called NUMBER(*).

Table 5-3. Row Number Functions

ANSI	SQL Anywhere	Sybase ASE	MS SQL Server	Oracle	Informix
	NUMBER(*)			ROWNUM	

Oracle ROWNUM   ROWNUM is based on the order of the rows when the *first* set of query results are returned. (ORDER BY clauses take effect *after* the numbers are assigned.) The ROWNUM of any particular row varies from time to time, depending on the query conditions. Don't confuse ROWNUM with a related Oracle feature, ROWID (see "Using ROWID to Remove Duplicates" in Chapter 4).

To get neatly numbered report lines on Oracle, try a query like this:

Oracle

```
SQL> select custnum, fname, rownum
  2  from customer;

CUSTNUM    FNAME                    ROWNUM
---------  --------------------  ---------
111222222  geoff lowell                  1
111223333  ruby                          2
111333333  phillip                       3
111334444  felipe                        4
111444444  kimiko                        5
223456789  SAM                           6
777777777                                7
777777778  merit                         8
776677778  pete pete                     9
776667778  Pete                         10
923457789  lauren                       11
999456789  LI-REN                       12

12 rows selected.
```

However, if you add an ORDER BY (or another feature that creates intermediate results), the ROWNUM values aren't useful. That is because the ORDER BY is imposed after the ROWNUM.

Oracle

```
SQL> select custnum, fname, rownum
  2  from customer
  3  order by fname;
```

```
CUSTNUM    FNAME                    ROWNUM
---------  --------------------  ---------
223456789  SAM                           6
999456789  LI-REN                       12
776667778  Pete                         10
111334444  felipe                        4
111222222  geoff lowell                  1
111444444  kimiko                        5
923457789  lauren                       11
777777778  merit                         8
776677778  pete pete                     9
111333333  phillip                       3
111223333  ruby                          2
777777777                                7

12 rows selected.
```

In *Oracle8: The Complete Reference* (Osborne McGraw-Hill, Oracle Press, 1999), authors George Koch and Kevin Loney suggest creating a view to put the data in the order you want and then selecting from the view, adding the ROWNUM column. This example applies the technique to the customer table. You want to show the row numbers in fname order. Notice that the view has a GROUP BY clause, since ORDER BY is not allowed in a CREATE VIEW statement. The GROUP BY puts the view data in fname order.

Oracle
```
SQL> create view test1
  2  as
  3  select custnum, fname
  4  from customer
  5  group by fname, custnum;

View created.
```

When you query the view without imposing any order, you see the rows in fname order (uppercase followed by lowercase).

Oracle

```
SQL> select custnum, fname
  2  from test1;

CUSTNUM   FNAME
--------- --------------------
223456789 SAM
999456789 LI-REN
776667778 Pete
111334444 felipe
111222222 geoff lowell
111444444 kimiko
923457789 lauren
777777778 merit
776667778 pete pete
111333333 phillip
111223333 ruby
777777777

12 rows selected.
```

Adding ROWNUM assigns a number to each row. The ORDER BY is not necessary in this case—it simply echoes the action of the CREATE VIEW GROUP BY.

Oracle

```
SQL> select custnum, fname, rownum
  2  from test1
  3  order by fname;

CUSTNUM   FNAME                           ROWNUM
--------- --------------------------- ---------
223456789 SAM                                  1
999456789 LI-REN                               2
776667778 Pete                                 3
111334444 felipe                               4
111222222 geoff lowell                         5
111444444 kimiko                               6
923457789 lauren                               7
777777778 merit                                8
776667778 pete pete                            9
```

```
111333333 phillip                        10
111223333 ruby                           11
777777777                                12
```

12 rows selected.

NUMBER(*)   The NUMBER(*) function in Adaptive Server Anywhere allows you to create row numbers for output.

NUMBER does not have the Oracle ORDER BY limitation, because the numbers are assigned after all other processing. Nonetheless, Adaptive Server Anywhere documentation urges caution when using the NUMBER function and suggests the AUTOINCREMENT feature instead for some uses. (See "Comparing Autonumbering Systems" at the beginning of this chapter for more on this topic.)

Here's an example.

Adaptive Server Anywhere

```
select  custnum, fname, number (*)
from customer
```

```
custnum    fname                   number(*)
=========  ===================     ===========
111222222 geoff lowell                       1
111333333 phillip                            2
223456789 SAM                                3
777777778 merit                              4
776667778 Pete                               5
999456789 LI-REN                             6
111223333 ruby                               7
111334444 felipe                             8
111444444 kimiko                             9
777777777 (NULL)                            10
776667778 pete pete                         11
923457789 lauren                            12
```

[12 rows]

Without sorting, the rows are in no particular order. When you add an ORDER BY clause, the rows change order and so do the NUMBER values. The example database on ASA is set up to be case insensitive, hence the sort order ("Sort Order" in "Case" in Chapter 2 gives more information on sorting).

Adaptive Server Anywhere

```
select  custnum, fname, number (*)
from customer
where fname between 'a' and 'm'
order by fname
```

```
custnum    fname                    number(*)
=========  ====================  ============
111334444  felipe                           1
111222222  geoff lowell                     2
111444444  kimiko                           3
923457789  lauren                           4
999456789  LI-REN                           5
```

[5 rows]

Check your system documentation to make sure you understand how (and if) your implementation handles built-in result row numbers. Be sure to consider performance implications.

Your Numbers

You can create row numbers on the fly with an unequal self-join and a COUNT. (Review self-joins and unequal joins in "Finding Near-Duplicates" in Chapter 4.)

Adaptive Server Anywhere

```
select count(*) as num, c1.fname
from customer c1, customer c2
where c2.fname <= c1.fname
group by c1.fname
order by num
```

```
        num fname
=========== =====================
          1 SAM
          2 felipe
          3 geoff lowell
          4 kimiko
          5 lauren
          6 LI-REN
          7 merit
          8 Pete
          9 pete pete
         10 phillip
         11 ruby
```

[11 rows]

Why does this work? We've seen before how Cartesian joins, equal joins, and unequal joins do their jobs (Figure 4–2). A join that includes both matches and ordered nonmatches gives output as in Figure 5–2.

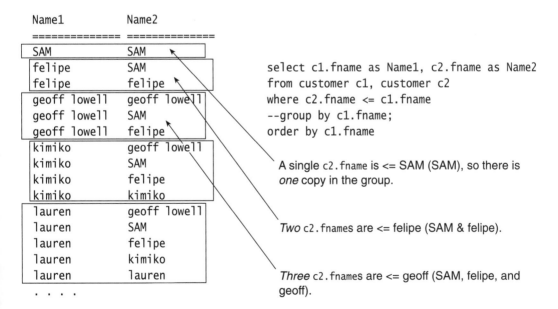

```
Name1           Name2
=============== ===============
SAM             SAM
felipe          SAM
felipe          felipe
geoff lowell    geoff lowell
geoff lowell    SAM
geoff lowell    felipe
kimiko          geoff lowell
kimiko          SAM
kimiko          felipe
kimiko          kimiko
lauren          geoff lowell
lauren          SAM
lauren          felipe
lauren          kimiko
lauren          lauren
. . . .
```

```
select c1.fname as Name1, c2.fname as Name2
from customer c1, customer c2
where c2.fname <= c1.fname
--group by c1.fname;
order by c1.fname
```

A single c2.fname is <= SAM (SAM), so there is *one* copy in the group.

Two c2.fnames are <= felipe (SAM & felipe).

Three c2.fnames are <= geoff (SAM, felipe, and geoff).

Figure 5–2. Creating Row Numbers

When you add GROUP BY and COUNT, you get row numbers. (Some systems also require an ORDER BY.)

Adaptive Server Anywhere

```
select count(*), c1.fname
from customer c1, customer c2
where c2.fname <= c1.fname
group by c1.fname
order by c1.fname
```

```
  count(*) fname
=========== ====================
          1 SAM
          2 felipe
          3 geoff lowell
          4 kimiko
          5 lauren
          6 LI-REN
          7 merit
          8 Pete
          9 pete pete
         10 phillip
         11 ruby
```

```
[11 rows]
```

This is an interesting exercise, but remember, it has nothing to do with permanent numbering. In this simple form, it works for unique data only. When you try the same code on customer.city (a column with duplicate data) you get these confusing results:

Adaptive Server Anywhere

```
select count(*), c1.city
from customer c1, customer c2
where c2.city <= c1.city
group by c1.city
```

```
count(*) city
========== ====================
         2 Berkeley
        20 reading
        14 NY
         8 Boston
         5 Macedon
        12 Silver Spring
         8 Oakland
        11 Seattle
         1 Austin
```

[9 rows]

A little research reveals that a DISTINCT is helpful, as the following partial results show. There is one Austin row, two Berkeley rows, three Boston rows, four Macedon rows, and so on.

Adaptive Server Anywhere

```
select distinct c1.city, c2.city
from customer c1, customer c2
where c2.city <= c1.city
order by c1.city
```

```
city                 city
==================== ====================
Austin               Austin
Berkeley             Austin
Berkeley             Berkeley
Boston               Austin
Boston               Berkeley
Boston               Boston
Macedon              Austin
Macedon              Berkeley
Macedon              Boston
Macedon              Macedon
NY                   Austin
NY                   Berkeley
NY                   Boston
NY                   Macedon
NY                   NY
[partial results]
```

The final query, with GROUP BY, puts the DISTINCT inside the COUNT. This allows you to tally unique occurrences of c1.city for each c2.city.

Adaptive Server Anywhere

```
select count(distinct c1.city), c2.city
from customer c1, customer c2
where c2.city >= c1.city
group by c2.city

count(distinct c1.city) city
======================= =====================
                      1 Austin
                      2 Berkeley
                      3 Boston
                      4 Macedon
                      5 NY
                      6 Oakland
                      7 Reading
                      8 Seattle
                      9 Silver Spring

[9 rows]
```

The order of your results may vary. DISTINCT can be a performance loser. (Read more about tuning it in "Sorting with DISTINCT and UNION" in Chapter 6.)

Finding the Top *N*: Six Approaches

Why would you want to find the top (or bottom) *N*? Perhaps you need to send special offers to the best five customers or prune the lowest-selling three products or give a 10% discount to the biggest ten purchases. You don't want to display the whole list of customers or products or sales totals to get this information. Here are six quite different methods to try.

- Row limits and ORDER BY
- Row numbers and HAVING
- Subquery
- Nested Subqueries
- Aggregates and many copies
- Cursors

As noted earlier in this chapter in the section "Locating the High Value," these techniques may not be available in your SQL dialect. Do some testing before you rely on any one of them.

Row Limits and ORDER BY

Let's say you want to see the products with the highest three prices. If your system has a way of specifying the number of rows to display (see in "Row Counts of Various Sorts" in this chapter), you can set it to 3 and then order the results in descending price order. Don't forget to turn ROWCOUNT off—it stays in effect until you change it or log out.

> *Adaptive Server Anywhere*
> **set rowcount 3**
>
> [command completed]
>
> select name, price
> from product
> order by **price desc**
>
> | name | price |
> |====================|==========|
> | memory8 | 400.00 |
> | z_connector | 149.00 |
> | memory tripler | 119.99 |
>
> [3 rows]
>
> **set rowcount 0**
>
> [command completed]

Row Numbers and HAVING

Here's another way to find the top five customers or lowest-selling three products or biggest ten purchases. Specifically, we're using row numbers with HAVING to list the five highest product prices.

```
          P2                      P1
==================== ====================
     400.0000            400.0000
     149.0000            149.0000
     400.0000            149.0000
     119.9900            119.9900
     149.0000            119.9900
     400.0000            119.9900
      89.9900             89.9900
     119.9900             89.9900
     149.0000             89.9900
     400.0000             89.9900
          .  .  .  .
```

The highest P1 price is less than
no P2 price and equal to 1.

The next highest P1 price is less
than 1 P2 price and equal to 2.

Figure 5–3. Row Numbers and HAVING

This is similar to the "Your Numbers" technique for row numbers in that it involves a self-join and a GROUP BY with COUNT. It adds a new element to the combination—a HAVING clause—to limit the number of rows returned (Figure 5–3). However, this neat solution brings the possibility of more problems. For example, you'd expect this code to return five rows, but you get only four.

Adaptive Server Anywhere
```
select count ( p2.price) as Num, p1.price as Price
from product p1, product p2
where p1.price <= p2.price
group by Price
having count(p2.price) <= 5
```

```
    Num        Price
=========== ==========
      4        89.99
      3       119.99
      2       149.00
      1       400.00
```

[4 rows]

What's going on? A look at the data without the HAVING shows the under-lying data and reminds us that price is not necessarily unique. (You can deactivate or comment out the HAVING clause by preceding it with double dashes.)

Adaptive Server Anywhere
```
select count ( p2.price) as Num, p1.price as Price
from product p1, product p2
where p1.price <= p2.price
group by Price
--having count(p2.price) <= 5
```

Num	Price
===	===
105	19.99
48	20.00
13	29.00
24	29.99
30	39.99
7	49.00
12	49.99
4	89.99
3	119.99
2	149.00
1	400.00

[11 rows]

As in the earlier section "Creating Row Numbers," when there are duplicate values, adding a DISTINCT in the COUNT changes the results.

Adaptive Server Anywhere
```
select count ( distinct p2.price ) as Num, p1.price as Price
from product p1, product p2
where p1.price <= p2.price
group by Price
--having count(distinct p2.price) <= 5
```

Num	Price
===========	==========
11	19.99
10	20.00
9	29.00
8	29.99
7	39.99
6	49.00
5	49.99
4	89.99
3	119.99
2	149.00
1	400.00

[11 rows]

To get the top five, remove the comment sign from the HAVING clause. If results are in ascending order, add an ORDER BY DESC.

Adaptive Server Anywhere

```
select count ( distinct p2.price) as Num, p1.price as Price
from product p1, product p2
where p1.price <= p2.price
group by Price
having count(distinct p2.price) <= 5
order by Price desc
```

Num	Price
===========	==========
1	400.00
2	149.00
3	119.99
4	89.99
5	49.99

[5 rows]

Basically, this says that only one p2.price is less than or equal to $400.00, two p2.prices are less than or equal to $149.00, and so on. (Your system may require p1.price rather than the column display alias, Price, in the GROUP BY clause.)

The process breaks down into the following steps.

1. Evaluate all the rows in the table, using the WHERE clause to choose which ones to include in the groups.

2. Build a work table with the columns in the GROUP BY list, plus one more column for each aggregate.

3. Load the groups into the work table.

4. Calculate the aggregates for each group.

5. Apply the HAVING clause to govern GROUP rows that show up in the final results.

Subquery

Here's another method for finding the top five customers or lowest-selling three products or biggest ten purchases without displaying all the data from the relevant tables. Once again, the example finds the five highest prices in the product table.

This correlated subquery (in two slightly different versions) works on most systems. Like the self-join, it compares the table to itself. The outer query feeds the first qualifying row to the inner query, where it is analyzed to see if it meets the inner query conditions, and the inner query returns results to the outer query. Then the outer query passes the next qualifying row to the inner query. See "Subqueries" in Chapter 3 for an illustration of how this works.

Adaptive Server Anywhere

```
select distinct price
from product p1
where
     (select count(*)
      from product p2
      where p1.price < p2.price)    <=5
order by price

     price
==========
     49.99
     89.99
    119.99
    149.00
    400.00

[5 rows]
```

Oracle
```
SQL> select distinct price
  2  from product p1
  3    where 5 >
  4      (select count(*)
  5       from product p2
  6       where p1.price < p2.price )
  7  order by p1.price;

   PRICE
---------
   49.99
   89.99
  119.99
     149
     400

5 rows selected.
```

To see product names as well as prices, add product.name to the outer query.

Nested Subqueries

Still in pursuit of the five highest prices (or three best customers, or 15 longest-running machines), try another technique: subqueries inside subqueries (Figure 5–4). In this method, you find the maximum price in a subquery and feed it to an outer query. The outer query uses this value to find the next lowest maximum value. The number of nested subqueries depends on *N*.

Conceptually, you start with the innermost query. After processing it, your SQL engine passes the result back to the next query (as a constant) and resolves the query. The first MAX finds the highest value.

Adaptive Server Anywhere
```
select max(price)
from product

max(product.price)
==================
           400.00

[1 row]
```

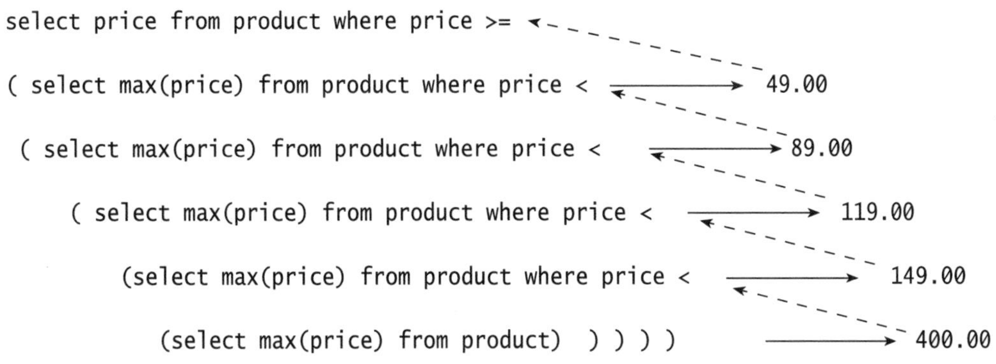

```
select price from product where price >= ◄-_
                                               `-_
( select max(price) from product where price <  ◄───────► 49.00
                                                  `-_
  ( select max(price) from product where price <   ◄──────►  89.00
                                                     `-_
    ( select max(price) from product where price <   ◄─────►  119.00
                                                        `-_
      (select max(price) from product where price <    ──────►  149.00
                                                         ◄─-_
        (select max(price) from product)  ) ) ) )    ──────►  400.00
```

```
        price
    ===========
         49.99
         49.99
         89.99
        119.99
        149.00
        400.00
         49.99
        149.99
```

Figure 5-4. Nested Subqueries

Using this highest value in the WHERE clause, the next query calculates a new maximum, and so on.

Adaptive Server Anywhere
```
select max(price)
from product
where price < 400

max(product.price)
===================
           149.00

[1 row]

select max(price)
from product
where price < 149
```

```
max(product.price)
==================
            119.99
```

[1 row]

The price $49.00 shows up twice in the results because there are two products with that price. If you add a DISTINCT in the SELECT clause, you'll get down to five values. Of course, if you are using unique values, there is no problem. This probably isn't a very good choice when you're looking for performance, since your engine will have to check the table once for each value. However, if your system is optimized to handle a MIN or a MAX with a clustered index, it can be surprisingly fast.

Aggregates and Many Copies

Here's a different use of aggregates to find the top *N* prices.

This is another query you should check for performance issues on your system. Essentially, you use table aliases to create *N* versions of the table (here *N* is 5, so you have copies of the product table labeled p1 through p5). You find the highest price in each table but set conditions in the WHERE clause requiring that p1.price is greater than p2.price and so on down the line. In the end, you have a list of the top *N* prices.

Adaptive Server Anywhere

```
select max(p1.price), max(p2.price), max(p3.price), max(p4.price), max(p5.price)
from product p1, product p2, product p3, product p4, product p5
where p1.price > p2.price and
      p2.price > p3.price and
      p3.price > p4.price and
      p4.price > p5.price
```

```
max(p1.price) max(p2.price) max(p3.price) max(p4.price) max(p5.price)
============= ============= ============= ============= =============
      400.00        149.00        119.99         89.99         49.99
```

[1 row]

Check how your database system handles multiple aggregates in the SELECT list. You'll probably find a table scan for each item. Even systems that are optimized to return a single MIN or MAX with good speed may go into slow motion when trying to handle multiple aggregates in the SELECT list.

Cursors

Here's the last method for locating the top five prices (or oldest 25 products on the shelf or best three hours for offering a sale). A cursor is a kind of bridge between relational database set processing and traditional row processing. It generates a result set and then goes through the results row by row.

Acceptable elements and performance vary a great deal from system to system. You may need to put the code inside a stored procedure or access it through ESQL. Be sure to check your vendor's documentation for explanations and examples. And beware! Cursors are often overused because the SQL programmer hasn't learned to think in sets but is very good at row-by-row processing. (If your only tool is a hammer, a lot of problems look like nails.) You can often get much better performance by turning a cursor into a set query. Look for cases where a predecessor has used a cursor to perform the same action over and over—these are good candidates for conversion.

Here's a simple cursor built on Adaptive Server Enterprise. (It won't run on other systems without modification.) It creates a query (DECLARE CURSOR)—the command must run by itself. Then it OPENs (runs) the query. Each FETCH brings back a row and moves the pointer to the next row.

Adaptive Server Enterprise

```
declare top5 cursor
for
select name, price
from product
order by price desc

[command completed]

open top5

fetch top5
```

```
name                    price
----                    ------------------------
memory8                                   400.00
```

fetch top5

```
name                    price
----                    ------------------------
z_connector                               149.00
```

A more complex treatment requires variables to hold values (created with DECLARE, a different command than DECLARE CURSOR), a counter (@num), and looping (WHILE). These three elements are Transact-SQL extensions.

Adaptive Server Enterprise

```
declare top5_2 cursor
for
select name, price
from product
order by price desc

[command completed]

declare @name varchar(20), @price smallmoney, @num tinyint
select @num = 1
open top5_2
while @num <6
    begin
        fetch top5_2 into @name, @price
        print 'Num is %1! Name is %2! and price is %3!', @num, @name, @price
        select @num = @num + 1
    end
```

The cursor produces results like this:

Adaptive Server Enterprise

```
Num is 1 Name is memory8 and price is 400.00
Num is 2 Name is z_connector and price is 149.00
Num is 3 Name is memory tripler and price is 119.99
Num is 4 Name is landlord logs and price is 89.99
Num is 5 Name is tax time and price is 49.99
```

To make this piece of code realistic, you'd have to add error handling. If you no longer need the cursor, you can free up the resources with CLOSE and DEALLOCATE statements.

Adaptive Server Enterprise

```
close top5
deallocate cursor top5
close top5_2
deallocate cursor top5_2
```

Picking Every Nth

Let's say you want to look at every third row or sample every eighth customer or generate some random test data by picking every tenth first name to combine with a small set of last names.

Here you can use the by-now-familiar combination of unequal self-joins, GROUP BY, COUNT, and HAVING with a new feature, modulo. Basically, you generate invisible row numbers and then use modulo *N* in the HAVING clause to find every *N*th row. (You'll find details on modulo in the next section.)

Adaptive Server Anywhere

```
select c1.fname, c1.custnum
from customer c1, customer c2
where c1.custnum >= c2.custnum
group by c1.fname, c1.custnum
having mod( count(*) , 5) = 0
```

```
fname                 custnum
==================== =========
kimiko               111444444
merit                777777778
```

```
[2 rows]
```

As Figure 5–5 shows, these two rows actually do represent every fifth row. (Different systems may display the results in different order.)

To understand how this works, take a look at the MOD (modulo) function.

```
fname                custnum
==================== =========
geoff lowell         111222222
ruby                 111223333
phillip              111333333
felipe               111334444
kimiko               111444444
SAM                  223456789
Pete                 776667778
pete pete            776677778
(NULL)               777777777
merit                777777778
lauren               923457789
LI-REN               999456789
```

```
select c1.fname, c1.custnum
from customer c1, customer c2
where c1.custnum >= c2.custnum
group by c1.fname, c1.custnum
--having mod( count(*) , 5) = 0
```

```
fname                custnum
==================== =========
kimiko               111444444
merit                777777778
```

Figure 5-5. Modulo

What Modulo Is

Modulo finds the remainder after division. On many systems, the syntax is

```
MOD ( expression, divisor )
```

The Transact-SQL dialect uses the percent sign (%) to represent modulo.

```
expression % divisor
```

On Transact-SQL systems, the previous example looks like this (the results are the same):

Transact-SQL

```
select c1.fname, c1.custnum
from customer c1, customer c2
where c1.custnum >= c2.custnum
group by c1.fname, c1.custnum
having count(*)  % 5 = 0.
```

Table 5-4. Modulo

ANSI	ASA	ASE	MS SQL Server	Oracle	Informix
	MOD (num_expr, int) REMAINDER (num_expr, int)			MOD (num_expr, int)	MOD (num_expr, int)
		num_expr % int	num_expr % int		

Table 5-4 summarizes these differences. Check your system manuals to see what your SQL engine allows as valid datatypes for modulo, and whether or not it returns fractions.

Here are some examples of how modulo works:

- mod(18, 4) = 2—18/4 = 4, remainder 2
- mod(18, 6) = 0—18/6 = 3, remainder 0
- mod(18, 7) = 4—18/7 = 2, remainder 4

Translate the examples into code, and you'll get something like this (add FROM dual to the query if you're using Oracle; FROM any small table if you are using another system that does not allow queries without a FROM clause):

Adaptive Server Anywhere

```
select mod(18,4) as mod4, mod(18, 6) as mod6, mod (18, 7) as mod7

 mod4    mod6    mod7
======  ======  ======
     2       0       4

[1 row]
```

On Transact-SQL, the code looks like this:

Transact-SQL

```
select 18 % 4  as mod4, 18 % 6 as mod6, 18 % 7 as mod7

mod4         mod6         mod7
-----------  -----------  -----------
2            0            4

(1 row(s) affected)
```

Modulo in WHERE and HAVING

For finding rows, use modulo in the WHERE or HAVING clause. For example, which rows in the orderdetail table have units divisible by a particular number? Start by checking values in the unit column in the orderdetail table:

Adaptive Server Anywhere

```
select distinct unit
from orderdetail
```

```
   unit
======
      1
      2
      5
      6
   2222
   3333
     25
      7
     20
```

[9 rows]

Finding the "Evens," Every Third, Every Fifth   To find the rows with an even number of units, write code like this, figuring that anything divided by 2 with a remainder of 0 must be even:

Adaptive Server Anywhere

```
select distinct unit
from orderdetail
where mod (unit, 2) = 0
```

```
   unit
======
      2
      6
   2222
     20
```

[4 rows]

To find units divisible by 3 or 5, just modify the divisor in the modulo function.

Adaptive Server Anywhere

```
select distinct unit
from orderdetail
where mod(unit, 3) = 0
```

```
  unit
======
     6
  3333
```

```
[2 rows]
```

```
select distinct unit
from orderdetail
where mod(unit, 5) = 0
```

```
  unit
======
     5
    25
    20
```

```
[3 rows]
```

Offsetting, or Changing the Starting Point To start counting at a different point, vary the value in the WHERE clause, changing the modulo (result) value from 0 to 1 or 2 or *N*. This allows you to get random but evenly distributed data, handy for testing.

Adaptive Server Anywhere

```
select distinct unit
from orderdetail
where mod(unit, 5) = 1
```

```
  unit
======
     1
     6
```

```
[2 rows]
```

```
select distinct unit
from orderdetail
where mod(unit, 5) = 2

   unit
  ======
      2
      7
   2222

[3 rows]

select distinct unit
from orderdetail
where mod(unit, 5) = 3

   unit
  ======
   3333

[1 row]
```

The last query reads, "Find units that when divided by 5 have a remainder of 3." (3333/5 = 666 with 3 left over.)

Back to Nth Row

Why does the modulo have to be combined with a self-join and a GROUP BY? Why not just use the modulo function on some numeric column? (Depending on how your system handles datatypes, you may have to convert c1.custnum to an integer datatype before you can use the modulo function on it.)

Adaptive Server Anywhere

```
select c1.fname, c1.custnum
from customer c1, customer c2
where c1.custnum >= c2.custnum
group by c1.fname, c1.custnum
having mod (convert (int, c1.custnum ) , 3) = 0
```

```
fname                   custnum
====================    =========
geoff lowell            111222222
phillip                 111333333
kimiko                  111444444
(NULL)                  777777777
lauren                  923457789
LI-REN                  999456789

[6 rows]
```

The results show that you're getting rows with `custnum` divisible by 3—not every third row (there are only 12 rows in the table!). To get every *N*th row, you need a row number of some sort. If you have a built-in counter, use it. Otherwise, try the self-join, GROUP BY, HAVING method. Be sure to check performance implications on your system before you commit.

Correlated Subquery

Another version of the every *N*th query involves a correlated subquery. (For more on this topic, see "Correlated and Noncorrelated Subqueries" in Chapter 3.)

Adaptive Server Anywhere

```
select c1.fname, c1.custnum
from customer c1
where exists
      (select max(c2.fname)
      from customer c2
      where c1.custnum >= c2.custnum
      having mod( count(*),  5 ) = 0 )
```

```
fname                   custnum
====================    =========
merit                   777777778
kimiko                  111444444

[2 rows]
```

Generating a Running Total

Stepping away from the top *N*, we jog on to the running total. Like many of the
examples in this chapter, it uses GROUP BY, an unequal self-join, and an aggregate. This time, the aggregate is SUM. The example adds each price in the
product table to a running total. Note that you display fname and price from the
first copy of the table, but the total is based on the second copy of the table.
That is, you add up all the values in the second copy of the table that are less
than or equal to the value in the first table.

Adaptive Server Anywhere

```
select p1.name, p1.price, sum(p2.price)
from product p1, product p2
where p2.name <= p1.name
group by p1.name, p1.price
order by sum(p2.price)
```

name	price	sum(p2.price)
blood & guts	29.99	29.99
bug stories	20.00	49.99
bugbane	49.00	98.99
C++ for kids	39.99	138.98
cook & book	19.99	158.97
home poll kit	19.99	178.96
how multi is media?	20.00	198.96
landlord logs	89.99	288.95
memory manager	19.99	308.94
memory tripler	119.99	428.93
memory8	400.00	828.93
money master	29.00	857.93
more paper dolls	19.99	877.92
mortgage minder	39.99	917.91
nt guru	20.00	937.91
paper dolls	19.99	957.90
star systems	39.99	997.89
tax time	49.99	1047.88
teach yourself greek	49.99	1097.87
typing test	29.99	1127.86
z_connector	149.00	1276.86

[21 rows]

Your system may not require an ORDER BY.

A SUM query shows the running total final value to be correct.

Adaptive Server Anywhere
```
select sum(price)
from product

sum(product.price)
==================
          1276.86
```

[1 row]

If what you need is a grand total, avoid the running total technique. The simpler SUM query is much more efficient, in terms of performance.

Why the running total technique works isn't obvious at all. Here's a step-by-step analysis with a smaller, simpler table, testjoin. If you've followed examples earlier in the book, it may look like this:

Adaptive Server Anywhere
```
select *
from testjoin

        num name
=========== =====
          1 one
          2 two
          3 one
```

[3 rows]

Modify the data so that the numeric and alphabetic data orders match.

Adaptive Server Anywhere
```
update testjoin set name = 'a' where num = 1
update testjoin set name = 'b' where num = 2
update testjoin set name = 'c' where num = 3
```

[3 rows]

```
select *
from testjoin

num          name
----------   -----
1            a
2            b
3            c

[3 rows]
```

Using the unequal self-join with GROUP BY and SUM, we get code like this:

Adaptive Server Anywhere

```
select t1.name, t1.num, sum(t2.num)
from testjoin t1, testjoin t2
where t2.name <= t1.name
group by t1.name, t1.num
order by sum(t2.num)

name          num sum(t2.num)
=====  ===========  ===========
a              1            1
b              2            3
c              3            6

[3 rows]
```

First, look at a cartesian product, where no join is specified, so every value of t1 is matched up with every value of t2. Group them, and mark out all rows where t1.name is greater than or equal to t2.name (the same as t2.name <= t1.name—turned backwards to make the chart easier to read; Figure 5–6).

In your hand-done groups, you can see that the sum for all qualifying a values is 1. The sum for b values is 3 (1 + 2), and the sum for c is 6 (1 + 2 + 3).

A variation on the running total uses a correlated subquery in the SELECT list. (Not all vendors support this feature.) The outer query displays name and num, and the subquery finds the sum of nums for that name, going in one direction only.

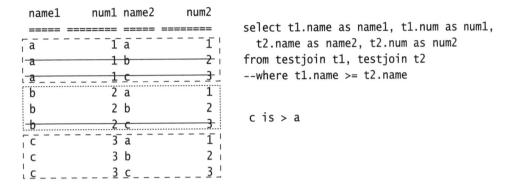

```
select t1.name as name1, t1.num as num1,
   t2.name as name2, t2.num as num2
from testjoin t1, testjoin t2
--where t1.name >= t2.name


 c is > a
```

Figure 5-6. Running Total

Adaptive Server Anywhere

```
select t1.name, t1.num,
     (select sum(t2.num)
      from testjoin t2
      where t2.name <= t1.name) as numSUM
from testjoin t1
order by numSUM
```

name	num	numSUM
=====	===========	===========
a	1	1
b	2	3
c	3	6

[3 rows]

You can get an idea of how this works by substituting a constant for the value in the inner query.

Adaptive Server Anywhere

```
--select t1.name, t1.num,
--(
select sum(t2.num)
     from testjoin t2
     where t2.name <= 'a'
-- )
-- from testjoin t1
```

```
sum(t2.num)
===========
          1
```

```
[1 row]
```

Substituting b and c in this code produces 3 and 6, respectively.

Translating for the original problem, you get this code (the 3 in the ORDER BY clause refers to the third element in the SELECT list).

Adaptive Server Anywhere

```
select p1.name, p1.price,
    (select sum(p2.price)
     from product p2
     where p2.name <= p1.name)
from product p1
order by 3
```

Summary

This chapter is all about numbers. It starts out with a summary of varying autonumbering techniques by system and goes on to examine finding the top value, numbering output rows, capturing the top or bottom N values, locating every Nth, and displaying running totals. It also provides lots of practice with subqueries, GROUP BY, aggregates, complex joins, and HAVING.

- How can you get unique numbers for new customers or parts? Depending on the SQL engine you use, it may be with a default, column property, or datatype in the CREATE TABLE statement, or with a separate object. The examples show autonumbering in the five familiar systems. This is just the starting point, of course—a list of related issues ends the section.
- Locating the high value has two approaches: nested aggregates in the HAVING clause and a FROM subquery. Not all SQL dialects support either of these techniques, so be sure to check your manuals. You can also play around with ordering results and then limiting the number of rows displayed.
- Your vendor may supply a built-in row number for numbering display rows. These often have limitations, and you may choose to "row your own" with unequal self-joins, GROUP BY, and COUNT.

- Finding the top five (or bottom two) means looking at a number of different approaches. The core method uses unequal self-joins, GROUP BY, COUNT, and a HAVING clause comparing the COUNT to the number of rows you want to see—row numbers with one more feature. Other solutions to the top N question use subqueries, aggregates, and cursors.
- Picking every fifth or third row takes advantage of the combined power of unequal self-joins, GROUP BY, COUNT, and HAVING with the modulo function. It is a good tool to use when generating data for tests.
- The running total method uses unequal self-joins, GROUP BY, and SUM.

Chapter 6

Tuning Queries

In This Chapter

- Defining the Basic Problem
- Understanding the Optimizer and Associated Tools
- Managing the WHERE Clause
- Creating Covering Indexes
- Joining Columns
- Sorting with DISTINCT and UNION
- Choosing Between HAVING and WHERE
- Looking at Views
- Forcing Indexes

Perform, #%&#@!

Can you influence database performance by the SQL you choose? Yes, you can. Mostly, this means knowing what indexes you have and how SQL code does or does not take advantage of them.

Of course, there are many other factors—database design, hardware configuration, system architecture, network setup—that have profound effects on performance. While it's true that a poorly written query can slow performance by invalidating relevant indexes, it's equally certain that a really well-crafted query cannot overcome fundamental system limitations.

Unfortunately, SQL tuning is never cut-and-dried. It's a constant weighing of one factor against another, requiring endless measuring and attention and frequent changes. In addition, you won't find the msdpn database much use in testing different approaches to queries. Most optimizers ignore indexes when the data set is very small and simply read the tables sequentially (do table scans). Review the queries in this section to make sure you understand the principles of writing efficient SQL, but be sure to test specifics on your system with something much closer to real data.

Understanding indexes and writing queries to take advantage of indexes can give you the best performance improvements on an existing database. These are the steps you go through when you start thinking about query performance:

1. Find out what kind of work your database is tuned for and what it looks like—the tables, views, and other objects in it. An entity-relationship diagram is very helpful. If you don't have one, use system tools to sketch out the major tables.

2. Get a list of indexes for the tables you'll be using via system catalogs, GUI interfaces, or commands.

3. Look into the details of your optimizer and identify tools for seeing how the optimizer handles different queries.

4. Armed with these tools, examine specific "slow" queries. First of all, make sure they are returning the correct results.

5. Review the WHERE clause. Are relevant indexes useful? Up to date? Is any construction nullifying an available index? Could you use a covering index?

6. Check joins—are join columns compatible?

7. Is there any unnecessary or redundant action? Are DISTINCT and UNION overused? Do you see HAVING used like WHERE? Are queries complicated by going through views?

There is a list of index/query areas to consider in the chapter summary.

Since index and optimizer tools vary greatly from system to system (they are not SQL commands), you'll find brief instructions on using the Adaptive Server Anywhere tools in this chapter—just enough to let you follow the examples if you are using the software on the CD. For details on Adaptive Server Anywhere (or basics on any other system), you're on your own!

Defining the Basic Problem

Proper indexing can have a huge effect on database efficiency. Just like an index in a book, an index in a database makes it easy to find data. Instead of paging through the book, hoping to find information about Emu Sisters Productions, you can go directly to the location the index gives you. Now think about what happens when you remove Chapter 3 from a book or add 20 pages to Chapter 7. The book index is invalidated from the point of change on and needs to be rebuilt.

In much the same way, adding, removing, and changing rows in a database leads to index maintenance tasks. Even a relatively small edit, such as changing Emu Sisters to E-Gals, is likely to cause some index differences, as the shorter size of the new entry affects the page splits. If you are changing book text or database rows all the time and you have very detailed indexes, you'll need to get the text pages and index back in synch. So what's good for one kind of work (finding information/querying/decision support) is bad for another (modifying information/updating, inserting, and deleting/transaction processing).

It's not just indexes that show this dichotomy. Database design, storage allocations, memory, and many other choices reflect the work a database is supposed to do. These decisions are beyond the scope of this book, and you're best off looking at information specifically for the system you are using.

However, returning to the question of indexes, there are some general rules the SQL writer can follow to improve performance (at least with sorted or B-tree indexes, common in many systems). First, find out what indexes you have and put together WHERE clauses that can use the indexes rather than WHERE clauses that can't use the indexes. Often, the difference is minor. For example, in just about every system, the queries in Figure 6–1 will give different performance, assuming an index on prodnum and a nontrivial number of rows.

Why? IN processes (a form of OR) are often slow, requiring multiple reads of the table. BETWEEN is easier for most SQL engines to handle. After all, it's just a range. With an index, it's a matter of finding the low boundary and following the index until encountering the high value.

Adaptive Server Anywhere

```
select prodnum, type, price          select prodnum, type, price
from product                         from product
where prodnum in (104, 105, 106, 107)    where prodnum between 104 and 107
```

```
      prodnum type              price
      =========== ============ ============
          104 education        49.99
          105 game             19.99
          106 hardware        149.00
          107 application      39.99
```

better
performance with
BETWEEN

Figure 6-1. WHERE and Performance

Once you have general guidelines on efficient SQL, you can look for places where you can substitute faster syntax for slower. Sometimes you won't have the option—often IN (or some other "slow" choice) is the best answer. However, as you review code you've written yourself or inherited, you'll find places where you can improve performance with relatively minor changes.

Understanding the Optimizer and Associated Tools

To see how query variants affect performance, you need two things: information about indexes and a way to see the choices the optimizer made. Most systems provide tools for both these functions, but they vary widely.

Getting Information on Indexes

You'll always be able to find out what indexes are connected to a particular table, through the meta-data system catalogs if nothing else (see "Getting Meta-Data from System Catalogs" in Chapter 7). For example, in Adaptive Server Anywhere, a quick survey of the system catalogs reveals two likely suspects: sysindex and systable. A first try at a query to locate indexes for a particular table might look like this:

Adaptive Server Anywhere
```
select sysindex.index_name, systable.table_name
from sysindex, systable
where sysindex.table_id = systable.table_id
    and table_name = 'product'
```

```
index_name                table_name
====================  ==================================
prodix                    product
pricex                    product
```

[2 rows]

(See "Writing Queries Using System Catalogs" in Chapter 7 for more examples of generating this kind of code.)

In Adaptive Server Enterprise and MS SQL Server, an easy way to investigate indexes is the sp_helpindex stored procedure (the output from the two RDBMSs is not identical). It tells you the names of the indexes and the columns in each.

("Nonclustered" is a type of Transact-SQL index, with pointers from the bottom row of the index to the data—the index and data are not in the same order. This contrasts to a clustered index, in which the index and data are in the same order.)

Adaptive Server Enterprise

```
exec sp_helpindex product
```

index_name	index_description	index_keys	ix_max_rows_per_page
prodix	nonclustered, unique located on default	prodnum	0
pricex	nonclustered located on default	price	0

```
(2 rows affected)
```

In many systems, including the Adaptive Server Anywhere on this book's CD, the index information source of choice is a graphical user interface (GUI) tool. Since you may not be much of an ASA user but would like to follow along, here are basic instructions on using ASA Sybase Central for index information (see the help files for details). If you're using another system, the tools and commands will look different but will probably supply very similar information—the name of the index, the columns that make it up, the order in which the columns appear, and the index type.

Open Sybase Central and click *Connect* under the *Tools* button (Figure 6–2). Choose *Adaptive Server Anywhere.* Fill in the forms for the *Login* and *Database* tabs for msdpn (Figure 6–3), logging in as DBA with a password of SQL (both must be uppercase) and substituting your *msdpnb.db* address you used for *Database file* for the *C:/SQLBook* line.

After you click *OK,* you'll see your server (here *msdpn,* with the terminal icon) listed in the Sybase Central window (Figure 6–4). Click it and then click the database-owner combination you want to use—*msdp(DBA)*—with the disk icon. You'll see a list of objects (Figure 6–5). Click *Tables.* From the detailed list of tables and views, click the table name you want (say, product) and then *Indexes* (Figure 6–6). Pick the index you want. Use the tabs on the window to get details.

There is information on the msdpn indexes in "Table Details" in Chapter 1.

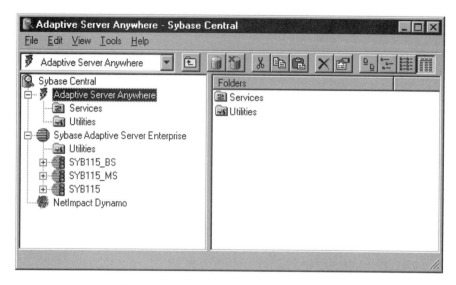

Figure 6-2. Connecting on Sybase Central

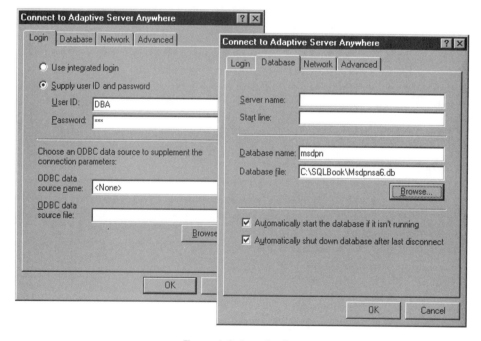

Figure 6-3. Logging In

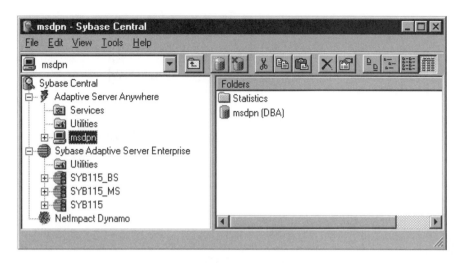

Figure 6-4. Choosing a Database

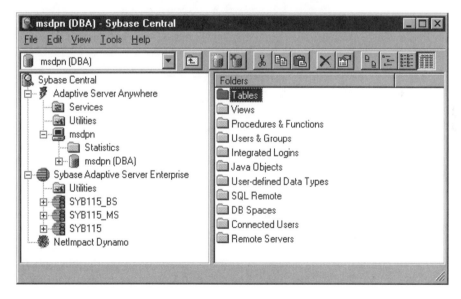

Figure 6-5. Listing Objects

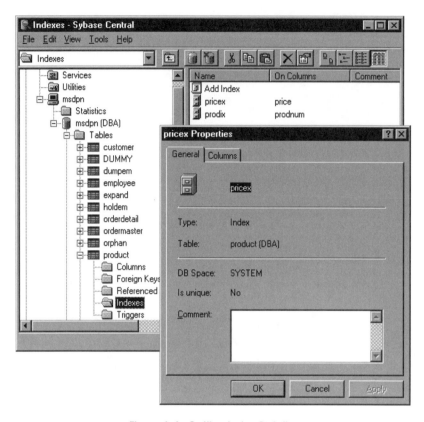

Figure 6–6. Getting Index Details

Checking the Optimizer

To check your work, you need to know a little about your optimizer, the part of the SQL engine that decides how to process a query. A cost-based optimizer looks at processing options and chooses the one that is "cheapest" in terms of time. If your system is cost-based, you may need to run commands that make sure the statistics on data are current (see Table 6–2). In a rule-based system, the optimizer makes choices based on a set of ranked guidelines.

Most systems support a command or a tool that shows you what the optimizer is doing. In Adaptive Server Anywhere, the software included on the disk, there is one of each.

- The command is the PLAN function, which takes a query (in quotes) as its argument. For a list of related commands, see Table 6–1.
- The tool is the Performance Monitor on Sybase Central (an option under *Statistics*).

If you're following along with the Adaptive Server Anywhere software included on the CD, you may need to send PLAN results to an output file in order to read more than the first line. To do this, end the query with a semicolon and follow it with an OUTPUT TO line naming a file in which to store the query results, and a FORMAT line prescribing the format of columns in the output file. The following examples illustrate this method.

Adaptive Server Anywhere

```
select plan
( 'select prodnum, type, price, description  from product
                    where prodnum in (1104, 1105, 1106, 1107)' );
output to out.txt
format text
```

The out.txt file (it could have any name) is located in the directory that holds the ASA database file. When you open the out.txt file, you'll see information on how the query was processed.

Adaptive Server Anywhere

```
Estimate 1 I/O operations (best of 2 plans considered)
Scan product sequentially
  Estimate getting here 21 times
  For _value_1 in (1104,1105,1106,1107)
```

If you change the IN phrase to a BETWEEN, the output is different.

Adaptive Server Anywhere

```
select plan
( 'select prodnum, type, price, description  from product
                    where prodnum between 1104 and 1107' );
output to out.txt
format text

Estimate 5 I/O operations
Scan product using unique index prodix
for rows where prodnum is between 1104 and 1107
  Estimate getting here 4 times
```

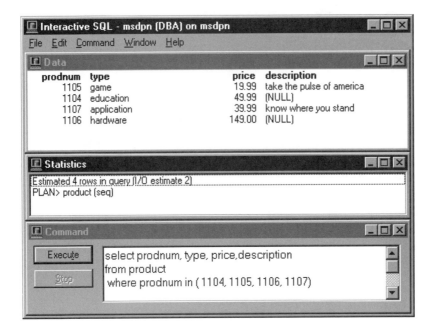

Figure 6-7. Interactive SQL Window

Without knowing much about the PLAN messages, you can see that the IN query doesn't use an index—it does a table scan. The BETWEEN query uses the prodix index. The first one goes somewhere 21 times, while the second makes just four trips.

You can get a shorter version of that information by looking at the ASA Interactive SQL Statistics window (Figures 6–7 and 6–8). Notice that the PLAN> line for the two queries is different. The first indicates a sequential scan of the table. The second shows index use. This is parallel to the PLAN results, and easier to read and generate. Figure 6–8 shows just the statistics part of the screen produced by the BETWEEN version of the query. Adaptive Server Anywhere provides more detailed performance information in the Sybase Central Performance Monitor.

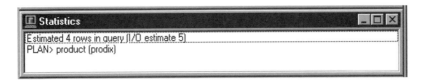

Figure 6-8. Statistics Pane of the Interactive SQL Window

Table 6-1. Monitoring Performance

ANSI	ASA	ASE	MS SQL Server	Oracle	Informix
	PLAN ('query')	SET SHOWPLAN ON SET NOEXEC ON	SET SHOWPLAN _ALL ON	EXPLAIN PLAN	SET EXPLAIN ON

For a summary of commands that keep tabs on the optimizer, see Table 6–1. You'll need to do some research before you can get much information from the output of any of these commands. You may find additional tools that are used at your site—GUI-based, third party, or home grown.

SQL Conventions

Before diving into performance in SQL queries, consider how your code looks. Code is easier to read and understand if you present it consistently. In some systems, reusability of cached code may depend on the various copies being identical. Differences as small as a single space character may be relevant. In addition, training time for new employees is shorter if they can expect consistent patterns. For your sanity, develop coding guidelines. Here are some common suggestions.

- Start each line with a SQL verb (SELECT, FROM).
    ```
    select prodnum, type, price
    from product
    where prodnum between 104 and 107
    ```

- Indent continued lines.
    ```
    select prodnum, type, price
    from product
    where prodnum between 104 and 107
        and price >50.00
    ```

- Be consistent in naming tables and columns—don't make some table names singular and others plural, don't use case randomly, and don't call one column *pubdate* and a related column in another table *pub_date.*
- If you use table aliases, stick to the same ones, and don't use non-mnemonic aliases such as *a*, *b*, and *c* for *supplier, product, customer.*
- Put in lots of comments: the date, your name, what the query or script is about—everything you'd want to know.

Managing the WHERE Clause

The WHERE clause is the place to start your search for SQL you can change to get better performance. You already know what indexes you have. Now look at the optimizer plan for a problem query and see if the indexes are getting used or if the optimizer is searching the table row by row.

Why a Table Scan?

Just because you have an index on a column doesn't mean your optimizer will use it.

- If the amount of data is trivial (as in the msdpn tables), a search using an index may not be faster than a table scan and the optimizer may choose not to use the index.
- If the query includes all rows in the table (no WHERE clause), the optimizer does a table scan.
- If you're retrieving a lot of data from the table, an index may give no advantage.
- If the optimizer does not have accurate information on data distribution, it may pick the wrong index or no index at all.
- If you include certain elements in the WHERE clause, you may make the index unavailable.

Of these elements, only the last two are under your control.

Data Distribution Statistics

First, check your system documents to see if the DBA needs periodically to run a command to keep the optimizer current (UPDATE STATISTICS in Transact-SQL and Informix, ANALYZE in Oracle). Microsoft SQL Server also supports a command that tells you when the command was last run (STAT_DATE—there's more information on it in "Using System Functions" in Chapter 7). See Table 6–2 for a list of commands associated with index statistics. The SQL Anywhere ESTIMATE command is included in the table, but it works differently than the UPDATE STATISTICS or ANALYZE commands, allowing the user to give the optimizer hints on data distribution.

Table 6-2. Index Statistics

ANSI	SQL Anywhere	SAE	MS SQL Server	Oracle	Informix

		`UPDATE STATISTICS`	`UPDATE STATISTICS`
			
			`STATS_DATE`
				`ANALYZE`	`UPDATE STATISTICS`

	`ESTIMATE`				

Disabling an Index with a Bad WHERE

Second, don't disable a valid index by the way you construct your WHERE clause. The easiest elements to optimize are comparison operators (=, >, <, and variants) or operators that can be translated to comparison operators (BETWEEN and some LIKE clauses).

Anything else may make your indexes unavailable. Here are some suspicious areas to investigate. Since architecture and optimizers vary so much, you'll have to check your system documentation to find out just how these areas affect (or don't affect!) your queries.

- Comparing columns in the same table
- Choosing columns with low-selectivity indexes
- Doing math on a column before comparing it to a constant
- Applying a function to column data before comparing it to a constant
- Finding ranges with BETWEEN
- Matching with LIKE
- Comparing to NULL
- Negating with NOT
- Converting values
- Using OR
- Finding sets of values with IN
- Using multicolumn indexes

Comparing Columns in the Same Table

In many systems, comparing columns in the same table makes an index useless. For example, consider matching the empnum column to a string constant versus matching it to another column, bossnum. The two queries return the same results.

Adaptive Server Anywhere

```
select fname, lname, empnum, bossnum
from employee
where empnum = bossnum

select fname, lname, empnum, bossnum
from employee
where empnum = '443232366'
```

fname	lname	empnum	bossnum
Scorley	Blake-Pipps	443232366	443232366

```
[1 row]
```

With a nontrivial number of rows, the first query scans the table sequentially. The second uses the empix index. If you test this query on another system, you may not see this difference, because the employee table is so small. However, it's clear that an index on empid helps find the employee with a particular identification number and is less useful in finding one with the same number as the boss. Why? Because a constant (443232366) is constant. An index points to a known value, not an unknown value.

Using Nonselective Indexes

A unique index is 100% selective. Every index entry points to a single location in the data. A nonselective index is just the opposite—each index entry points to multiple data locations. You can think of selectivity as roughly the number of distinct index entries divided by the number of data rows. Optimizers don't get much advantage from nonselective indexes, and they often don't use them.

Returning to the book index comparison, imagine an index that listed every occurrence of the word "and." Because "and" is so common, you'd find an index reference to just about every page in the book. Using the index does not make finding "and" faster than paging through the book, because "and" has low selectivity.

Consider attributes such as gender, where there are only two choices. There's no point indexing this kind of column unless the data distribution is very skewed. If 90% of the employees are male and 10% are female, the optimizer might use the index where gender is female. It would not use it in searches for males.

Doing Math on a Column

Another WHERE clause element to watch out for is doing math on an indexed column before comparing it to a constant. The index can find the column value but not the column value * 2. To test this out on the msdpn database on the Adaptive Server Anywhere CD, run these two queries.

Adaptive Server Anywhere

```
select prodnum, price
from product
where price * 2 > 200

select prodnum, price
from product
where price  > 100
```

```
    prodnum      price
=========== ===========
       2111     119.99
       1106     149.00
       1794     400.00
```

[3 rows]

The first one does a table scan. The second takes advantage of the pricix index. This change is relatively easy to enforce, thanks to our good friend Ms. Algebra. Unadorned indexed columns on the left! Computations on the right! Get in the habit of changing WHERE clauses as in Figure 6–9.

```
WHERE price +5 < 20        ⟶        WHERE price < 15

WHERE price - 400 = 0      ⟶        WHERE price = 400

WHERE price -2 = 117       ⟶        WHERE price = 119
```

Figure 6-9. Calculation in the WHERE Clause

Using Functions

Functions have the same effect on an indexed column in a WHERE clause as math does. The index points to a value but understands nothing about calculations or functions. You already know that a search for employees by number uses the empix index.

Adaptive Server Anywhere

```
select fname, lname, empnum, bossnum
from employee
where empnum = '443232366'
```

If you modify the column name (empnum) with a substring function, even one that does exactly the same match and produces the same results, you'll get a table scan.

Adaptive Server Anywhere

```
select fname, lname, empnum, bossnum
from employee
where substr(empnum, 1, 9) = '443232366'
```

fname	lname	empnum	bossnum
Scorley	Blake-Pipps	443232366	443232366

[1 row]

Here's another example. The first query does a table scan. The second uses the empid index.

Adaptive Server Anywhere

```
select fname, lname, empnum, bossnum
from employee
where empnum || ' ' || fname = '443232366 Scorley'

select fname, lname, empnum, bossnum
from employee
where empnum = '443232366'  and fname = 'Scorley'
```

```
fname                   lname                   empnum     bossnum
===================== ===================== ========= =========
Scorley                 Blake-Pipps             443232366 443232366
```

[1 row]

Finding Ranges with BETWEEN

If there is an index on a column, BETWEEN will not disable it. BETWEEN is treated as a pair of comparison operators. The low value must precede the high value.

The first of the following queries uses the prodix index on prodnum. The second uses the index on price.

> ### *Adaptive Server Anywhere*
> ```
> select prodnum, name
> from product
> where prodnum between '1110' and '1357'
> ```
>
> ```
>      prodnum name
> =========== =====================
>         1110 star systems
>         1255 bug stories
>         1357 nt guru
> ```
>
> [3 rows]
>
> ```
> select prodnum, name, price
> from product
> where price between 300 and 400
> ```
>
> ```
>      prodnum name                      price
> =========== ===================== ==========
>         1794 memory8                   400.00
> ```
>
> [1 row]

NOT BETWEEN is not as easy to resolve with an index—an index points to a specific value. In the following case, you get a table scan.

Adaptive Server Anywhere

```
select prodnum, name, price
from product
where price not between 10 and 100
```

```
    prodnum name                        price
========== ==================== ==========
      2111 memory tripler             119.99
      1794 memory8                    400.00
      1106 z_connector                149.00
```

[3 rows]

Matching with LIKE

Most systems can take advantage of an index with LIKE as long as you provide the first character in the pattern (see "Matching Patterns" in Chapter 2). To follow this example, start by creating an index on the name columns of customer, last name first.

Adaptive Server Anywhere

```
create unique index custnmix
on customer (lname, fname)

select lname, fname
from customer
where lname like 'Pe%'
```

The SQL engine translates the LIKE into a range comparison and is able to take advantage of the index.

Adaptive Server Anywhere

```
select lname, fname
from customer
where lname >= 'Pe' and lname < 'Pf'
```

```
lname                fname
==================== ====================
Peters               Pete
```

[1 row]

However, the picture is different if you start with a wildcard. The optimizer does not use an index—the index cannot point to an unknown value.

Adaptive Server Anywhere

```
select lname, fname
from customer
where lname like '%ete%'
```

You get the same answer, of course, but the method is a table scan.

Comparing to NULL

Adaptive Server Anywhere uses the index on product.price in both the following queries, but not all systems do. Check vendor documentation to find out how nulls and indexes relate. If your system takes the "a null is not equal to anything" dictum into the realm of indexes, you may want to campaign for defaults instead of nulls at design time.

Adaptive Server Anywhere

```
select prodnum, price
from product
where price = 49.99
```

```
select prodnum, price
from product
where price is null
```

Another issue to check out is whether or not null returns a value in an IN. The following query may return one or two rows, depending on how your system handles null values in this situation.

Adaptive Server Anywhere

```
select prodnum, price
from product
where price in (null, 400.00)
```

Negating with NOT

A related area is how NOT and negatives such as <> and != affect index use. Indexes, after all, point to entries. What do they know about nonentries? The two following queries return the same results here (they could return quite disparate results with different data). The first uses the custnmix on last and first names. The second does not.

Adaptive Server Anywhere
```
select lname, fname
from customer
where lname = 'WONG'

select lname, fname
from customer
where lname not between ' ' and 'W'
```

```
lname                 fname
==================== ====================
WONG                 LI-REN
```

Get in the habit of converting NOT phrases when you can (Figure 6–10). In most cases, you'll be better off looking for rows with prices greater than zero rather than rows with prices not equal to zero. In addition to its effect on index uses, negative logic is sometimes hard to understand and therefore open to error.

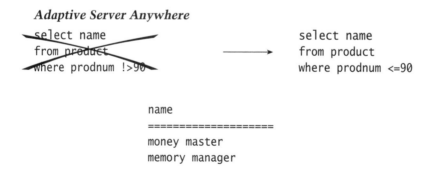

Figure 6-10. Negatives in WHERE

Converting Values

Conversions, like math or functions, can disable an index, and this is true for autoconversions the system handles as well as conversions you perform. For starters, keep the conversion on the right side of the equation, if possible (Figure 6–11).

In ASE, character data defined to allow null is actually stored as VARCHAR data, so joining two columns that differ only in whether or not they allow nulls may cause a conversion. The optimizer cannot use an index on the converted column. In Oracle, some autoconversions deactivate an index, others don't. Check your vendor documentation for details.

You'll find information about convert functions in "Converting Dates (and Other Datatypes)" in Chapter 2.

Using OR

An OR clause returns results if any one of the conditions is true (A = 1 or B > A or C = 3). If the columns in an OR clause have indexes, the optimizer can use the relevant indexes or do a table scan. Using the indexes means dumping results from each clause into an intermediate table and then removing duplicates from the intermediate table (Figure 6–12).

In a cost-based system, it's important that the table statistics be up to date. Otherwise, the optimizer may make the wrong choice.

If the ORed columns do not have indexes or the optimizer chooses not to use the indexes, you'll see a table scan (Figure 6–13).

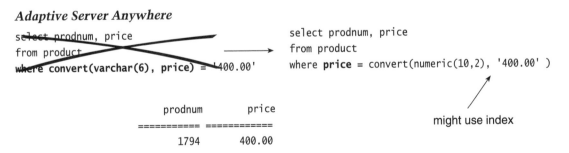

Adaptive Server Anywhere

```
select prodnum, price
from product
where convert(varchar(6), price) = '400.00'
```

```
select prodnum, price
from product
where price = convert(numeric(10,2), '400.00' )
```

might use index

```
        prodnum        price
    ============ ============
            1794       400.00
```

Figure 6-11. Conversions in WHERE

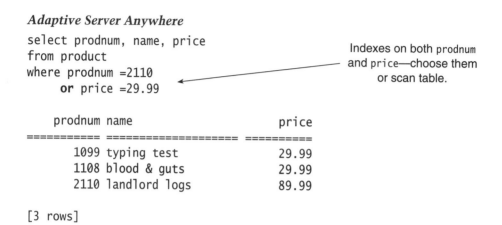

Figure 6-12. OR Processing: Indexes

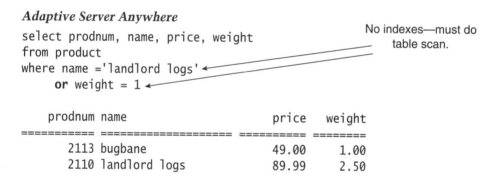

Figure 6-13. OR Processing: No Indexes

Finding Sets of Values with IN

Many third-party front-end applications overuse IN, sometimes employing it to find a single value or to return values in a range (Figure 6–14). This can be a problem, as IN is a form of OR processing, and tends to be expensive. If you are lucky, an IN with multiple terms can be re-stated as a range. This works only when the elements in the IN are the only ones in the range. If there were a $200 price in the second Figure 6–14 query, the BETWEEN translation would not be equivalent to the IN version.

Adaptive Server Anywhere

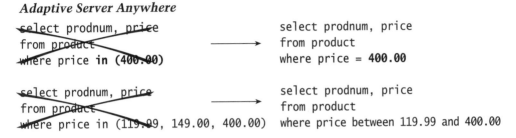

```
select prodnum, price                    select prodnum, price
from product                  ------->    from product
where price in (400.00)                   where price = 400.00

select prodnum, price                     select prodnum, price
from product                  ------->    from product
where price in (119.99, 149.00, 400.00)   where price between 119.99 and 400.00
```

Figure 6-14. IN

Check IN clauses carefully. Could you do the same work with a simple equals comparison? With a range?

Using Multicolumn Indexes

In many cases, indexes consist of two or more columns (Figure 6–15). The ord-prodix index in orderdetail is an example: it includes the ordnum and prodnum columns, in that order, and the order matters. The optimizer can use the index to find ordnum or combinations of ordnum and prodnum, but it can't follow pointers to go directly to prodnum values. Think of a phone book entry. It helps you find all the subscribers surnamed Smith and all the Smiths with Heather as a first name. It's no good for finding people with an unknown last name whose first name is Heather, though.

When you construct WHERE clauses, keep in mind the order of the columns in the index. Order of columns in the SELECT list has no effect.

Creating Covering Indexes

If you take multicolumn index awareness a step further, you can greatly boost performance in some situations: when all the data you need is in the index, the optimizer may retrieve it from the index without going to the data pages. This index is sometimes called a "covering" index and can be a big plus. Why? Because index entries are shorter than data rows and there are more of them on a page; the SQL engine can get to the covering index faster than to the data.

To use a covering index, you must meet the following conditions.

- Every column in the SELECT list and every column in every other clause (WHERE, ORDER BY, GROUP BY, HAVING) must be in the index.

Adaptive Server Anywhere

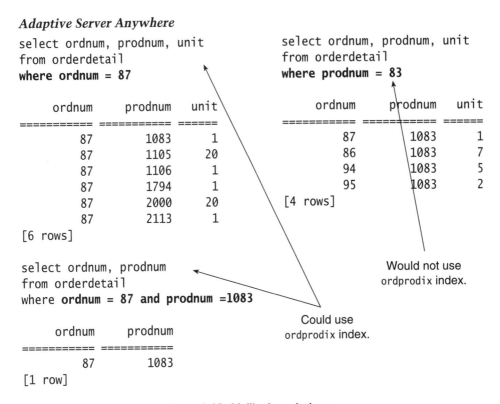

```
select ordnum, prodnum, unit
from orderdetail
where ordnum = 87
```

ordnum	prodnum	unit
87	1083	1
87	1105	20
87	1106	1
87	1794	1
87	2000	20
87	2113	1

[6 rows]

```
select ordnum, prodnum
from orderdetail
where ordnum = 87 and prodnum =1083
```

ordnum	prodnum
87	1083

[1 row]

```
select ordnum, prodnum, unit
from orderdetail
where prodnum = 83
```

ordnum	prodnum	unit
87	1083	1
86	1083	7
94	1083	5
95	1083	2

[4 rows]

Would not use
ordprodix index.

Could use
ordprodix index.

Figure 6-15. Multicolumn Indexes

- The index must not be disabled by functions or math or conversions—or any of the constructions covered earlier in this chapter.
- The WHERE clause must use columns in the order in which they appear in the index (it can go directly to a specific ordnum or combination of ordnum and prodnum but not to prodnum alone, as discussed in "Using Multicolumn Indexes" at the end of the previous section).

For example, to resolve a query including only the orderdetail ordnum and prodnum columns, everything you're asking for (prodnum and ordnum) is in the ordprodix index in ordnum order. If you specify ordnum or ordnum and prodnum in the WHERE clause, the SQL engine can find the index rows that contain that value and return results from there, never touching the data pages.

Adaptive Server Anywhere

```
select prodnum, ordnum
from orderdetail
where ordnum = 84
```

prodnum	ordnum
1099	84
1255	84
2050	84

[3 rows]

A less efficient variation results when all the columns in the query are in the index but you specify only a nonleading column (prodnum) in the WHERE clause. The SQL engine may resolve the query by reading the entire index sequentially. In some performance-monitoring tools, this is identified as an index scan, parallel to a table scan but faster.

Adaptive Server Anywhere

```
select prodnum, ordnum
from orderdetail
where prodnum = 1099
```

prodnum	ordnum
1099	84
1099	89

[2 rows]

But back to the leading column situation: if you add a column that is not part of the index (here unit), the optimizer will still be able to use the index, but it'll have to get the nonindex values from the data pages (Figure 6–16). The same thing happens when you add nonindex conditions to the WHERE clause. The index no longer "covers" the query.

You can cover queries by understanding your indexes and avoiding adding extra columns to your SELECT list. Don't do a SELECT * if all you want is the product number! Remember, the index covers the query only if *everything* in the SELECT and WHERE clauses is in the index, if you haven't disabled the index, and if you pay attention to order in multicolumn indexes.

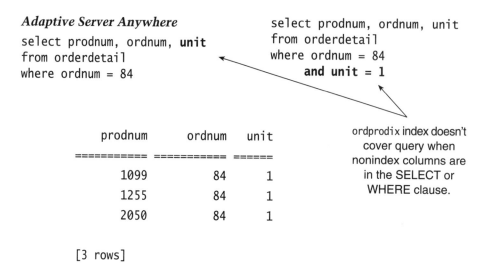

Adaptive Server Anywhere

```
select prodnum, ordnum, unit
from orderdetail
where ordnum = 84
```

```
select prodnum, ordnum, unit
from orderdetail
where ordnum = 84
and unit = 1
```

ordprodix index doesn't cover query when nonindex columns are in the SELECT or WHERE clause.

```
   prodnum        ordnum     unit

=========== =========== ======
      1099            84        1
      1255            84        1
      2050            84        1
```

[3 rows]

Figure 6-16. Covering Indexes

Joining Columns

All the previous hints on WHERE clause construction also apply to joins. Watch out for joins with functions or math on one or both sides. Avoid datatype mismatches, even subtle ones.

In addition, experiment with redundant joins. For example, if you join three tables, two joins are adequate. Adding a third may give the optimizer more options. In this example, backorder is a new table, similar to orderdetail, but it has one more column.

Adaptive Server Anywhere

```
create table backorder
(
ordnum        int       not null,
prodnum       int       not null,
unit          smallint  not null,
shipdate      date          null,
backnotedate  date      not null
)

[table created]
```

```
create unique index bkopix on backorder(ordnum, prodnum)

[index created]

insert into backorder
select ordnum, prodnum, unit, shipdate, '1999-09-14'
from orderdetail
where shipdate is null


[15 rows]
```

The standard join between three tables looks like this:

Adaptive Server Anywhere

```
select om.ordnum
from ordermaster om, orderdetail od, backorder bo
where om.ordnum = od.ordnum
      and od.ordnum = bo.ordnum
      and om.ordnum = 81
```

Adding one more loop to complete the circle may help some optimizers by providing more choices. The results of the two queries are the same.

Adaptive Server Anywhere

```
select om.ordnum
from ordermaster om, orderdetail od, backorder bo
where om.ordnum = od.ordnum
    and od.ordnum = bo.ordnum
    and bo.ordnum = om.ordnum
    and om.ordnum = 81


    ordnum
===========
        81
        81
        81


[3 rows]
```

Sorting with DISTINCT and UNION

Sorting shows up in a number of places in addition to the ORDER BY clause. Here, check how it works in DISTINCT, UNION, and WHERE.

DISTINCT

Some SQL users automatically throw a DISTINCT into every query (Figure 6–17). Don't do it unless you really need to get rid of duplicates! DISTINCT means that results are generated and then sorted.

In addition, DISTINCT can serve as a cover-up for "broken" queries. Don't reach for a DISTINCT every time you get multiples instead of singles. Think through the logic first. Make sure your query is really asking the question you have in your mind.

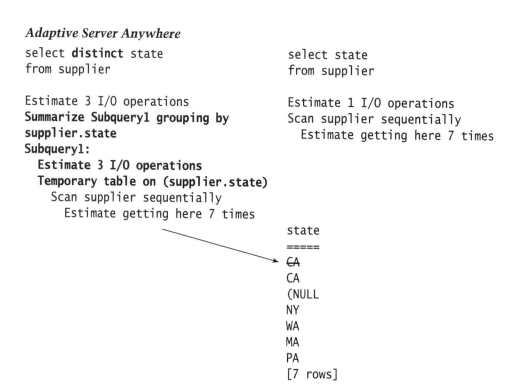

Adaptive Server Anywhere

```
select distinct state
from supplier

Estimate 3 I/O operations
Summarize Subquery1 grouping by
supplier.state
Subquery1:
  Estimate 3 I/O operations
  Temporary table on (supplier.state)
    Scan supplier sequentially
      Estimate getting here 7 times
```

```
select state
from supplier

Estimate 1 I/O operations
Scan supplier sequentially
    Estimate getting here 7 times
```

```
state
=====
CA
CA
(NULL
NY
WA
MA
PA
[7 rows]
```

Figure 6-17. DISTINCT

When DISTINCT means more work, and no real increase in result coherence, do without it. This doesn't mean to avoid DISTINCT—it's a very useful element. It just means to weigh the cost against the advantage.

UNION

In the same way, use UNION ALL rather than UNION unless you need to eliminate duplicates. UNION returns rows from each query included in the statement, puts them in a work table, and then sorts them to remove duplicates. UNION ALL skips the last step. (Information on UNION appears in Chapter 3.)

Here's a UNION ALL query and the ASA PLAN it generated:

Adaptive Server Anywhere

```
select plan ('
select name, state
from supplier
union all
select lname, state
from customer ')

Estimate 5 I/O operations
Take all rows from Subquery1,Subquery2
Subquery1:
  Estimate 1 I/O operations
  Scan supplier sequentially
    Estimate getting here 7 times
Subquery2:
  Estimate 3 I/O operations
  Scan customer sequentially
    Estimate getting here 12 times
```

Following is the plan for the same query with the ALL removed. Without knowing anything about PLAN messages, it's clear that UNION takes more processing than UNION ALL. An additional subquery is listed, for example.

Adaptive Server Anywhere

```
Estimate 11 I/O operations
Summarize Subquery1 grouping by expr,expr
Subquery1:
  Estimate 11 I/O operations
  Temporary table on (expr,expr)
    Take all rows from Subquery2,Subquery3
Subquery2:
  Estimate 1 I/O operations
  Scan supplier sequentially
    Estimate getting here 7 times
Subquery3:
  Estimate 3 I/O operations
  Scan customer sequentially
    Estimate getting here 12 times
```

In this case, the two queries actually produce the same results. You see differences only if the UNIONed queries contain duplicate result rows.

Adaptive Server Anywhere

```
name                  state
==================== =====
Connectix Co.         CA
Soft Stuff            CA
Total Recall          (NULL
Hi Finance!           NY
TrendMaster           WA
Above Average Arts    MA
Emu Sister Prdctns    PA
McBaird               CA
aziz                  MA
khandasamy            NY
mokoperto             MA
Peters                NY
WONG                  MD
archer                CA
le blanc              MA
sato                  WA
deathmask-z           MA
rs                    TX
Menendez              NY

[19 rows]
```

WHERE

Some Oracle references suggest avoiding a sort by using a meaningless condition on a WHERE clause, forcing the data into some order. Let's say you want to see customers in last-name order. There is a unique index on customer number. You add one (not unique, given the nature of names) on lname fname. In this section, there is a leading space on lname rs and fname SAM.

Oracle
```
SQL> create index custnmix on customer(lname, fname);

Index created.
```

A query with no WHERE or ORDER BY clause shows data in this order:

Oracle
```
SQL> select lname, fname, custnum
  2  from customer;
```

LNAME	FNAME	CUSTNUM
McBaird	geoff lowell	111222222
archer	ruby	111223333
aziz	phillip	111333333
le blanc	felipe	111334444
sato	kimiko	111444444
khandasamy	SAM	223456789
deathmask-z		777777777
mokoperto	merit	777777778
rs	pete pete	776677778
Peters	Pete	776667778
Menendez	lauren	923457789
WONG	LI-REN	999456789

```
12 rows selected.
```

Without using an ORDER BY, add a WHERE clause on the column in question (lname), assuming that there are no conflicting WHERE conditions that call for some other index and the indexed column does not use nulls. Oracle (and some other systems) may produce results in lname order. If you get the results you want, use your performance tools to measure the difference between this technique and using ORDER BY. However, this technique can fail if the indexes change. Be sure to document it and note it's a trick.

Oracle

```
SQL>  select lname, fname, custnum
  2   from customer
  3   where lname >= ' ';
```

LNAME	FNAME	CUSTNUM
rs	pete pete	776677778
McBaird	geoff lowell	111222222
Menendez	lauren	923457789
Peters	Pete	776667778
WONG	LI-REN	999456789
archer	ruby	111223333
aziz	phillip	111333333
deathmask-z		777777777
khandasamy	SAM	223456789
le blanc	felipe	111334444
mokoperto	merit	777777778
sato	kimiko	111444444

12 rows selected.

Choosing Between HAVING and WHERE

WHERE puts conditions on the table rows, determining which should be returned. HAVING puts conditions on grouped result rows. The processing order is as follows:

1. Select rows with WHERE.

2. Divide rows into sets with GROUP BY.

3. Calculate aggregate values for each group.

4. Eliminate unwanted group result rows with HAVING.

Any rows you can remove with WHERE, rather than HAVING, make your query more efficient. There are fewer rows to group and fewer to aggregate. In

Adaptive Server Anywhere

```
select type, count(*)
from product


group by type
having type <> 'book'
```

```
select type, count(*)
from product
where type <> 'book'
group by type
```

```
type              count(*)
============ ===========
application          8
game                 4
education            4
hardware             2

[4 rows]
```

Figure 6-18. WHERE and HAVING

Figure 6–18 it makes sense to remove books before rather than after grouping and counting. You save a lot of work.

Use HAVING to limit group result rows, as in the following query:

Adaptive Server Anywhere

```
select type, count(*)
from product
group by type
having count(*) > 5
```

```
type              count(*)
============ ===========
application          8

[1 row]
```

Looking at Views

When you write a query on a view, the view is translated into its underlying SELECT statements. If you need information from one table but go through a multitable view to get it, you'll pay a price.

Adaptive Server Anywhere

```
create view ordervu
as
select od.ordnum, od.prodnum,substr( p.name,1, 20) as name,
       p.price * od.unit as cost
from orderdetail od, product p
where od.prodnum = p.prodnum

[view created]
```

To find the name of a particular product, you might write a query like this:

Adaptive Server Anywhere

```
select distinct   prodnum, name
from ordervu
where prodnum = 2050

    prodnum name
=========== ====================
       2050 tax time

[1 row]
```

It gives you exactly the results you want, but a look at the PLAN output is daunting.

Adaptive Server Anywhere

```
Estimate 13 I/O operations
Summarize Subquery1 grouping by orderdetail.prodnum,expr
Subquery1:
  Estimate 13 I/O operations (best of 2 plans considered)
  Temporary table on (orderdetail.prodnum,expr)
    Scan product AS p sequentially
      Estimate getting here 21 times
      Scan orderdetail AS od sequentially
        Estimate getting here 693 times
```

Removing DISTINCT cuts down on the processing a bit, but it also returns multiple copies of the product number and name. It shows one row for every order that includes the product number 2050.

Adaptive Server Anywhere

```
select  prodnum, name
from ordervu
where prodnum = 2050

     prodnum name
 =========== ====================
        2050 tax time
        2050 tax time
        2050 tax time
        2050 tax time
        2050 tax time
        2050 tax time
        2050 tax time

[7 rows]

Estimate 5 I/O operations (best of 2 plans considered)
Scan product AS p sequentially
   Estimate getting here 21 times
   Scan orderdetail AS od sequentially
      Estimate getting here 693 times
```

Compare the ordervu view PLANs to the product table PLAN for essentially the same query.

Adaptive Server Anywhere

```
select  prodnum, name
from product
where prodnum = 2050

     prodnum name
 =========== ====================
        2050 tax time

Estimate 4 I/O operations
Scan product using unique index prodix
for rows where prodnum equals 2050
   Estimate getting here 1 times
```

Don't use a view if all the data you want is in a single underlying table, and don't make frequently queried views unnecessarily complex.

Forcing Indexes

Many systems permit overriding the optimizer's choices by forcing use of a specified index. This is a good tool for testing, particularly when you are exploring how the optimizer behaves. It gives you a way to see how different indexes work with the same data.

However, hardwiring your queries to use a particular index is dangerous. You lose flexibility. When the data changes, you're tied to the index that worked best last Tuesday—quite possibly not the right choice today. If you decide to force index choices, be sure to document the decision and the cause in the code, and plan to check the SQL regularly. There are plenty of stories about queries that were slow until an expert was called in. Performance improved!. . .for a while. . .and then dropped to abysmal. Another expert removed the index forcing elements, cleaned up some messy WHERE clauses, avoided a view, eliminated a sort, and ended up with longer-lasting improvements.

Summary

This chapter is about making sure your SQL is as effective as possible from a performance point of view. Optimizers vary a lot, so use this information as a starting point, and remember, there are many other factors that can influence performance.

- Make sure you understand what indexes you have.
- Next, find out what tools let you look at the optimizer's choices.
- Once you know your indexes and have a way of finding out whether or not they are being used in a particular query, check the WHERE clause in problem queries. There are many ways you can structure a WHERE clause to invalidate available queries. Often, you can fix a performance problem by making a simple change.
- Indexes that cover queries (contain all the information you need for the results) can be very useful. There are some strict rules to follow, however, in both creating and using them.
- Good joins are critical to relational database performance. Joins have many of the strictures of ordinary WHERE clauses.
- Sorting always means another pass: get the data, then put it in order. Understand when you may be doing unnecessary sorting (with DISTINCT and UNION) and avoid it.
- HAVING and WHERE are not the same. WHERE eliminates rows before you form groups. HAVING limits the group results. Doing WHERE work in HAVING can slow performance down.

- Views are handy, but they may be expensive. Understand the cost of view queries, and create views accordingly.
- Many systems provide ways to go around the optimizer in index choice. Be cautious when you do this.

Asking Performance Questions

Don't come out of this chapter feeling that you shouldn't use functions or DISTINCT or views. Instead, train yourself to look for the fastest way to achieve what you want.

Start by asking the big questions:

- Does the query return useful results?
- Is it lacking anything? Does it bring back extraneous information?
- Is it still needed? Could it be run less frequently or against smaller amounts of data?
- Is the sense that this query is "slow" realistic? Why?

Next, get some information on the indexes.

- Are there indexes on columns frequently used in queries?
- Is the index on the right column or group of columns?
- Is the optimizer using the indexes?
- Are there unused indexes?

If the optimizer is not using existing indexes, find out why.

- Does the optimizer have up-to-date information on the indexed column's statistics?
- Does a table scan make more sense than using an index (lots of rows coming back)?
- Is the query written so that it invalidates an available index (math, functions, conversions on indexed columns)?
- Is IN used where a range or an equal sign would return the same results?
- Are the columns in multicolumn indexes in the wrong order—built on fname, lname when queries usually look for lname?

Finally, look for ways you can speed up processing.

- Would it help to add an index?
- Could indexes that are never used be dropped?
- Could common queries benefit from covering indexes?
- Are there unnecessary DISTINCTs?
- Does the query use UNION where UNION ALL would work?
- Are views more complex than necessary?
- Are hardwired index choices now less than optimal?

Chapter 7

Using SQL to Write SQL

In This Chapter

- Getting Meta-Data from System Catalogs
- Using System Functions
- Writing SQL with SQL
- Creating Test Data with SQL

Systematically Speaking

One of the definitions of a relational database is that it contains meta-data: information about itself and about user-created objects in system catalogs (usually implemented as system tables, though in some cases they are views). The system catalog names and the way you access them can vary widely from DBMS to DBMS. However, whatever your system, you should be able to use the system catalogs in SQL queries to find much useful information, such as:

- User, group, and role definitions
- Column, table, constraint, and index connections
- Space use
- Error messages
- Language and character set data
- Configuration specifics

Don't even dream of editing system catalogs! That's the job of a seasoned expert and then only when there is no other alternative. Depending on how your system is set up, you may not be able to query all system catalogs. However, you'll usually have read access to the ones important to your work.

Some vendors have functions that can help you handle system information—translating user numbers to user names, for example. These system functions pull information out of system catalogs.

You can use the information you get from system catalogs, system functions, and user tables to generate SQL. These techniques are particularly handy for DBA tasks—they assure up-to-date information while saving time. Once you are satisfied with the SQL-generating queries, you can set them up to run automatically, cleaning junk out of the database nightly, updating customer permissions on a regular basis, checking log size, and so on. You can use many of the same techniques for creating test data.

Getting Meta-Data from System Catalogs

System catalogs often have a name element, such as "sys," that makes them easy to find. To work with system catalogs, you need to be familiar with them. This means:

1. Get a list of the system catalogs. You can do this by querying the database, using vendor tools, or consulting documentation.

2. Figure out what columns each contains. Here again, you have your choice of querying system tables or using vendor-provided tools.

3. Decide how to use the information. For example, you might join the catalog that contains table data and the one that holds index information to produce a report on tables and their indexes.

Exactly what the system table names are, what information each contains, and how the columns join varies from system to system, but all vendors provide this capability, and you can use it to create queries. However, you may find that GUI tools your vendor supplies are easier to use for many questions about your system. The advantage of using SQL queries is that you can embed them in scripts and run them from the operating system. You can also send the output to other applications.

Listing System Catalogs

Since all the information about your system is stored in system catalogs, you can query the system catalogs to get a list of themselves. Here are examples of partial system catalog lists on our familiar RDBMSs—Adaptive Server Anywhere, Microsoft SQL Server, Oracle, and Informix. As you compare the queries, notice that the catalog names and structures differ, but the type of information is similar.

Adaptive Server Anywhere For compatibility with Adaptive Server Enterprise, Adaptive Server Anywhere contains two sets of system tables: its own (uppercase) and ASE (lowercase). Here is a query that retrieves both types of system tables from the first part of the alphabet, using the ASA system catalog SYSTABLE:

Adaptive Server Anywhere

```
select table_name
from systable
where table_name between 'sysa' and 'sysd'

table_name
===============================
sysalternates
SYSARTICLE
SYSARTICLECOL
SYSARTICLECOLS
SYSARTICLES
sysauditoptions
sysaudits
SYSCAPABILITIES
SYSCAPABILITY
SYSCAPABILITYNAME
SYSCATALOG
syscharsets
SYSCOLAUTH
SYSCOLLATION
SYSCOLLATIONMAPPINGS
SYSCOLPERM
SYSCOLUMN
SYSCOLUMNS
syscolumns
syscomments
sysconfigures
sysconstraints
syscurconfigs

[23 rows]
```

To see nonsystem tables, you can look for those that do not start with "sys" or those that belong to a particular user. For example, if you want to see everything

DBA owns, use a query like this, joining `systable` and `sysuserperm` to get the user name associated with the table:

Adaptive Server Anywhere
```
select t.table_name, t.table_id ,t.creator, up.user_name
from systable t, sysuserperm up
where t.creator = up.user_id  and up.user_name = 'DBA'
order by table_name
```

```
table_name          table_id creator user_name
================    ======== ======= ========
customer                 191       1 DBA
dumpem                   224       1 DBA
employee                 217       1 DBA
expand                   219       1 DBA
holdem                   221       1 DBA
orderdetail              216       1 DBA
ordermaster              218       1 DBA
product                  188       1 DBA
supplier                 220       1 DBA
testjoin                 222       1 DBA
testseq                  225       1 DBA

[11 rows]
```

Once you know the system catalog and user table names, explore their structure with Sybase Central. It provides graphical information on columns and indexes. "Getting Information on Indexes" in Chapter 6 should get you started.

Transact-SQL (Sybase Adaptive Server Enterprise and Microsoft SQL Server) Adaptive Server Enterprise and Microsoft SQL Server store one copy of each kind of system table in the `master` database (the Sybase and Microsoft table lists and contents are not the same, although the methods are). Each user database also contains a subset of these tables. Here's a list of some of the system tables in the Microsoft SQL Server `master` database:

Transact-SQL
```
select name
from master.dbo.sysobjects
where name between 'sysa' and 'sysd'
```

```
name
--------------------------------
sysallocations
sysalternates
sysaltfiles
syscacheobjects
syscharsets
syscolumns
syscomments
sysconfigures
sysconstraints
syscurconfigs
syscursorcolumns
syscursorrefs
syscursors
syscursortables

(14 row(s) affected)
```

To list nonsystem (user) tables, use the msdpn database rather than the master database, and specify type in your query. (Type U is for user tables, type S for system tables, type V for views.)

Transact-SQL
```
select name
from msdpn.dbo.sysobjects
where type = 'U'

name
-----------------------------------------------------------------
product
orderdetail
test
testn
customer
employee
ordermaster
expand
supplier
testjoin
testseq

(11 row(s) affected)
```

To find out what columns each table has, use the sp_help stored procedure (the Adaptive Server Enterprise and Microsoft SQL Server displays are not identical—and only part of the ASE report follows).

Sybase Adaptive Server Enterprise

```
exec sp_help syscolumns
```

Name	Owner	Type
syscolumns	dbo	system table

Data_located_on_segment	When_created
system	Jan 1 1900 12:00AM

Column_name	Type	Length	Prec	Scale	Nulls	Default_name	Rule_name	Identity
id	int	4	NULL	NULL	0	NULL	NULL	0
number	smallint	2	NULL	NULL	0	NULL	NULL	0
colid	tinyint	1	NULL	NULL	0	NULL	NULL	0
status	tinyint	1	NULL	NULL	0	NULL	NULL	0
type	tinyint	1	NULL	NULL	0	NULL	NULL	0
length	tinyint	1	NULL	NULL	0	NULL	NULL	0
offset	smallint	2	NULL	NULL	0	NULL	NULL	0
usertype	smallint	2	NULL	NULL	0	NULL	NULL	0
cdefault	int	4	NULL	NULL	0	NULL	NULL	0
domain	int	4	NULL	NULL	0	NULL	NULL	0
name	sysname	30	NULL	NULL	0	NULL	NULL	0
printfmt	varchar	255	NULL	NULL	1	NULL	NULL	0
prec	tinyint	1	NULL	NULL	1	NULL	NULL	0
scale	tinyint	1	NULL	NULL	1	NULL	NULL	0
remote_type	int	4	NULL	NULL	1	NULL	NULL	0
remote_name	varchar	30	NULL	NULL	1	NULL	NULL	0

index_name	index_description	index_keys	index_max_rows_per_page
syscolumns	clustered, unique on system	id,number,colid	0

. . .

```
[partial results]
```

Adaptive Server Enterprise and Microsoft SQL Server also have GUI tools you can use to get information about system and user tables—Sybase Central and SQL Server Enterprise Manager, respectively.

Oracle   Oracle stores system information in views, classified as USER (the current user), ALL (all users, PUBLIC), or DBA (database administrator), depending on the level of permission associated with the view. You can check the central view called DICTIONARY (or DICT) to get a list. Here's a query to locate early-alphabet USER system views—object names are stored in uppercase, so that's what you need to use in the WHERE clause, when you are looking for a match:

> ***Oracle***
>
> ```
> SQL> select table_name
>   2  from dict
>   3  where table_name between 'USER_A' AND 'USER_D';
>
> TABLE_NAME
> ------------------------------
> USER_ALL_TABLES
> USER_ARGUMENTS
> USER_AUDIT_OBJECT
> USER_AUDIT_SESSION
> USER_AUDIT_STATEMENT
> USER_AUDIT_TRAIL
> USER_CATALOG
> USER_CLUSTERS
> USER_CLUSTER_HASH_EXPRESSIONS
> USER_CLU_COLUMNS
> USER_COLL_TYPES
> USER_COL_COMMENTS
> USER_COL_PRIVS
> USER_COL_PRIVS_MADE
> USER_COL_PRIVS_RECD
> USER_CONSTRAINTS
> USER_CONS_COLUMNS
>
> 17 rows selected.
> ```

To see nonsystem tables, query the CAT (CATALOG) view.

```
SQL>  select table_name
   2    from cat
   3    where table_type = 'TABLE' and table_name not like '%$'

TABLE_NAME
------------------------------
CUSTOMER
DUAL
EMPLOYEE
EXPAND
ORDERDETAIL
ORDERMASTER
PRODUCT
SUPPLIER
TESTJOIN
TESTNUM
TESTSEQ

11 rows selected.
```

To get information on the columns in a table, use the Oracle SQL Plus DESCRIBE command. It lists the columns in a table, their NULL status, and their datatypes.

Oracle

```
SQL> describe USER_COLL_TYPES;
```

Name	Null?	Type
TYPE_NAME	NOT NULL	VARCHAR2(30)
COLL_TYPE	NOT NULL	VARCHAR2(30)
UPPER_BOUND		NUMBER
ELEM_TYPE_MOD		VARCHAR2(7)
ELEM_TYPE_OWNER		VARCHAR2(30)
ELEM_TYPE_NAME		VARCHAR2(30)
LENGTH		NUMBER
PRECISION		NUMBER
SCALE		NUMBER
CHARACTER_SET_NAME		VARCHAR2(44)

Informix   Informix system catalogs have a tabid of 99 or less.

Informix

```
select tabname, tabid
from systables
where tabid <100 and tabname between 'sysa' and 'sysd'
order by tabname
```

```
tabname                 tabid

sysblobs                   20
syschecks                  13
syscolauth                  5
syscoldepend               15
syscolumns                  2
sysconstraints             11
```

[6 rows]

To get a list of user tables, look for ones with an id above 99.

Informix

```
select tabname, tabid
from systables
where tabid > 99
```

```
tabname                 tabid
------------------------------
supplier                  108
customer                  101
ordermaster               106
expand                    107
product                   110
testjoin                  111
employee                  112
orderdetail               113
testseq                   114
```

[9 rows]

To see the structure of a table, use the GUI IECC, the dbschema utility, or the *Info* option of the dbaccess utility.

Writing Queries Using System Catalogs

Take time to get to know your system catalogs. They are an invaluable source of information. Once you learn how to use them, you'll never feel really lost in a new database. Even without a sketch of the database tables, columns, and indexes, you have the means to understand your environment. Although the details vary from vendor to vendor, the method is consistent.

Here's a query, using four Adaptive Server Anywhere system tables, that, for a given table name or set of table names, tells you the index names, the columns in the indexes, and their order. In this case, you learn that ordermaster has one index consisting of a single column and orderdetail has one index made up of two columns.

To get this information for all tables in the database, remove the last condition of the WHERE clause.

Adaptive Server Anywhere

```
select t.table_name,
  i.index_name, c.column_name,
  ic.sequence
from systable t, sysindex i, sysixcol ic, syscolumn c
where t.table_id = i.table_id
  and i.table_id =ic.table_id
    and i.index_id = ic.index_id
    and c.column_id = ic.column_id
    and c.table_id = ic.table_id
    and t.table_name like 'order%'

table_name  index_name column_name sequence
=========== ========== =========== ==========
ordermaster ordix       ordnum      0
orderdetail ordprodix   ordnum      0
orderdetail ordprodix   prodnum     1

[3 rows]
```

You could also get this information from the GUI Sybase Central tool that comes with Adaptive Server Anywhere (see "Getting Information on Indexes" in Chapter 6).

If you're not using ASA, you'll need to modify the query quite a bit, using your vendor's system catalogs. Here's an example, using Oracle:

Oracle

```
SQL>  select ui.table_name, ui.index_name, ui.index_type,
   2        uic.column_name, uic.column_position
   3    from user_indexes ui, user_ind_columns uic
   4    where uic.index_name = ui.index_name
   5        and ui.table_name like 'ORDER%';
```

TABLE_NAME	INDEX_NAME	INDEX_TYPE	COLUMN_NAME	COLUMN_POSITION
ORDERMASTER	ORDIX	NORMAL	ORDNUM	1
ORDERDETAIL	ORDPRODIX	NORMAL	ORDNUM	1
ORDERDETAIL	ORDPRODIX	NORMAL	PRODNUM	2

```
3 rows selected.
```

In any DBMS, if multiple user tables have the same name, you'll need to add an owner-name column or condition.

Using System Functions

Unlike character, number, convert, and conditional functions, system functions concern the environment and get information from system catalogs or the host machine. Here, they are divided into two groups:

- Functions that identify a user, session, version, or other administrative element
- Functions that display the current date, time, or timestamp

Both kinds of system functions are useful in queries.

Getting Administrative Information

You often need to know who or where you are, particularly if you have multiple database identities or help other users. These functions (Table 7–1) can help you nail reality down.

Table 7-1. System Functions

ANSI	ASA	ASE	MS SQL Server	Oracle	Informix
current_USER	USER_ID USER_NAME	USER_ID USER_NAME	CURRENT_USER USER_ID USER_NAME	USER UID	USER
SYSTEM_USER	SUSER_ID SUSER_NAME	SUSER_ID SUSER_NAME	SYSTEM_USER SUSER_ID SUSER_NAME		
SESSION_USER			SESSION_USER		
	DB_NAME DB_ID	DB_NAME DB_ID	DB_NAME DB_ID		DBSERVERNAME DBSITENAME
	OBJECT_NAME OBJECT_ID	OBJECT_NAME OBJECT_ID	OBJECT_NAME OBJECT_ID		
		HOST_NAME HOST_ID	HOST_NAME HOST_ID		DBINFO ('dbhostname')
	SELECT @@VERSION	SELECT @@VERSION	SELECT @@VERSION	SELECT * FROM v$version	SELECT DBINFO ('VERSION', 'MAJOR'), DBINFO('VERSION', 'MINOR') FROM systables

What do you do with the system functions? On the simplest level, use them to produce reports about your environment. This query tells you who you are and where and when you are logging in.

Adaptive Server Anywhere

```
select 'System user ' || suser_name()
    || ' using database ' || db_name() ||  ' logging in on '
    || convert(char(20),getdate())

'Systemuser'||suser_name(
============================================================================
System user DBA using database msdpn logging in on jul 06 2000 12:50PM

[1 row]
```

Often, the functions are useful in translating system catalog codes into strings. A query of the Adaptive Server Anywhere sysobjects table for user (type U) table names and their owners (uids) looks like this:

Adaptive Server Anywhere

```
select name, uid,  type
from sysobjects
where type = 'U'
```

```
name                        uid type
========================    === ====
RowGenerator                  3 U
rs_lastcommit                 4 U
rs_threads                    4 U
ul_user                       3 U
ul_table                      3 U
ul_script                     3 U
ul_connection_script          3 U
ul_table_script               3 U
ul_scripts_modified           3 U
EXCLUDEOBJECT                 3 U
customer                      1 U
orderdetail                   1 U
ordermaster                   1 U
product                       1 U
supplier                      1 U
```

```
[15 rows]
```

If you decide that you want only the tables that belong to the DBA, you can figure out the uid with a query like this, using the USER_NAME function (or its equivalent) to translate the uid into a name:

Adaptive Server Anywhere

```
select distinct  uid,  user_name(uid)
from sysobjects
order by uid
```

```
uid    user_name(sysobjects.uid)
======  =====================
     0 SYS
     1 DBA
     3 dbo
     4 rs_systabgroup
```

[4 rows]

Then you can modify your query.

Adaptive Server Anywhere
```
select name, user_name( uid ),  type
from sysobjects where type = 'U' and user_name(uid) = 'DBA'
```

```
name                     user_name(sysobjects.uid) type
=================  ========================= ====
customer           DBA                       U
orderdetail        DBA                       U
ordermaster        DBA                       U
product            DBA                       U
supplier           DBA                       U
```

[5 rows]

Here's another example. Microsoft SQL Server supports a system function (STATS_DATE) that tells you when statistics for a given index were last updated (see Table 6–2 for more information on UPDATE STATISTICS). The function takes two arguments: the table identification number and the index identification number. Here, the Transact-SQL OBJECT_ID function translates a table name to its identification number. The value "2" for the index number is based on a query of sysindexes and sysobjects.

Microsoft SQL Server
```
select stats_date(object_id('ordermaster'), 2)
```

```
--------------------------
2000-01-25 13:17:58.120
```

(1 row(s) affected)

```
update statistics ordermaster

select stats_date(object_id('ordermaster'), 2)


--------------------------
2000-03-23 16:28:24.397

(1 row(s) affected)
```

Finding Today's Date

Another set of system functions deals with today's date. The functions are use-ful as defaults (say for dating orders or customer support calls) and in calculations (subtract the order date from today's date, if the product hasn't shipped yet, to find out how old it is). Here's where to look for other date information:

- Convert functions (including those for dates) are in "Converting Dates (and Other Datatypes)" in Chapter 2.
- Functions for adding and subtracting dates are in "Doing Math on Dates" in Chapter 2.
- Techniques for matching dates are in "Finding Dates" in Chapter 2.
- Commands for setting the default date format are in "Defining Default Date Format" in Appendix B.

Adaptive Server Anywhere presents two date "constants," CURRENT DATE and CURRENT TIME. One retrieves the date, the other the time. ASA also sup-ports the Transact-SQL GETDATE function, which returns both date and time.

As you can see from the results, it's possible to set different formats for the different date elements. Here DATE data (current date) is in the default YYYY-MM-DD format, while DATETIME and TIMESTAMP data (GETDATE(), order-date) use the name of the month followed by the day and year.

Adaptive Server Anywhere

```
select  current date, current time, getdate(), orderdate
from ordermaster
where ordnum between 81 and 85
```

```
current date current time   getdate(*)                orderdate
============ ==============  =========================  ====================
2000-06-02   13:52:34.260   Jun 02 2000 13:52:34   Jan 02 1999 02:30:00
2000-06-02   13:52:34.260   Jun 02 2000 13:52:34   Jan 02 1999 00:00:00
```

[2 rows]

Informix offers two possibilities: TODAY and CURRENT. The first displays the date only; the second produces date and time.

Informix

```
select today as Date, current as DateTime, orderdate
from ordermaster
where ordnum between 81 and 85
```

```
Date        DateTime                 orderdate
----------  -----------------------  ---------
06/02/2000  2000-06-02 17:18:50.000  1999-01-02 02:30
06/02/2000  2000-06-02 17:18:50.000  1999-01-02 00:00
```

[2 rows]

Adaptive Server Enterprise uses just one function, GETDATE().

Adaptive Server Enterprise

```
select getdate() as DateTime, orderdate
from ordermaster
where ordnum between 81 and 85
```

```
DateTime              orderdate
====================  ====================
Jun 02 2000 17:22:17  Jan 02 1999 02:30:00
Jun 02 2000 17:22:17  Jan 02 1999 00:00:00
```

(2 row(s) affected)

Microsoft SQL Server supports GETDATE and CURRENT_TIMESTAMP.

MS SQL Server

```
select getdate(), current_timestamp, orderdate
from ordermaster
where ordnum between 81 and 85
```

		orderdate
2000-06-02 17:25:12.990	2000-06-02 17:25:12.990	1999-01-02 02:30:00.000
2000-06-02 17:25:12.990	2000-06-02 17:25:12.990	1999-01-02 00:00:00.000

(2 row(s) affected)

The Oracle function is SYSDATE.

Oracle

```
SQL> select sysdate as DateTime, orderdate
  2  from ordermaster
  3  where ordnum between 81 and 85;
```

DATETIME	ORDERDATE
02-JUN-00	02-JAN-99
02-JUN-00	02-JAN-99

2 rows selected.

From this example, it might seem that Oracle's SYSDATE function reports only the date, not the time. Actually, it reports date or date and time or time alone, depending on how you have defined the default date. This topic is covered in "Notes on Environment and Display" in Appendix B.

Table 7–2 summarizes how you can tell the systems used in this book to display today's date. If you have a different system, the chances are that you have a different method. Check your documentation for details.

Inserting Today's Date

Here's how you can add date information to a row on INSERT. You could also set up a default in your CREATE TABLE statement, using the system date function.

Table 7-2. Today's Date

ANSI	ASA	ASE	MS SQL Server	Oracle	Informix
CURRENT_DATE CURRENT_TIME CURRENT_TIMESTAMP	CURRENT DATE CURRENT TIME GETDATE	 GETDATE	 CURRENT_TIMESTAMP GETDATE	 SYSDATE	TODAY CURRENT

Adaptive Server Anywhere

```
insert into orderdetail
select 100, 1083, 4, getdate()
from orderdetail
```

```
[1 row]
```

```
insert into orderdetail
select 101, 1083, 4, current date
from orderdetail
```

```
[1 row]
```

```
select *
from orderdetail
where ordnum  >99
```

```
      ordnum      prodnum   unit shipdate
   =========== =========== ====== ==================
          100        1083      4 Jun 22 2000 16:00
          101        1083      4 Jun 22 2000 00:00
```

```
[2 rows]
```

Don't forget to remove the rows, if you added them.

Adaptive Server Anywhere

```
delete from orderdetail
where ordnum >99
```

```
[2 rows]
```

Writing SQL with SQL

You can use system catalogs and system functions to generate SQL. After all, the system catalogs contain information about your database. Commands based on current system catalog data incorporate the most recent changes.

GRANTing Permissions

Imagine that you have added a new user to your Adaptive Server Anywhere database, and you want to give that user permission to use some tables. If you know that users are listed in a system table (here, sysusers—check your vendor's documentation for the equivalent) and tables are named in another (sysobjects), you can write a query to create SQL statements to grant table use to new users. Here is how you construct the query.

In the SELECT clause, create the SQL command. Use

- text elements (GRANT SELECT ON, in quotes).
- system table column names (sysobjects.name, sysusers.name).

In the WHERE clause, qualify the rows.

- Specify new users (here, new users have numbers above 5).
- Identify the type of objects you want to grant use of (here, user tables; type "U").
- Include information on ownership if needed (the UID function translates the user identification number in sysobjects to a name, and the WHERE clause checks to make sure the name is "DBA").

The combination of text elements, values from system tables, and manipulation of information by system functions produces code you can use. To follow along, use the "Users and Groups" option in Sybase Central to add a user (Figure 6–5 should help you get started).

Adaptive Server Anywhere
```
select 'GRANT SELECT ON', sysobjects.name, 'TO', sysusers.name
from sysusers, sysobjects
where sysobjects.type = 'U'
    and user_name (sysobjects.uid) = 'DBA' and sysusers.uid >5
```

```
'GRANT SELECT ON' name                'TO' name
================== ============= ==== ===========================
GRANT SELECT ON    customer       TO   newbie
GRANT SELECT ON    product        TO   newbie
GRANT SELECT ON    orderdetail    TO   newbie
GRANT SELECT ON    employee       TO   newbie
GRANT SELECT ON    ordermaster    TO   newbie
GRANT SELECT ON    supplier       TO   newbie

[6 rows]
```

If you concatenate the columns together (see Table 2–1 for details), the output looks more like a script.

Adaptive Server Anywhere
```
select 'GRANT SELECT ON ' || sysobjects.name || ' TO ' || sysusers.name
from sysusers, sysobjects
where sysobjects.type = 'U'
and user_name (sysobjects.uid) = 'DBA' and sysusers.uid >5

'GRANT SELECT ON ' || sysobje
=====================================================
GRANT SELECT ON customer TO newbie
GRANT SELECT ON product TO newbie
GRANT SELECT ON orderdetail TO newbie
GRANT SELECT ON employee TO newbie
GRANT SELECT ON ordermaster TO newbie
GRANT SELECT ON supplier TO newbie

[6 rows]
```

Now you can run the output as SQL statements.

Adaptive Server Anywhere
```
GRANT SELECT ON customer TO newbie
GRANT SELECT ON orderdetail TO newbie
GRANT SELECT ON ordermaster TO newbie
GRANT SELECT ON product TO newbie
GRANT SELECT ON supplier TO newbie

[Grant complete]
```

Removing Junk Objects

Here's another application: getting rid of junk tables. You want to clean up all the test tables you generated while trying things out, so you write a SQL query that looks for user tables with the word "test" embedded in the name. In Adaptive Server Anywhere, the table to start with is sysobjects. Your implementation may use a different name.

Adaptive Server Anywhere

```
select 'DROP TABLE' , name
from sysobjects
where type = 'U' and name like '%test%'


'DROP TABLE' name
============ =========================================
DROP TABLE   testjoin
DROP TABLE   testchar
DROP TABLE   test
DROP TABLE   test2

[4 rows]
```

The related query on Oracle is almost the same, except for a different table name, a different column name, and the need to keep the LIKE match upper-case, because that's how object names are stored.

Oracle

```
SQL> select 'DROP TABLE', table_name
  2  from cat
  3  where table_name like '%TEST%';

'DROPTABLE TABLE_NAME
---------- ------------------------------
DROP TABLE TEST
DROP TABLE TEST2
DROP TABLE TESTCHAR
DROP TABLE TESTJOIN

4 rows selected.
```

Get the idea? Although the system table names and column names are different, they contain similar information. You can use the system tables to generate lots of workaday SQL: permission scripts and cleanup scripts are just the beginning.

Adding Line Breaks   If you want a semicolon or "go" between lines, try adding the CHAR function to the select list. CHAR(10) represents the carriage return character. (You may not be able to see how this works if you are using a GUI tool. Try saving the output file to an ASCII-format file—it'll make more sense.)

First, get familiar with how CHAR and ASCII work. ASCII translates a character to its ASCII representation.

Sybase Adaptive Server Anywhere
```
select ascii('a')

ascii('a')
==========
        97

[1 row]
```

CHAR does the opposite.

Sybase Adaptive Server Anywhere
```
select char(98)

"char"(98)
==========
b

[1 row]
```

ASCII and its sister function, CHAR, are available in many SQL engines; see Table 7–3 for more information. The ASCII value of new line is 10. When you concatenate DROP TABLE to the table name and then to a CHAR(10) linefeed and semicolon, the code and results look like this:

Table 7–3. ASCII and CHAR

ANSI	ASA	ASE	MS SQL Server	Oracle	Informix
	ASCII	ASCII	ASCII	ASCII	
	CHAR	CHAR	CHAR	CHR	

Adaptive Server Anywhere

```
select 'DROP TABLE' , name, char(10)  ||  ';' as x
from sysobjects
where type = 'U' and name like '%test%'
```

```
'DROP TABLE' name
===========  =========================================================
DROP TABLE   testjoin
;
DROP TABLE   testchar
;
DROP TABLE   test
;
DROP TABLE   test2
;
```

Creating Test Data with SQL

You can use similar techniques to create test data. Let's say you need more rows in the customer table. Since you have a unique index, you can't just insert more copies of the existing rows. You have to modify the customer numbers so that each row will have a different one. Here's where convert functions come in handy. You change the character datatype to a numeric one and add some value—here, 11. (See Table 2–9 for more information on available functions.)

Adaptive Server Anywhere

```
select custnum, cast (custnum +11 as integer)
from customer
order by custnum
```

```
custnum    customer.custnum+11
=========  ===================
111222222          111222233
111223333          111223344
111333333          111333344
111334444          111334455
111444444          111444455
223456789          223456800
776667778          776667789
776677778          776677789
777777777          777777788
777777778          777777789
923457789          923457800
999456789          999456800

[12 rows]
```

Now, in order to use the changed customer number, you have to convert it back to a CHAR(9).

Adaptive Server Anywhere

```
insert into customer (custnum,
 lname, address, city, state, postcode,
 areacode, phone, status)
select cast ( cast (custnum +11 as integer) as char(9) ),
 lname, address, city, state, postcode,
areacode, phone, '4'
from customer

[12 rows]
```

You can continue inserting the rows back into the table in this way until you have the table size you want. You may need to vary the number you add to custnum.

Adaptive Server Anywhere

```
insert into customer (custnum,
 lname, address, city, state, postcode,
 areacode, phone, status)
```

```
select cast ( cast (custnum +21 as integer) as char(9) ),
 lname, address, city, state, postcode,
  areacode, phone, '4'
from customer

insert into customer (custnum,
 lname, address, city, state, postcode,
 areacode, phone, status)
select cast ( cast (custnum +30 as integer) as char(9) ),
 lname, address, city, state, postcode,
 areacode, phone, '4'
from customer

insert into customer (custnum,
 lname, address, city, state, postcode,
 areacode, phone, status)
select cast ( cast (custnum +35 as integer) as char(9) ),
 lname, address, city, state, postcode,
 areacode, phone, '4'
from customer
```

To remove extra rows, just look for those that have a 4 in the status column.

Adaptive Server Anywhere
```
delete from customer
where status = 4
```

Summary

This chapter covers some advanced techniques for writing queries.

- System catalogs vary a lot across RDBMSs. Their names and column lists have little in common. However, they all contain system meta-data, and you can query them.
- System functions give access to environment information, such as user identity, host name, today's date, and current software version. They help untangle codes in system tables, translating an object ID, for example, to an object name.

- Generating SQL with SQL is a powerful technique. It is particularly useful in administrative tasks, such as managing permissions and cleaning up. You use system tables and system functions to retrieve up-to-the-minute data in query format. Then you run the queries.
- Last of all, there are some examples of using SQL to generate test data. You often want tables or rows to try things out on, and it's easiest to use existing data as a starting point. However, you want to be careful not to corrupt it.

Appendix A

Understanding the Sample DB: msdpn

In This Appendix

- Describing the database
- Collecting the CREATE Scripts
- Explaining the INSERT Scripts
- Experimenting and Transaction Management
- Removing Data and Objects: DROP and DELETE Commands

MegaSysDataProNet Co

For consistency, there's just one example set in the book, the msdpn database. It models the business of MegaSysDataProNet Co, a completely imaginary but soon-to-be-profitable high-tech e-commerce endeavor. MSDPN Co sells software, toys, educational materials, hardware, and so on over the Net. It has six tables. All are short and have lots of text columns. The tables hold data about customers, suppliers, products, sales, and employees. Many tables that a real business would have are missing, of course, and the amount of data in each table is trivial. Nonetheless, you can use the msdpn tables to test most of the problems addressed in the book.

You'll find a full description of the database in "Understanding the msdpn Database" in Chapter 1, along with listings of the data in each table. Scripts for creating and filling the database are in this appendix and on the CD.

Figure A–1 shows the entity-relationship diagram for the msdpn database, with tables, their primary keys, and how the tables relate to each other.

- customer contains customer name, address, phone, and status information.
- supplier gives similar information on the product makers.
- product holds information about the item, including its price.
- employee stores information about staff.
- ordermaster represents the top level of an order.
- orderdetail is the order line item table.

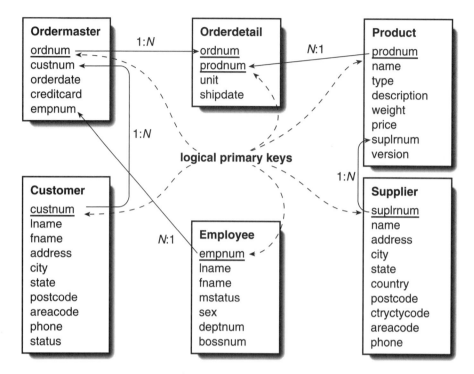

Figure A-1. msdpn Database Entity-Relationship Diagram

Table names are bold and in slightly larger script than column names. Underlined columns are unique identifiers (logical primary keys). Each table has a unique index built on its unique identifier (logical primary key). In one case (orderdetail), two columns (ordnum and prodnum) are required for uniqueness.

The arrows show the relationships between the tables. Checking the ordermaster and orderdetail tables, you can see that each row in ordermaster may have multiple related rows in orderdetail. Each row in orderdetail has only one related row in ordermaster. This parent-child relationship is described as 1:*N*.

Collecting the CREATE Scripts

The CREATE scripts for the RDBMSs used in the book are all pretty much the same, except for minor differences in datatype names (see Appendix B) and null use. They are included in their full form for your convenience here and also (in a slightly different form) on the CD that comes with the book.

If you are using ASA, the RDBMS that comes on the CD, you don't have to create anything. The tables are loaded and ready to go. You may want to review the CREATE script to get information about the tables.

If you're working with another system, you may be able to use the scripts provided to create the msdpn tables there.

Datatypes for a particular implementation are picked mostly for ease of understanding and portability—they may not be the best choices in a production environment. For example, Adaptive Server Anywhere treats CHAR and VARCHAR as the same type. Nonetheless, the ASA script uses both CHAR and VARCHAR because there is a distinction in other systems.

The scripts for each system create the six tables and their indexes. Some systems and tools require you to execute one command at a time. Others allow you to run the whole script as a single batch (a bunch of commands terminated with a "go" or a semicolon or the tool execute key) or as a series of batches. Because requirements for terminator signals vary, even within an RDBMS, they are not included in the scripts in this chapter.

Once the tables and indexes are in place, use the INSERT script (next section) to add data.

Experimentation is the best way to learn. Don't be afraid to play with the tables. If you want to restore a table to its original form, you can delete all rows ("DROP and DELETE Commands") and insert a new batch of data with the relevant INSERT script.

Adaptive Server Anywhere

The msdpn database is created with SQL Anywhere utilities. If you are using the Adaptive Server Anywhere software on the CD that comes with the book, the database is already created and the tables installed. When you remove or change a table, you can use the script to re-create it. To refresh all the tables, drop all six (see "Removing Data and Objects: DROP and DELETE Commands" for the DROP commands), then copy the CREATE script into the Interactive SQL window and execute it in one piece. When all tables are created, load the data with the INSERT script on the CD ("Explaining the INSERT Scripts").

If your version of ASA allows MONEY datatype, you can substitute that for DECIMAL(8,2).

```
/*
set option public.Scale = 2;
set option public.Precision = 10;
*/


create table customer
(
custnum      char(9)        not null,
lname        varchar(20)    not null,
fname        varchar(20)        null,
address      varchar(40)    not null,
city         varchar(20)    not null,
state        char(2)        not null,
postcode     char(10)       not null,
areacode     char(3)        not null,
phone        char(7)        not null,
status       char(1)            null
)
create unique index custix on customer(custnum)

create table supplier
(
suplrnum     smallint       not null,
name         varchar(20)    not null,
address      varchar(20)    not null,
city         varchar(20)    not null,
state        char(2)            null,
country      varchar(20)    not null,
postcode     varchar(10)    not null,
ctryctycode  varchar(7)         null,
areacode     char(3)            null,
phone        char(7)            null
)
create unique index suppix on supplier(suplrnum)

create table product
(
prodnum      int            not null,
name         varchar(20)    not null,
type         varchar(12)        null,
description  varchar(50)        null,
```

```
weight       decimal(6,2) not null,
price        numeric(8,2)     null,
suplrnum     smallint     not null,
version      varchar(8)       null
)
create unique index prodix on product(prodnum)
create index pricex on product(price)

create table ordermaster
(
ordnum      int           not null,
custnum     char(9)       not null,
orderdate   timestamp     not null,
creditcard  varchar(20)   not null,
empnum      char(9)       not null
)
create unique index ordix on ordermaster(ordnum)

create table orderdetail
(
ordnum      int           not null,
prodnum     int           not null,
unit        smallint      not null,
shipdate    date              null
)
create unique index ordprodix on orderdetail(ordnum, prodnum)

create table employee
(
empnum       char(9)      not null,
lname        varchar(20)  not null,
fname        varchar(20)      null,
mstatus      tinyint          null,
sex          tinyint          null,
deptnum      int          not null,
bossnum      char(9)      not null
)
create unique index empix on employee(empnum)
```

Sybase Adaptive Server Enterprise

The changes here are minor.

- The DATE datatype becomes DATETIME throughout (SMALLDATETIME would work too).
- The price column in the product table uses the MONEY datatype.
- Since ASE supports multiple databases, use GUI tools or the CREATE DATABASE statement (from the master database) to set up the msdpn database. Then make msdpn active (with your GUI interface or the USE command) and run the CREATE script and INSERT script ("Explaining the INSERT Scripts") from there.

```
create table customer
(
custnum      char(9)       not null,
lname        varchar(20)   not null,
fname        varchar(20)       null,
address      varchar(40)   not null,
city         varchar(20)   not null,
state        char(2)       not null,
postcode     char(10)      not null,
areacode     char(3)       not null,
phone        char(7)       not null,
status       char(1)           null
)
create unique index custix on customer(custnum)

create table supplier
(
suplrnum     smallint      not null,
name         varchar(20)   not null,
address      varchar(20)   not null,
city         varchar(20)   not null,
state        char(2)           null,
country      varchar(20)   not null,
postcode     varchar(10)   not null,
ctryctycode  varchar(7)        null,
areacode     char(3)           null,
phone        char(7)           null
)
create unique index suppix on supplier(suplrnum)
```

```
create table product
(
prodnum      int           not null,
name         varchar(20)   not null,
type         varchar(12)       null,
description  varchar(50)       null,
weight       decimal(6,2)  not null,
price        money             null,
suplrnum     smallint      not null,
version      varchar(8)        null
)
create unique index prodix on product(prodnum)
create index pricex on product(price)

create table ordermaster
(
ordnum       int           not null,
custnum      char(9)       not null,
orderdate    datetime      not null,
creditcard   varchar(20)   not null,
empnum       char(9)       not null
)
create unique index ordix on ordermaster(ordnum)

create table orderdetail
(
ordnum       int           not null,
prodnum      int           not null,
unit         smallint      not null,
shipdate     datetime          null
)
create unique index ordprodix on orderdetail(ordnum, prodnum)

create table employee
(
empnum       char(9)       not null,
lname        varchar(20)   not null,
fname        varchar(20)       null,
mstatus      tinyint           null,
sex          tinyint           null,
```

```
deptnum       int          not null,
bossnum       char(9)      not null
)
create unique index empix on employee(empnum)
go
```

Microsoft SQL Server

The Sybase Adaptive Server Enterprise script works without change, as do the general instructions for creating the msdpn database—although the GUI tools are different.

Oracle

One difference between Oracle and other vendors is the use of VARCHAR2 instead of VARCHAR.

```
--If you use SQL Plus to create the tables, read the script in with
-- START filename (when filename is in Oracle/bin) or
-- START filename_full_path

create table customer
(
custnum       char(9)      not null,
lname         varchar2(20) not null,
fname         varchar2(20)      null,
address       varchar2(40) not null,
city          varchar2(20) not null,
state         char(2)      not null,
postcode      char(10)     not null,
areacode      char(3)      not null,
phone         char(7)      not null,
status        char(1)           null
)
;
create unique index custix on customer(custnum);
```

```
create table supplier
(
suplrnum      number            not null,
name          varchar2(20)  not null,
address       varchar2(20)  not null,
city          varchar2(20)  not null,
state         char(2)               null,
country       varchar2(20)  not null,
postcode      varchar2(10)  not null,
ctryctycode varchar2(7)           null,
areacode      char(3)               null,
phone         char(7)               null
)
;
create unique index suppix on supplier(suplrnum)
;

create table product
(
prodnum       number            not null,
name          varchar2(20)  not null,
type          varchar2(12)          null,
description varchar2(50)          null,
weight        number(6,2)   not null,
price         number(8,2)           null,
suplrnum      number            not null,
version       varchar2(8)           null
)
create unique index prodix on product(prodnum)
create index pricex on product(price)

create table ordermaster
(
ordnum        number            not null,
custnum       char(9)           not null,
orderdate     date              not null,
creditcard    varchar2(20)  not null,
empnum        char(9)           not null
)
create unique index ordix on ordermaster(ordnum)
```

```
create table orderdetail
(
ordnum      number      not null,
prodnum     number      not null,
unit        number      not null,
shipdate    date          null
)
create unique index ordprodix on orderdetail(ordnum, prodnum)

create table employee
(
empnum      char(9)       not null,
lname       varchar2(20) not null,
fname       varchar2(20)   null,
mstatus     number         null,
sex         number         null,
deptnum     int         not null,
bossnum     char(9)     not null
)
create unique index empix on employee(empnum)
```

Informix

Informix does not allow null in CREATE TABLE statements. It supports a
MONEY datatype.

```
create table customer
(
custnum     char(9)       not null,
lname       varchar(20)   not null,
fname       varchar(20)          ,
address     varchar(40)   not null,
city        varchar(20)   not null,
state       char(2)       not null,
postcode    varchar(10)   not null,
areacode    char(3)              ,
phone       varchar(7)           ,
status      char(1)

)
create unique index custix on customer(custnum)
```

```
create table supplier
(
suplrnum    int            not null,
name        varchar(20)    not null,
address     varchar(20)    not null,
city        varchar(20)    not null,
state       char(2)                 ,
country     varchar(20)    not null,
postcode    varchar(10)    not null,
ctryctycode varchar(7)              ,
areacode    char(3)                 ,
phone       varchar(7)
)
create unique index suppix on supplier(suplrnum)

create table product
(
prodnum     int            not null,
name        varchar(20)    not null,
type        varchar(12)             ,
description varchar(50)             ,
weight      decimal(6,2)   not null,
price       money(8,2)              ,
suplrnum    int            not null,
version     varchar(8)
)
create unique index prodix on product(prodnum)
create index pricex on product(price)

create table employee
(
empnum      char(9)        not null,
lname       varchar(20)    not null,
fname       varchar(20)             ,
mstatus     smallint                ,
sex         smallint                ,
deptnum     smallint       not null,
bossnum     char(9)        not null
)
create unique index empix on employee(empnum)
```

```
create table ordermaster
(
ordnum      int           not null,
custnum     char(9)       not null,
orderdate   datetime year to minute        not null,
creditcard  varchar(20)   not null,
empnum      char(9)       not null
)
create unique index ordix on ordermaster(ordnum)

create table orderdetail
(
ordnum      int           not null,
prodnum     int           not null,
unit        int           not null,
shipdate    date
)
create unique index ordprodix on orderdetail(ordnum, prodnum)
```

Explaining the INSERT Scripts

The INSERT statements have one limitation: date format. This applies only to the ordermaster and orderdetail tables. The generic section includes INSERT statements for customer, supplier, and product. The vendor-specific scripts contain insert scripts for ordermaster and orderdetail.

The product script also requires one minor change for Oracle users.

INSERT INTO customer

```
insert into customer
values ('111222222', 'McBaird', 'geoff lowell',
  '89 Hillcrest St.' ,'Berkeley', 'CA', '94608',
  '510', '5552234', null)

insert into customer
values ('111223333', 'archer', 'ruby',
  '444 37th St #3', 'Oakland', 'CA', '94609',
  '510', '5551111', '2')
```

```
insert into customer
values ('111333333', 'aziz', 'phillip',
 '92 Arch St.' ,'reading', 'MA', '01867',
 '617', '5551333', '1')

insert into customer
values ('111334444', 'le blanc', 'felipe',
 '2 Jacob Way #8', 'reading', 'MA', '01867',
 '617', '5551111', '3')

insert into customer
values ('111444444','sato','kimiko',
 'the highlands','Seattle','WA','98104',
 '206','5552233', '3')

insert into customer
values ('223456789','khandasamy',' SAM',
 '123 Lane St.','NY','NY','10028',
 '212','2231234','2')

insert into customer
values ('777777777','deathmask-z', null,
 'Old Foundry Block 2','Boston','MA','02110',
 '617','5557777', null)

insert into customer
values ('777777778','mokoperto', 'merit',
 'Old Foundry Block 2','Boston','MA','02110',
 '617','5557777','1')

insert into customer
values ('776677778','rs',' pete pete',
 'New Trail 6','Austin','TX','78730',
 '512','5557777','2')

insert into customer
values ('776667778','Peters','Pete',
 '45 N. Maine','Macedon','NY','14502',
 '800','5557777','2')
```

```
insert into customer
values ('923457789','Menendez', 'lauren',
 '158 Beach St.','NY','NY','11215',
  '917','1231235', '3')

insert into customer
values ('999456789','WONG', 'LI-REN',
 '12 Main St.','Silver Spring','MD','20906',
  '301','1231235', '3')
```

INSERT INTO supplier

```
insert into supplier
values (111, 'Connectix Co.',
 '333 North Ave', 'S.F.', 'CA','USA',  '94130',
  null, null, null)

insert into supplier
values (222, 'Soft Stuff',
 '373 Java Ave', 'San Jose', 'CA', 'USA', '95128',
 null,'408', '5554223')

insert into supplier
values (333, 'Total Recall',
 '42 Norton St.', 'Tokyo', null, 'JAPAN',  '143',
 '81-3','376', '13111')

insert into supplier
values (444, 'Hi Finance!',
 '53 5th Ave', 'NY', 'NY', 'USA', '10028',
 null, '201', '5554434')

insert into supplier
values (555, 'TrendMaster',
 '9 Nopar Ct.', 'Seattle', 'WA', 'USA', '98104',
 null, '206', '5552233')

insert into supplier
values (666, 'Above Average Arts',
 '33 West St.', 'Boston', 'MA', 'USA', '02110',
 null, '617', '5554223')
```

```
insert into supplier
values (777, 'Emu Sister Prdctns',
 '7 Forge Ave', 'Philadelphia', 'PA', 'USA', '97212',
 null, '215', '5557433')
```

INSERT INTO product

For Oracle, & is a variable marker. When you insert rows into the Oracle version of product, avoid problems with & in either of these ways:

- Change the & in phrases like "cook & book" so that you have something like "cook + book" or "cook n book."
- Turn off variable substitution with SET SCAN OFF. You can turn it back on with SET SCAN ON.

```
insert into product
values (2000, 'cook & book', 'application',
 'record your recipes',
2.50, 19.99, 555, 'Super 6.')

insert into product
values (2047, 'paper dolls', 'game',
 'create & dress dolls',
 2.50, 19.99, 666, '10.1.01')

insert into product
values (2049, 'more paper dolls', 'game',
 'create & dress dolls',
 2.50, 19.99, 666,'10.1.01' )

insert into product
values (2050, 'tax time', 'application',
 '1995 edition',
 2.50, 49.99, 444, null)

insert into product
values (2111, 'memory tripler', 'application',
  '50% or more',
 -1.00, 119.99, 333, '6.5_a')
```

```
insert into product
values (1084, 'memory manager', 'application',
 null,
 -1.00, 19.99, 333, '10.1_6.5')

insert into product
values (1099, 'typing test', 'education',
 null,
 2.50, 29.99, 666, null)

insert into product
values (1105, 'home poll kit', 'game',
 'take the pulse of america',
 2.50, 19.99, 555, 'Super 6.')

insert into product
values (1110, 'star systems', 'education',
 'scientific horoscopes',
 1.50, 39.99, 555, 'Super 6.')

insert into product
values (2113, 'bugbane', 'application',
 null,
 1.00, 49.00, 222, null)

insert into product
values (1794, 'memory8', 'hardware',
 '8 Meg mem',
 -1.00, 400.00, 333, '6.5_a')

insert into product
values (1083, 'money master', 'application',
 'pers checking',
 5.80, 29.00, 444, '1.2')

insert into product
values (1104, 'teach yourself greek', 'education',
 null,
 2.50, 49.99, 666, null)
```

```
insert into product
values (1107, 'mortgage minder', 'application',
 'know where you stand',
 1.50, 39.99, 444, null)

insert into product
values (1108, 'blood & guts', 'game',
 null,
 2.50, 29.99, 666, null)

insert into product
values (1109, 'C++ for kids', 'education',
 null,
 2.50, 39.99, 666, '1.1')

insert into product
values (1255, 'bug stories', 'book',
 null,
 3.0, 20.00, 777, '2.2')

insert into product
values (1357, 'nt guru', 'book',
 null,
 3.00, 20.00, 777, '2.2')

insert into product
values (1457, 'how multi is media?', 'book',
 null,
 3.00, 20.00, 777, '10.1')

insert into product
values (2110, 'landlord logs', 'application',
 null,
 2.50, 89.99, 444, '1.3')

insert into product
values (1106, 'z_connector', 'hardware',
 null,
 2.2, 149.00, 111, '1.1')
```

INSERT INTO employee

```
insert into employee
values ('123232345', 'Miller', 'Hamid', 1, 1, 1, '223232366')

insert into employee
values ('223232366', 'Chang', 'laurna', 1, 2, 1, '443232366')

insert into employee
values ('111223333', 'archer', 'ruby', 1, 2, 1, '223232366')

insert into employee
values ('923457789', 'Menendez', 'lauren', 1, 1, 1, '223232366')

insert into employee
values ('222222221', 'Bloomfeld', 'Bill', 2, 1, 1, '443232366')

insert into employee
values ('443232366', 'Blake-Pipps', 'Scorley', 2, 2, 1, '443232366')
```

INSERT INTO ordermaster

Dates are always a problem, since different systems have different default formats. However, most allow you to change the display. This gives you two ways to handle the date issue.

- Check your system to see if it supports the date format in the script, and if it does, change the default date format until it matches the format in the script.
- Edit the date data in the script so that it conforms to your system's needs (see "Notes on Environment and Display" in Appendix B for examples).

To set the date format on Adaptive Server Anywhere, use code like this, depending on whether you are setting the display for yourself or for other users.

Adaptive Server Anywhere

```
set option dba.Date_format = 'Mmm dd yyyy';
set option public.Date_format = 'Mmm dd yyyy';
set option dba.timestamp_format = 'Mmm dd yyyy HH:NN:SS pp';
set option public.timestamp_format = 'Mmm dd yyyy HH:NN:SS pp';
```

For Oracle, you can set the date format thus:

Oracle
```
SQL> alter session
  2  set nls_date_format = 'Mon DD YYYY hh:mi am';

Session altered.
```

For Microsoft SQL Server, the SET command allows you to input dates in the script format. However, the command does not affect display.

Microsoft SQL Server
```
set dateformat 'mdy'
```

Here's the INSERT script. Make sure you decide how to handle dates before you run it.

```
insert into ordermaster
values (81, '223456789', 'Jan 2 1999 02:30 am', '1222222232224222', '123232345')

insert into ordermaster
values (85, '111334444', 'Jan 2 1999', '7777 7777 7777 7777', '123232345')

insert into ordermaster
values (86, '777777779', 'Jan 2 1999', '7777 7777 6663', '111223333')

insert into ordermaster
values (87, '111333333', 'Jan 2 1999', '00001111222233334444', '111223333')

insert into ordermaster
values (89, '111222222', 'Jan 2 1999', '1234333331114123', '923457789')

insert into ordermaster
values (90, '111444444', 'Jan 2 1999', '111112111121111', '923457789')

insert into ordermaster
values (91, '111223333', 'Jan 2 1999', '1111222233334444', '923457789')

insert into ordermaster
values (92, '777777778', 'Jan 2 1999', '777766661234X', '222222221')
```

```
insert into ordermaster
values (93, '111334444', 'Jan 05 1999 02:30 pm', 'X7777 7777', '222222221')

insert into ordermaster
values (94, '777777778', 'Jan 2 1999', '777766661234X', '222222221')

insert into ordermaster
values (95, '923456789', 'Jan 3 1999', '3131 7777 7777 7777', '443232366' )

insert into ordermaster
values (99, '776677778', 'Jan 2 1999', '1222222232224222', '923457789')
```

INSERT INTO `orderdetail`

This table also has a date column. See "INSERT INTO `ordermaster`" for ideas on how to handle dates on different systems.

```
insert into orderdetail
values (84, 1099, 1, null)

insert into orderdetail
values (84, 1255, 1, null)

insert into orderdetail
values (86, 2000, 2, null)

insert into orderdetail
values (81, 1357, 1, null)

insert into orderdetail
values (87, 1106, 1, null)

insert into orderdetail
values (87, 2113, 1, 'Jan 4 1999')

insert into orderdetail
values (87, 1794, 1, null)

insert into orderdetail
values (87, 1083, 1, null)
```

```
insert into orderdetail
values (91, 2111, 5, 'Jan 3 1999')

insert into orderdetail
values (89, 1199, 1, 'Jan 4 1999')

insert into orderdetail
values (89, 2050, 2, 'Jan 4 1999')

insert into orderdetail
values (85, 1794, 1, 'Jan 2 1999')

insert into orderdetail
values (90, 2110, 1, 'Jan 2 1999')

insert into orderdetail
values (95, 1255, 1, null)

insert into orderdetail
values (95, 1108, 1, null)

insert into orderdetail
values (95, 1105, 1, null)

insert into orderdetail
values (99, 2047, 6, null)

insert into orderdetail
values (99, 2050, 2222, null)

insert into orderdetail
values (92, 2050, 3333, null)

insert into orderdetail
values (93, 1105, 1, null)

insert into orderdetail
values (94, 1108, 1, null)

insert into orderdetail
values (81, 2050, 5, 'Jan 01 1999')
```

```
insert into orderdetail
values( 84, 2050, 1, 'Jan 05 1999' )

insert into orderdetail
values ( 85, 2050, 25, 'Jan 05 1999' )

insert into orderdetail
values( 86, 1083, 7, 'Jan 05 1999' )

insert into orderdetail
values( 91, 1107, 7, 'Jan 05 1999' )

insert into orderdetail
values( 93, 2050, 5, 'Jan 05 1999' )

insert into orderdetail
values( 94, 1083, 5, 'Jan 05 1999' )

insert into orderdetail
values( 95, 1083, 2, 'Jan 05 1999' )

insert into orderdetail
values ( 86,1105, 20, 'Jan 05 1999' )

insert into orderdetail
values ( 87,1105, 20, 'Jan 05 1999' )

insert into orderdetail
values ( 87, 2000, 20, 'Jan 05 1999' )

insert into orderdetail
values ( 81, 1106, 2, 'Jan 05 1999')
```

Experimenting and Transaction Management

RDBMS transaction management is a huge topic. In essence, it assures that each transaction is atomic, consistent, isolated, and durable (ACID) .

Here, we're just looking at the SQL transaction commands. They give you a way to try commands that change data, check the results, and cancel (roll back) the transaction if you don't like what you got. On our sample system, you follow these steps.

1. Run BEGIN TRANsaction.

2. Make changes with UPDATE, INSERT, or DELETE.

3. Check the changes.

4. Save changes you like with a COMMIT TRANsaction, reverse ones you don't like with a ROLLBACK.

Here's an example. You want to change one employee's first name in your records, but you forget the WHERE clause and instead change *everyone's* name.

Adaptive Server Anywhere

```
begin tran

update employee
set fname = 'flora'

[6 rows updated]

select fname, lname
from employee
```

fname	lname
====================	====================
flora	Miller
flora	Chang
flora	archer
flora	Menendez
flora	Bloomfeld
flora	Blake-Pipps

```
[6 rows]
```

Because you started out with a BEGIN TRAN, you can neatly undo the UPDATE with a ROLLBACK.

Adaptive Server Anywhere

```
rollback

select fname, lname
from employee
```

```
fname                 lname
==================== ====================
Hamid                Miller
laurna               Chang
ruby                 archer
lauren               Menendez
Bill                 Bloomfeld
Scorley              Blake-Pipps

[6 rows]
```

This code works on Sybase ASE and Microsoft SQL Server, too. Actually,
Adaptive Server Anywhere (unlike the Transact-SQL systems) does not require
a BEGIN TRAN in order to do a ROLLBACK. You can roll back after executing
a data modification statement. Changes are reversed back to the most recent
COMMIT. In order to know where you are, use explicit COMMIT commands
or start data modification statements with BEGIN.

The following example shows a ROLLBACK on Oracle immediately after an
UPDATE with no BEGIN needed.

Oracle
```
SQL> update employee
  2  set fname = 'flora' ;

6 rows updated.

SQL> select distinct fname
  2  from employee;

FNAME
--------------------
flora

1 row selected.

SQL> rollback;

Rollback complete.

SQL> select distinct fname
  2  from employee;
```

```
FNAME
--------------------
Bill
Hamid
Lorna
Scorley
lauren
ruby

6 rows selected.
```

Transaction management commands vary from system to system, as shown in Table A–1. Other issues that affect transactions are mode and isolation level. Check your system documentation for details.

Table A-1. Transaction Commands

ANSI	ASA	ASE	MS SQL Server	Oracle	Informix

	BEGIN
	  TRANsaction
	  [tran_name]
		BEGIN
		  TRANsaction
		  [tran_name]
			BEGIN
			  TRANsaction
			  [tran_name |
			  @tran_variable]
				
				SET TRANSACTION
					BEGIN
					  [WORK]

COMMIT
[WORK]
	COMMIT
	  TRANsaction
	  [tran_name]
	
	COMMIT [WORK]
		COMMIT
		  [TRANsaction|
		  WORK]
		  [tran_name]
			COMMIT
			  TRANsaction
			  [tran_name |
			  @tran_variable]
			
			COMMIT [WORK]
				COMMIT	COMMIT
					[WORK]

ROLLBACK [WORK]	ROLLBACK [WORK]	ROLLBACK {TRANsaction | WORK} [tran_name | save_name]	ROLLBACK [TRANsaction [tran_name |@tran_variable| save_name | @save_variable]]	ROLLBACK [WORK] {TO [SAVEPOINT] save_name] | |[FORCE text]}	ROLLBACK [WORK]

	SAVEPOINT
	[save_name]
		SAVE
		  TRANsaction
		  save_name
			SAVE
			  TRANsaction
			  {save_name |
			  @save_variable}
				SAVEPOINT	

Removing Data and Objects: DROP and DELETE Commands

If you don't use transaction control commands and your experiments with the msdpn tables make them too unlike the tables described in the book, you have three choices.

- Remove the entire database and start over again, loading in the CREATE and INSERT scripts.
- Remove troublesome tables with the DROP TABLE command and re-create with those tables' individual CREATE and INSERT scripts.
- Remove data only with DELETE and reload with the relevant INSERT script.

Remove Database

In most cases, you'll do this with a GUI interface, a utility, or a nonstandard command. The advantage of removing the whole database is that it gives you a chance to start over: you can set up your storage and logs anew. You also get to purge all the extra objects you created while experimenting.

DROP Commands

DROP TABLE removes table definition, data, and related indexes. Then use the CREATE and INSERT scripts (in whole or part) to set the tables up again in their original form. Commands to remove the six tables and their indexes look like this:

```
drop table customer

drop table supplier

drop table product

drop table ordermaster

drop table orderdetail

drop table employee
```

DELETE FROM Command

To keep the table structure and indexes but remove all data, use the DELETE command. Then load a fresh set of data with all or part of the INSERT script. Commands to delete all data look like this:

```
delete from customer

delete from supplier

delete from product

delete from ordermaster

delete from orderdetail

delete from employee
```

Summary

This appendix contains information about the sample database msdpn and the scripts that create it.

- A brief description of the database and an entity-relationship diagram start things off. (There are more details in Chapter 1.)
- Next there is a collection of CREATE scripts, one per RDBMS. They also appear on the CD, in slightly different form.
- There is only one version of the INSERT script. It works on all the sample systems, except with dates and terminators. There you may have to do some editing.
- Experimenting is an important part of learning SQL. You can use transaction commands to roll back unsuccessful operations.
- If you forget to use transaction commands or the database or table needs big changes, you can DROP entire tables and start over again or just remove the data with DELETE and reload.

Appendix B

Comparing Datatypes and Functions

In This Appendix

- Datatype Comparison
- Function Comparison
- Join Syntax Comparison
- Notes on Environment and Display

Comparatively Speaking . . .

This appendix presents material you've seen before in a different format. It pulls together information scattered throughout the book as an abbreviated syntax reference.

The datatype and function charts don't tell you everything you need to know. They do give an idea of where to start looking in your documentation, and there are times when that can be very useful. Datatype names vary, and so do function names. Be warned: identical names do not mean identical definitions. To get a real understanding of datatypes and SQL functions available on your system, check the vendor's documentation and do some experiments.

In the same way, the join and outer join variants discussed in the book are summarized in a chart. ANSI and some RDBMSs support more options than are shown here.

Finally, there are some commands for managing the environment and displays (particularly for numbers and dates) that you may find useful.

Datatype Comparison

Table B–1 shows datatype names used in the msdpn database by vendor. Where a particular datatype is used for compatibility with one offered by another vendor, it is in italics. Some names have long and short versions (DECIMAL and

Table B-1. msdpn Datatypes

Element	ASA	ASE	MS SQL Server	Oracle	Informix
fixed character, max size *n*	CHAR(n)	CHAR(n)	CHAR(n)	CHAR(n)	CHAR(n)
variable character, max size *n*	VARCHAR(n)	VARCHAR(n)	VARCHAR(n)	VARCHAR2(n)	VARCHAR(n)
date and time information	*DATETIME* *SMALLDATETIME* TIMESTAMP	DATETIME SMALLDATETIME	DATETIME SMALLDATETIME	DATE	DATETIME
date information	DATE				DATE
time information	TIME				INTERVAL
whole numbers	INTeger SMALLINT TINYINT	INTeger SMALLINT TINYINT	INTeger SMALLINT TINYINT	*INTeger* *SMALLINT* NUMBER	INTeger SMALLINT
exact decimal	DECimal NUMERIC	DECimal NUMERIC	DECimal NUMERIC	*DECimal* *NUMERIC* NUMBER	DECimal NUMERIC
approximate numeric	FLOAT REAL DOUBLE PRECISION	FLOAT REAL DOUBLE PRECISION	FLOAT REAL DOUBLE PRECISION	*FLOAT* *REAL* *DOUBLE PRECISION* NUMBER	FLOAT SMALLFLOAT REAL DOUBLE PRECISION DECimal
currency	*MONEY* *SMALLMONEY*	MONEY SMALLMONEY	MONEY SMALLMONEY		MONEY

DEC): they are noted here with mixed case (DECimal). However, precision and scale for numeric datatypes are not included. Don't assume that the same name means identical characteristics. Check your documentation for details.

Adaptive Server Anywhere treats CHAR, VARCHAR, and LONG VARCHAR columns all as the same type.

Oracle's base real numeric datatype is NUMBER for whole numbers and NUMBER (precision, scale) for decimal numbers. However, Oracle accepts most numeric datatype names used by other systems, such as INT, SMALLINT, DECIMAL, FLOAT, REAL, and DOUBLE PRECISION, translating each into the appropriate NUMBER. Oracle has a VARCHAR datatype but urges customers to use VARCHAR2. VARCHAR is reserved for other uses.

Function Comparison

Tables B–2 through B–9 collect the tables scattered through the book. The information is grouped by topic:

- Character (string) functions
- Number functions
- Date functions
- Conditional functions
- Sequential number methods
- Row number and row id methods
- Tuning functions
- System functions

Character (String) Functions

These handy functions are useful both for displays and searches. Adaptive Server Anywhere's TRIM function removes both leading and trailing spaces.

Table B-2. Character (String) Functions

ANSI	ASA	ASE	MS SQL Server	Oracle	Informix
CHARacter_LENGTH (expr)	LENGTH (expr) DATALENGTH (expr) CHAR_LENGTH (expr)	DATALENGTH (expr) CHAR_LENGTH (expr)	LEN(expr) DATALENGTH (expr)	LENGTH (expr)	LENGTH (expr) CHAR_LENGTH (expr)
	COL_LENGTH ('table', 'column')	COL_LENGTH ('table', 'column')	COL_LENGTH ('table', 'column')		
char_expr || char_expr	char_expr + char_expr char_expr || char_expr STRING (char_expr, char_expr)	char_expr + char_expr	char_expr + char_expr	char_expr || char_expr CONCAT (char_expr , char_expr)	char_expr || char_expr

continued

Table B–2. Character (String) Functions (continued)

ANSI	ASA	ASE	MS SQL Server	Oracle	Informix
SUBSTRING (char_expr FROM start [FOR size])					SUBSTRING (char_expr FROM start [FOR size])
	SUBSTR (char_expr, start [, size])			SUBSTR (char_expr, start [, size])	SUBSTR (char_expr, start [, size])
	SUBSTRING (char_expr, start, size)	SUBSTRING (char_expr, start, size)	SUBSTRING (char_expr, start, size)		
					char_expr [start, end]
	REPEAT (char_expr, number)				
	REPLICATE (char_expr, number)	REPLICATE (char_expr, number)	REPLICATE (char_expr, number)		
	SPACE (number)	SPACE (number)	SPACE (number)		
				LPAD (expr, number [,expr])	LPAD (expr, number [, expr])
				RPAD (expr, number [, expr])	RPAD (expr, number [, expr])
UPPER(expr) LOWER(expr)	UPPER(expr) LOWER(expr) UCASE(expr) LCASE(expr)	UPPER(expr) LOWER(expr)	UPPER(expr) LOWER(expr)	UPPER(expr) LOWER(expr)	UPPER(expr) LOWER(expr)
				INITCAP(expr)	INITCAP(expr)

continued

Table B-2. Character (String) Functions (continued)

ANSI	ASA	ASE	MS SQL Server	Oracle	Informix
TRIM ([LEADING | TRAILING | BOTH] ['char'] FROM expr)	TRIM (expr) LTRIM (expr) RTRIM (expr)	LTRIM (expr) RTRIM(expr)	LTRIM (expr) RTRIM (expr)	LTRIM (expr [set]) RTRIM (expr [set])	TRIM ([LEADING | TRAILING | BOTH] ['char'] FROM expr)
POSITION	LOCATE CHARINDEX	CHARINDEX	CHARINDEX	INSTR	
	ASCII	ASCII	ASCII	ASCII	
	CHAR	CHAR	CHAR	CHR	
	SOUNDEX	SOUNDEX	SOUNDEX	SOUNDEX	
	DIFFERENCE	DIFFERENCE	DIFFERENCE		
	SIMILAR				

Number Functions

These aren't all the functions available, just the ones noted in the book.

Table B-3. Numeric Functions

ANSI	ASA	ASE	MS SQL Server	Oracle	Informix
	ROUND (num_expr, int)	ROUND (num_expr, int)	ROUND (num_expr, int)	ROUND (num_expr, int)	ROUND (num_expr, int)
	'TRUNCATE' (num_expr, int) TRUNCNUM (num_expr, int)			TRUNC (num_expr, int)	TRUNC (num_expr, int)

continued

Table B-3. Numeric Functions (continued)

ANSI	ASA	ASE	MS SQL Server	Oracle	Informix
	CEILING (num_expr)	CEILING (num_expr)	CEILING (num_expr)	CEIL (num_expr)	
	FLOOR (num_expr)	FLOOR (num_expr)	FLOOR (num_expr)	FLOOR (num_expr)	
	SIGN (num_expr)	SIGN (num_expr)	SIGN (num_expr)	SIGN (num_expr)	
	ABS (num_expr)	ABS (num_expr)	ABS (num_expr)	ABS (num_expr)	ABS (num_expr)
MOD (num_expr, int) REMAINDER (num_expr, int)				MOD (num_expr, int)	MOD (num_expr, int)
	num_expr % int	num_expr % int			

Date Functions

There are many date functions, and they vary greatly by vendor. Here is a sample.

Table B-4. Date Functions

ANSI	ASA	ASE	MS SQL Server	Oracle	Informix
CURRENT_DATE CURRENT_TIME CURRENT_TIMESTAMP	CURRENT DATE CURRENT TIME GETDATE	GETDATE	CURRENT_TIMESTAMP GETDATE	SYSDATE	TODAY CURRENT
date_expr + INTERVAL n unit date_expr - INTERVAL n unit	date_expr + n date_expr - n DATEADD DATEDIFF	DATEADD DATEDIFF	date_expr + n date_expr - n DATEADD DATEDIFF	date_expr + n date_expr - n MONTHS_BETWEEN	date_expr + INTERVAL n unit date_expr - INTERVAL n unit
INTERVAL date_expr unit	DAY MONTH YEAR DATENAME DATEPART	DATENAME DATEPART	DAY MONTH YEAR DATENAME DATEPART		DAY WEEKDAY MONTH YEAR

continued

Table B-4. Date Functions (continued)

ANSI	ASA	ASE	MS SQL Server	Oracle	Informix
CAST (expr AS [datatype | domain])	CAST (expr AS datatype) CONVERT (target datatype, expr [, datestyle])	CONVERT (target datatype, expr [, datestyle])	CAST (expr AS datatype) CONVERT (target datatype. expr [,datestyle])		CAST expr AS datatype expr :: datatype
	DATEFORMAT (expr, 'pattern') DATE ('expr')			TO_CHAR (expr, 'format')) TO_DATE (char_expr, 'format')	TO_CHAR(expr, 'format') TO_DATE (char_expr, 'format') DATE ('expr')

CAST and CONVERT work with all compatible datatype pairs, while TO_CHAR and TO_DATE are more limited. Informix supports CAST in some versions. Adaptive Server Anywhere supports many other date functions that can extract units, such as DAY, DAYNAME, DOW, HOUR, MONTH, and MONTHNAME.

Conditional Functions

These functions are grouped together because of their similar natures. There is an ANSI TRANSLATE function, but it is not the same as Oracle TRANSLATE.

Table B-5. Conditional Functions

ANSI	ASA	ASE	MS SQL Server	Oracle	Informix
CASE	CASE	CASE	CASE	DECODE	CASE DECODE
NULLIF	NULLIF	NULLIF	NULLIF		
COALESCE	COALESCE	COALESCE	COALESCE		
	ISNULL	ISNULL	ISNULL	NVL	NVL
				TRANSLATE	

Sequential Number Methods

These aren't set up in functions, but it makes sense to include them here, with other numbering capabilities.

Table B-6. Sequential Numbers

ANSI	ASA	ASE	MS SQL Server	Oracle	Informix
	DEFAULT AUTOINCRE-MENT in CREATE TABLE (also implemented as IDENTITY)	IDENTITY column property in CREATE TABLE	IDENTITY column property in CREATE TABLE	CREATE SEQUENCE seq, then INSERT seq.nextval	SERIAL datatype in CREATE TABLE INSERT 0 for SERIAL to get next number

Row Number and Row ID Methods

These are the leftovers, mostly from the chapter on numbering.

Table B-7. Row Number and Related Functions

ANSI	ASA	ASE	MS SQL Server	Oracle	Informix
	ROWCOUNT	ROWCOUNT	ROWCOUNT		
			TOP		FIRST
	NUMBER(*)			ROWNUM	
				ROWID	ROWID*

*Informix ROWID is different from Oracle ROWID. Notes appear in "Using ROWID to Remove Duplicates" in Chapter 4.

Tuning Functions

Many tuning options come from a utility or a GUI tool. These commands are related to performance, also.

Table B-8. Tuning Commands

ANSI	ASA	ASE	MS SQL Server	Oracle	Informix
	PLAN ('query')	SET SHOWPLAN ON SET NOEXEC ON	SET SHOWPLAN ALL ON	EXPLAIN PLAN	SET EXPLAIN ON
		UPDATE STATISTICS	UPDATE STATISTICS	ANALYZE	UPDATE STATISTICS
	ESTIMATE				
			STAT_DATE		

System Functions

These functions give you information about your environment.

Table B-9. Environment Functions

ANSI	ASA	ASE	MS SQL Server	Oracle	Informix
current_USER	USER_ID USER_NAME	USER_ID USER_NAME	CURRENT_USER USER_ID USER_NAME	USER UID	USER
SYSTEM_USER	SUSER_ID SUSER_NAME	SUSER_ID SUSER_NAME	SYSTEM_USER SUSER_ID SUSER_NAME		
SESSION_USER			SESSION_USER		
	DB_NAME DB_ID	DB_NAME DB_ID	DB_NAME DB_ID		DBSERVERNAME DBSITENAME
	OBJECT_NAME OBJECT_ID	OBJECT_NAME OBJECT_ID	OBJECT_NAME OBJECT_ID		
		HOST_NAME HOST_ID	HOST_NAME HOST_ID		DBINFO ('dbhostname')
	SELECT @@VERSION	SELECT @@VERSION	SELECT @@VERSION	SELECT * FROM v$version	SELECT DBINFO ('VERSION', 'MAJOR'), DBINFO('VERSION', 'MINOR') FROM systables

Join Syntax Comparison

The join variants noted in the book are listed in Table B–10. The ANSI standard specifies other joins (NATURAL, CROSS).

Table B–10. Join Syntax

ANSI	ASA	ASE	MS SQL Server	Oracle	Informix
SELECT select_list FROM t1 JOIN t2 ON t1.col=t2.col	SELECT select_list FROM t1 JOIN t2 ON t1.col=t2.col		SELECT select_list FROM t1 JOIN t2 ON t1.col=t2.col		
	SELECT select_list FROM t1, t2 WHERE t1.col=t2.col	SELECT select_list FROM t1, t2 WHERE t1.col=t2.col	SELECT select_list FROM t1, t2 WHERE t1.col=t2.col	SELECT select_list FROM t1, t2 WHERE t1.col=t2.col	SELECT select_list FROM t1, t2 WHERE t1.col=t2.col
SELECT select_list FROM t1 LEFT OUTER JOIN t2 ON t1.col=t2.col	SELECT select_list FROM t1 LEFT OUTER JOIN t2 ON t1.col=t2.col		SELECT select_list FROM t1 LEFT OUTER JOIN t2 ON t1.col=t2.col		SELECT select_list FROM t1, OUTER t2 WHERE t1.col=t2.col
	SELECT select_list FROM t1, t2 WHERE t1.col*=t2.col	SELECT select_list FROM t1, t2 WHERE t1.col*=t2.col	SELECT select_list FROM t1, t2 WHERE t1.col*=t2.col	SELECT select_list FROM t1, t2 WHERE t1.col=t2.col(+)	
SELECT select_list FROM t1 RIGHT OUTER JOIN t2 ON t1.col=t2.col	SELECT select_list FROM t1 RIGHT OUTER JOIN t2 ON t1.col=t2.col		SELECT select_list FROM t1 RIGHT OUTER JOIN t2 ON t1.col=t2.col		SELECT select_list FROM t2, OUTER t1 WHERE t1.col=t2.col
	SELECT select_list FROM t1, t2 WHERE t1.col=*t2.col	SELECT select_list FROM t1, t2 WHERE t1.col=*t2.col	SELECT select_list FROM t1, t2 WHERE t1.col=*t2.col	SELECT select_list FROM t1, t2 WHERE t1.col(+)=t2.col	

Notes on Environment and Display

This is a collection of odds and ends relating to the environment. In some cases, the commands are session-specific; you revert to the default every time you log in. In other cases, you have a temporary/permanent option.

Setting Number Formats

Some systems have built-in tools for formatting numbers. Oracle SQL Plus provides the (non-SQL) SET and COLUMN commands, and both have many options.

- SET controls aspects of the local environment, as well as elements focused on report production.
- COLUMN is limited to column and column heading formatting.

However, these capabilities do not translate to other Oracle software or to other SQL engines. They are great time savers if your environment is SQL Plus. (Jonathan Gennick's *Oracle SQL Plus: The Definitive Guide* [O'Reilly, 1999] gives many examples.)

A quick query, including different numeric datatypes, shows numeric values in default format. The price column is surprising: it includes no decimals for whole dollar values, making the numbers hard to read and compare.

Oracle

```
SQL> select  weight, price, unit
  2  from  product p, orderdetail od
  3  where p.prodnum = od.prodnum and price between 20 and 30;


   WEIGHT     PRICE      UNIT
 --------- --------- ---------
      2.5     29.99         1
        3        20         1
        3        20         1
      5.8        29         1
      2.5     29.99         1
        3        20         1
      2.5     29.99         1
      2.5     29.99         1
      5.8        29         7
      5.8        29         5
      5.8        29         2

11 rows selected.
```

You might try establishing an Oracle SQL Plus general number format with the SET command:

Oracle

```
SQL> set numformat 9,999,999.00
```

When you run the query again, it's obvious that SQL Plus applies the format to all numbers, not just decimals. Even integers develop decimal points.

Oracle

WEIGHT	PRICE	UNIT
2.50	29.99	1.00
3.00	20.00	1.00
3.00	20.00	1.00
5.80	29.00	1.00
2.50	29.99	1.00
3.00	20.00	1.00
2.50	29.99	1.00
2.50	29.99	1.00
5.80	29.00	7.00
5.80	29.00	5.00
5.80	29.00	2.00

11 rows selected.

But don't despair. Oracle SQL Plus lets you set different formats for each column with the COLUMN command.

Oracle

```
SQL> column weight format 999.9;
SQL> column price format 9,999.99;
SQL> column unit format 99;
SQL> select  weight, price, unit
  2  from   product p, orderdetail od
  3  where p.prodnum = od.prodnum and price between 20 and 30;
```

```
WEIGHT     PRICE UNIT
------  --------- ----
   2.5      29.99    1
   3.0      20.00    1
   3.0      20.00    1
   5.8      29.00    1
   2.5      29.99    1
   3.0      20.00    1
   2.5      29.99    1
   2.5      29.99    1
   5.8      29.00    7
   5.8      29.00    5
   5.8      29.00    2

11 rows selected.
```

Other interactive SQL systems have ways to control the environment, which sometimes include output appearance, but they don't all work the same. Be sure to check your documentation and try some experiments. You may find that you can define some elements—such as how nulls, dates, and numbers are displayed on a session (login), database, or server level.

Adaptive Server Anywhere supports a SET OPTION command (a SQL extension). Two options allow you to control the display of arithmetic operation results. PRECISION sets the maximum size of the result number. SCALE determines the number of digits to the right of the decimal point when the result is truncated to the maximum precision. The option does not affect how numbers are stored; that is determined by the scale and precision in the CREATE TABLE statement.

Adaptive Server Anywhere

```
set option public.Scale = 2
set option public.Precision = 6

select distinct price , price * 1.11111
from product
where price < 40
```

```
      price product.price*1.11111
 ==========  ====================
     19.99               22.21
     29.99               33.32
     39.99               44.43
     29.00               32.22
     20.00               22.22

 [5 rows]
```

Use scale and precision in the CREATE TABLE statement to start out right. For example, if you need a whole number, a decimal with two digits after the decimal point, and a decimal with four digits, most systems will accept syntax like this (see "Datatype Comparison" in this appendix for datatype names in other systems):

Adaptive Server Anywhere

```
create table testnum
 (whole int not null,
 dec2 decimal (15, 2)  not null,
 dec4 decimal (15, 4) not null )

[table created]
```

When you populate the table from existing price data, the CREATE TABLE definitions determine how the data is stored in the new table.

Adaptive Server Anywhere

```
insert into testnum
 select distinct price, price, price
 from product

select *
from testnum

       whole              dec2               dec4
 ===========  =================  =================
        19              19.99            19.9900
        20              20.00            20.0000
        29              29.00            29.0000
```

```
29          29.99          29.9900
39          39.99          39.9900
49          49.00          49.0000
49          49.99          49.9900
89          89.99          89.9900
119        119.99         119.9900
149        149.00         149.0000
400        400.00         400.0000
```

[11 rows]

Defining Display Precision

Transact-SQL provides a function (STR) that lets you define the display precision and scale of a number on the fly. For example, you can use it to make the price column scale expand from 2 to 4. Adaptive Server Anywhere also supports the function (see Table B–11). The precision is the total number of digits, while scale represents only digits to the right of the decimal.

```
STR (num_expr, precision, scale )
```

Adaptive Server Anywhere
```
select distinct price, str (price, 10, 4 )
from product
where price > 80.00
```

```
    price str(product.price,10,4)
========== ===================
    89.99      89.9900
   119.99     119.9900
   149.00     149.0000
   400.00     400.0000
```

[4 rows]

Table B-11. STR Function

ANSI	ASA	ASE	MS SQL Server	Oracle	Informix
	STR (num_expr, precision, scale)	STR (num_expr, precision, scale)	STR (num_expr, precision, scale)		

Defining Default Date Format

Most systems give you a way to define the default date format, often on a session (login) or server level. The options vary a lot, so check your system for specifics.

Here's an example of changing the date format for Oracle with a SQL Plus command.

Oracle

```
SQL> alter session set nls_date_format = 'dd Mon yyyy hh:mi am';
Session altered.

SQL>  select sysdate as DateTime, orderdate
   2  from ordermaster
   3  where ordnum between 81 and 85;

DATETIME               ORDERDATE
---------------------- --------------------
02 Jun 2000 05:29 pm 02 Jan 1999 02:30 am
02 Jun 2000 05:29 pm 02 Jan 1999 12:00 am

2 rows selected.
```

Adaptive SQL Anywhere allows you to set the date format for the dba, public, or a particular user.

Adaptive SQL Anywhere

```
set option dba.Date_format = 'Mmm dd yyyy hh:mm'
set option public.Date_format = 'Mmm dd yyyy hh:mm'
set option dba.timestamp_format = 'Mmm dd yyyy hh:mm'
set option public.timestamp_format = 'Mmm dd yyyy hh:mm'
```

```
select current date, current time, getdate(), orderdate
from ordermaster
where ordnum between 81 and 85
```

```
current date          current time    getdate(*)          orderdate
==============        =============   =============       =================
Jun 02 2000 00:00     17:32:10.363    Jun 02 2000 17:32   Jan 02 1999 02:30:00
Jun 02 2000 00:00     17:32:10.363    Jun 02 2000 17:32   Jan 02 1999 00:00:00
```

[2 rows]

Notice the difference between the CURRENT DATE and GETDATE output. The first is DATE data. Even when you add format for time to the display, CURRENT DATE does not display any values except 00:00 in the time area. That's because it does not store time values. GETDATE, on the other hand, is DATETIME datatype, holding TIMESTAMP information. It can display hour and minute values if the format allows.

Transact-SQL uses SET DATEFORMAT. However, this changes only the format allowed for inserts, not the display.

Table B–12 summarizes how you can tell the systems used in this book to set and display today's date. If you have a different system, chances are you have a different method. Check your documentation for details.

Table B-12. Setting Date Display Format

ANSI	ASA	ASE	MS SQL Server	Oracle	Informix
	SET OPTION dba.DATE_FORMAT 'format'	SET DATEFORMAT 'format'	SET DATEFORMAT 'format'	ALTER SESSION SET NLS_DATE_FORMAT 'format'	DBDATE environment variable

Summary

This appendix is mostly a summary of things you've seen before, brought together in a different format. It includes the following:

- Datatype comparison table
- SQL function comparison tables
- Join syntax comparison table
- Notes on environment and display

Appendix C

Using Resources

In This Appendix

- Books
- Web Sites
- Newsgroups

Books

General

Database Design for Mere Mortals: A Hands-On Guide to Relational Database Design by Michael J. Hernandez (1997: Addison-Wesley)

A Guide to the SQL Standard: A User's Guide to the Standard Database Language SQL, 4th edition, by Chris J. Date and Hugh Darwen (1997: Addison-Wesley)

Joe Celko's SQL for Smarties: Advanced SQL Programming by Joe Celko (1995: Morgan Kaufmann Publishers). There is a second edition out now.

Practical SQL Handbook: Using Structured Query Language, 3rd edition, by Judith S. Bowman, Sandra L. Emerson, and Marcy Darnovsky (1996: Addison-Wesley)

SQL: Implementing the SQL Foundation Standard by Paul J. Fortier (1999: Osborne McGraw-Hill)

SQL Queries for Mere Mortals by Michael J. Hernandez and John L. Viescas (2000: Addison-Wesley)

Understanding the New SQL: A Complete Guide by Jim Melton and Alan R. Simon (1993: Morgan Kaufmann Publishers, The Morgan Kaufmann Series in Data Management Systems)

Informix

Administering Informix Dynamic Server on Windows NT by Carlton Doe (1999: Prentice Hall, Informix Press)

Informix Basics by Glenn Miller (1999: Prentice Hall, Informix Press)

INFORMIX DBA Survival Guide, 2nd edition, by Joe Lumbley (1999: Prentice Hall, Informix Press)

Informix Guide to SQL: Reference and Syntax, 2nd edition, by Informix Software (1999: Prentice Hall, Informix Press)

Informix Performance Tuning, 2nd edition, by Elizabeth Suto (1997: Prentice Hall, Informix Press)

Informix Power Reference by Art Taylor (1998: Prentice Hall, Informix Press)

Programming Informix SQL/4GL, 2nd edition, by Cathy Kipp (1998: Prentice Hall, Informix Press)

Microsoft SQL Server

SQL Server 7 Developer's Guide by Michael Otey and Paul Conte (1998: McGraw-Hill)

(See the section on "Transact-SQL" for more books on SQL Server.)

mSQL/MySQL

MySQL and mSQL by Randy Jay Yarger and George Reese (1999: O'Reilly & Associates, Nutshell Series)

Oracle

Oracle 8: The Complete Reference by George Koch and Kevin Loney (1997: Osborne McGraw-Hill, Oracle Press)

Oracle 8 Dba Handbook by Kevin Loney (1998: Osborne McGraw-Hill, Oracle Press)

Oracle Performance Tuning by Mark Gurry and Peter Corrigan (1996: O'Reilly & Associates, Nutshell Handbook)

Oracle SQL High-Performance Tuning by Guy Harrison (1997: Prentice Hall)

Oracle SQL Plus: The Definitive Guide by Jonathan Gennick (1999: O'Reilly & Associates)

Sybase

Sybase Performance Tuning by Shaibal Roy and Marc Sugiyama (1996: Prentice Hall)

Sybase SQL Server Performance and Tuning Guide by Karen Paulsell (1996: International Thomson Publishing)

Sybase SQL Server Survival Guide by Jim Panttaja, Mary Panttaja, and Judy Bowman (1996: John Wiley and Sons)

(See "Transact-SQL" for more books on Sybase.)

Transact-SQL

Optimizing Transact-SQL: Advanced Programming Techniques by David Rozenshtein, Anatoly Abramovich, and Eugene Birger (1997: The Coriolis Group)

Transact-SQL Programming by Kevin Kline, Lee Gould, and Andrew Zanevsky (1999: O'Reilly & Associates, Nutshell Series)

Web Sites

Database Vendors

http://www.sybase.com

http://www.informix.com

http://www.oracle.com

http://www.microsoft.com

Other Offerings

These are sites you might want to check out, ones visited during the work on the book.

http://www.iiug.org

http://www.geocities.com/SiliconValley/File/2306/TechDesk.html

http://www.TDAN.com

http://www.orafaq.com

Newsgroups

comp.databases

(comp.databases has 28 subgroups, ranging from comp.databases.adabase to comp.databases.xbase.)

comp.databases.sybase

comp.databases.informix

comp.databases.ms-sqlserver

comp.databases.oracle (with subgroups marketplace, misc, server, and tools)

Index

@@VERSION, 252, 303
% (percent sign), 23, 24, 37, 58, 60
to represent modulo, 191
*/ (symbol for comment end), 10, 121
*= (Transact-SQL left outer join symbol),
   93
* (zero or more characters wildcard), 39
+ (Transact-SQL concatenate symbol),
   24–25
-- (symbol for comment line), 10
/* (symbol for comment start), 10, 121
:: (Informix symbol for CAST), 50
=* (Transact-SQL right outer join
   symbol), 93
? (single character) wildcard, 39
^ (caret) wildcard, 39
_ (underbar) wildcard, 37, 60
[ ] (square brackets) wildcard, 39
|| (ANSI concatenate symbol), 24–25

— A —

Abramovich, Anatoly, 77
ABS, 300
Adaptive Server Anywhere (ASA)
   character string functions used by,
      297–99
   conditional function used by, 301
   CREATE scripts in, 269–71
   datatypes used by, 296
   date function used by, 300–301
   environmental functions used by, 303

   join variants used by, 304
   number functions used by, 299–300
   row number and related functions,
      302
   sequential number methods used by,
      302
   tuning commands used by, 302–3
administrative information, getting,
   252–55
aggregates, 184–87
   nested, 164, 166, 184–87
ALTER TABLE, 110–11
   in adding FOREIGN KEY REFER-
      ENCES statement, 149
   CASCADE clause in, 149
American National Standards Institute
   (ANSI)
   character string functions, 297–99
   concatenate symbol (||), 24–25
   conditional function, 301
   date functions, 300–301
   environmental functions, 303
   join variants, 304
ANALYZE, 214, 303
AND, 121
ANSI. *See* American National Standards
   Institute (ANSI)
approximate numeric, 296
approximating numbers, 142–43
ASCII, 262, 263, 299
atomic, consistent, isolated, and durable
   (ACID) transactions, 288

CD-ROM WARRANTY

USING PRACTICAL SQL: THE SEQUEL CD

1. This CD contains

   - a 60-day trial version of Sybase Adaptive Server Anywhere
   - the msdpn sample database used in the book
   - files to create the msdpn tables on other DBMS systems (MS SQL Server, Oracle, Informix, and Sybase Adaptive Server Enterprise—software for these DBMSs is not, however, supplied on the CD)

2. To load Adaptive Server Anywhere, insert the CD in your drive. If an installation program does not come up immediately, choose the correct platform directory from the Anywhere directory (CE, Netware, Win16, or Win32) and start the setup.exe file. Follow the installation directions. For those short of space, Personal Server is the minimum. Sybase Central and Help files are useful additions.

3. Once you have installed Adaptive Server Anywhere, copy the msdpn6.db file from the CD to your hard drive.

4. Start Adaptive Server Anywhere/Interactive SQL (from the "Programs" menu on Windows, or according to the customs of your system).

5. The "Connect to Adaptive Server Anywhere" window opens. (If it does not, type "connect" in the "Command" pane at the bottom third of the Interactive SQL window and click "Execute". This will bring up the "Connect to Adaptive Server Anywhere" window.)

6. Type "DBA" (must be uppercase) in the login line, and "SQL" in the password line.

7. Without clicking the "OK" button, click the "Database" tab at the top of the form.

8. Type "msdpn" in the "Database name" line. Give the full path name of msdpn6.db in the "Database file" line. (See step 3. If you copied the msdpn6.db file to C:/SQL, for example, the address for "Database file" would be C:/SQL/msdpn6.db.).

9. Click "OK" at the bottom of the form. The heading in the top border of the "Interactive SQL" window indicates you are DBA, on msdpn. The msdpn database is already built and ready to go.

10. Type a sample query, such as "select * from employee" in the Interactive SQL "Command" pane. When you click the "Execute" button, the results appear in the "Data" pane at the top of the "Interactive SQL" window.

11. Use Sybase Central (It may be listed as "Manage Adaptive Server Anywhere" in the "Programs" menu.) for adding users, checking table column definitions, etc. Log into Sybase Central by picking the "Connect" option on the Sybase Central "Tools" menu. The "Connect to Adaptive Server Anywhere" window opens. Follow the steps described in steps 6-9 above.

12. CREATE and INSERT scripts are included in the dbcreates and dbinserts directories on the CD, and directions for using them are in the scripts and in Appendix A. Use these files if you want to restore after removing tables or deleting data.

13. Scripts for creating msdpn tables for other RDBMSs (Oracle, SQL Server, Informix, and Sybase ASE) are also included on the CD.